Vacations That Can Change Your Life

Vacations That Can Change Your Life

Adventures, Retreats and Workshops for the Mind, Body and Spirit

Ellen Lederman

 Sourcebooks, Inc.
Naperville, IL

Published by: Sourcebooks, Inc.
P.O. Box 4410, Naperville, Illinois 60567-4410
(630) 961-3900
FAX: 630-961-2168

Disclaimer:
Care has been taken to ensure that this publication was as accurate and
up-to-date as possible at the time of its most recent printing. Because of
the nature of such information, addresses, phone numbers, dates, and
other details are liable to change. We will be happy to receive correc-
tions, comments, and suggestions for future printings and editions.
Neither the author nor the publisher are associated in any way with any
of the programs listed in this book and make no warranties as to their
safety or stability. We therefore cannot accept responsibility for any con-
sequences arising from the use of this book...*please be safe.*

Library of Congress Cataloging-in-Publication Data

Lederman, Ellen
    Vacations that can change your life: adventures, retreats, and
workshops for the mind, body, and spirit / Ellen Lederman – 2nd ed.
        p.   cm.
    Includes index.
    ISBN 1-57071-391-X (alk. paper)
    1. Retreats—Directories.   2. Health resorts—Directories.
3. Vacation schools, Religious—Directories.   4. Vacations—
Directories.   5. Travel—Directories.   I. Title.
BL628.L43   1998
910'.25— dc21   98-7506
                                                           CIP

Printed and bound in the United States of America.

VHG Paperback — 10 9 8 7 6 5 4 3 2

TABLE OF CONTENTS

Dedication

For Andy

Acknowledgments

The author appreciates the information provided by
all the profiled programs and centers.

Thanks also to Andrew Lederman
for his technical support.

Introduction: Using This Book

*W*hat do you have to show for your last vacation?

If you're like most people: not much! The tan probably faded a few weeks after you came back. The relaxation you felt while you were away disappeared within a week or two of resuming your regular routine. All that remains of your investment (the time and money spent on the vacation) are the souvenirs you brought home.

T-shirts, ashtrays, and little plastic globes that "snow" when shaken may serve their purpose, but they don't have much of an impact on your life. Nothing is any different than it was before the vacation. You remain exactly as you were, thinking and feeling and doing the same old things.

But your next vacation can affect you in a meaningful and permanent way. Any of the possibilities in this book could transform your life. The skills learned or perspective gained will remain long after the actual experience has ended. Unlike standard travel which stresses passive sightseeing or sunbathing, these vacations demand active involvement of the mind/body/spirit. If you throw your whole self into one of these adventures, you can explore, discover, learn, heal, and grow.

There's no question that it's easier to continue your usual style of vacationing. Many people return to the same spot year after year for just this reason. Going back to a familiar beach or mountain resort eliminates the need for research and indepth planning. All that's required is a quick phone call to reserve your place. Or, if your chosen vacation is a little more complicated, a travel agent can provide advice and manage the details.

With the vacations in this book, you will need to expend a little more effort. Most travel agents haven't heard of the vast majority of the profiled vacations. You won't be able to pick up a travel magazine and see an ad for most of the retreats or workshops. Chances are your friends and neighbors haven't experienced these adventures and can't recommend any of them to you.

You'll also need to be prepared to venture past your normal comfort zone. Sticking with what you've always done in the past is much less risky than trying something new. It's safer and less stressful to know exactly what to expect. Even after reading about the vacations in this book and in any promotional material you may request, you still won't fully realize all that may occur or how the experience may affect you until you actually participate in one.

What you can expect is to be challenged in ways that aren't possible on standard vacations. In the place of a leisurely walk through a museum, you can choose to spend a week in more active pursuits that can expand your confidence and self-reliance such as kayaking through whitewater rapids. Instead of sitting on a beach, you can hike through a national forest as you learn backpacking and survival skills. Rather than just splashing around in the ocean, you can swim with the dolphins as part of a special program that enhances human creativity and communication.

On your previous vacations, probably the most intellectually challenging activity was flipping through a magazine or deciding on a restaurant for dinner. If you're ready to acquire skills and knowledge that last beyond your vacation, learning a foreign language or filmmaking can become your focus the next time you get away.

While you may have visited cathedrals on a European trip or even attended a religious service once or twice, it's likely that not a lot was asked of you spiritually on your last vacations. But the spiritual programs contained in this book actively promote spiritual/religious growth. Whether you're in need of a little renewal in your current faith or feel a compelling need to explore a new type of spirituality, you can get involved in a retreat that provides the environment and the support to explore the deepest parts of your soul.

Unlike your usual vacation which you spend entirely with family or friends (or sightsee among strangers with whom you never really interact), you'll need to extend yourself socially. Except for a few vacations where you meditate or participate in a solo backpacking vision quest in the desert, you'll encounter new people and share some intense experiences with them. While there are some vacations that are intended for you to share with a spouse, parent, or child, you may be participating in one on your own.

But don't let the demands and challenges scare you. You do have to invest yourself physically, emotionally, socially, intellectually, and spiritually, but you'll get much in return. The small amount of effort and time needed to learn more about the vacations which interest you is well worthwhile. It will ensure you of choosing the program that most meets your needs. The experiences you have will be transformational and will make a difference in the rest of your life.

And keep in mind that these experiences will also be enjoyable. You will not be giving up all the fun and relaxation of a more typical vacation. Even the most rigorous programs include some recreation. The majority of the centers, retreats, and adventures are held in very scenic locations by oceans, lakes, mountains, and farmland. You'll enjoy good food and make great new friends.

It's very possible that one of these programs will change your life in a very positive way. You might learn a new skill, develop a hobby, improve your health, or discover your spiritual side. Investigate and then enjoy what may be the vacation of a lifetime!

Using This Book

This book is only the first step of your quest for a transformational vacation. Each listing is purely informational and should not be construed as an endorsement (although testimonials from previous participants are used whenever available). Only you can determine which ones are right for you. Write for further information, compare brochures, call with questions, and make your own decision. You'll need to take into account such variables as cost, location, length of the program, type of accommodations, and so on. However, your major focus should be on the content, goals, and philosophy of the programs. Think about what skills or perspective you'd like to attain on your vacation and look for the program that best addresses these needs. Ask yourself whether you're primarily looking for:

- developing or maximizing your spirituality
- healing your mind or spirit
- healing your body
- maintaining/improving psychological health
- maintaining physical health
- maximizing your personal development and functioning
- maximizing your relationships
- learning a specific skill

If you find yourself unable to select one area because all options appeal to you, a holistic vacation is probably most appropriate since it can offer all the possibilities.

Listings are grouped into five chapters. Some of the vacations can fit under more than one chapter, but appear under the most relevant chapter for the sake of simplicity.

Chapter One profiles holistic vacations that address the "whole person" by fully integrating mind, body, and spirit. While all the listings in the book do this to some extent, the experiences in this section truly touch upon all three areas in equal measure.

The first part of the Holistic chapter focuses on Comprehensive Programs that use a full range and wide variety of interdisciplinary techniques and philosophies. Esalen in California is one of the largest and oldest examples of this type of vacation. Offerings include biofeedback, African spirituality, expressive play, massage, ecology, and meditation. Similar workshops, playshops, and seminars are available at other comprehensive holistic centers in Scotland, Greece, Chicago, New York, and California. Specific examples can range from a "Have Journal, Will Paddle" kayaking and journaling trip (incorporating personal growth and discovery with active physical demands) through Serenity By the Sea in Canada to Rhythm Exploration and Drum Building at Montana's Feathered Pipe Ranch (experiencing Native American traditions to explore one's inner rhythms while connecting to nature and others).

The second section of this chapter, Individual Disciplines, takes a more singular approach by focusing on vacations that specialize in one specific area such as bodywork, yoga, or sound and music. Examples include Hawaiian Pathways, where participants expand their awareness and self-mastery through ancient sacred Hawaiian arts of meditation, dance, chant, and massage, or Hellerwork Training where natural movement and expression is freed through exercises and work on the body's structure so that each participant's innate wholeness can be revealed.

Chapter Two contains listings with a spiritual focus. These vacations promote spirituality in a religious or philosophical sense.

The first section includes programs devoted to participatory programs. Some have a singular denominational focus, such as Pendle Hill in Pennsylvania with its Quaker orientation. Others, such as the intentional community of the Lama Foundation in New Mexico, offer programs which touch upon a variety of world religions, including Buddhism, Islam, Christianity, Judaism, and Sufism. Some provide a focused, isolated silent retreat experience (Mystic Journey Retreat Center in Alabama only serves one participant at a time), whereas others are larger in scope (such as the group tours to sacred sites and spiritual activities in Bali or Native American reservations). A few of the vacations are offered only once a year, such as Pennsylvania's Rainbow Experience with lectures and experiences like "Close Encounters of the Angelic Kind" where participants learn to walk, talk, laugh, and cry with their personal angels.

The second part profiles vacations that allow for the expression of spirituality through social action and service. By making a difference in the world, you can make a difference in your own life. You can develop the vision and commitment to continue working on the causes that are important to you long after the vacation has ended. Possibilities can range from clearing trails in national parks through the Appalachian Trail Club, building homes for low-income families throughout the United States and the world for Habitat for Humanity, canoeing down the Missouri River in Montana to study prairie dog colonies for the Foundation for Field Research, and teaching important skills while promoting volunteer assistance throughout the world by participating in Global Volunteers.

Any one of these spiritual vacations can change your perspective for the rest of your life. You can develop or strengthen your focus on what's really important and expand your thoughts and actions beyond the more mundane concerns of daily life.

Chapter Three describes adventures that heal the body or mind/spirit after abuse, trauma, substance abuse, or illness. Other listings are preventive in nature, helping physical and emotional health to be maintained and improved when there has not been any significant problems.

The first section addresses Mind/Spirit vacations. These programs optimize emotional well-being through both traditional mental health techniques such as psychoanalysis and alternative methods such as breathwork and re-experiencing the birth process. Among the many possibilities are the "Learning to Love Yourself" course at the Onsite program in Tucson which incorporates group therapy and experiential self-worth exercises, healing through analysis of dreams at Oregon's Aesculapia Wilderness Healing Retreat, and 12 Step programming during Sober Vacations' Caribbean cruises.

The second section profiles Body Programs. These programs can assist in weight reduction, decrease cholesterol and blood pressure, promote physical fitness, and control symptoms of diseases such as chronic pain, cancer, diabetes, heart disease, chronic fatigue syndrome, and immune disorders and allergies. A few are highly specialized, such as the Stop Smoking Recovery Programs in Florida. Some have a unique focus, such as ancient oil massages at the Canadian Pacific Oasis for Perfect Health, herbal teas at the New Life Health Center in Massachusetts, or enzyme-rich organic diets at Hippocrates Health Institute in Florida. Most of the programs offer a comprehensive approach like Duke University's Diet and Fitness Center in North Carolina, encompassing exercise, nutrition, education, and stress management.

Although the chapter is divided into two sections according to the primary focus, all the programs address the mind/spirit and the body. The Mind/Spirit vacations can include techniques that involve the body such as movement therapy and offer nutritious foods and exercise to ensure that participants don't neglect their physical health. The Body vacations incorporate training and activities such as meditation and positive thinking to maximize emotional health. Thus any of the programs can help you achieve optimal physical and emotional vitality. When you feel good, you can take better advantage of all that life has to offer.

Chapter Four focuses on self-improvement vacations. While all the vacations in the book can improve you in some way (whether learning a foreign language, establishing a lifelong exercise program, or acquiring a new spirituality), the programs in this chapter emphasize a more generalized growth as a human being. The attitudes and skills learned in the self-improvement vacations can make you more aware and confident of the person you really are. They can also help you become the best possible you.

The first part of the chapter is devoted to personal empowerment programs which can develop self-esteem, increase confidence, improve decision-making ability, and promote creativity. Many of the programs (such as Antelope Retreat and Education Center in Wyoming) incorporate wilderness training to establish a sense of self-sufficiency and find your personal vision of what you want yourself and your life to be. Other programs, such as the one week Avatar course held in numerous locations throughout the United States and abroad, help to discreate (cause to vanish or self-destruct) limiting beliefs that only serve to restrict life and cause discomfort. Unique programs include California's Camp Winnarainbow teaching performing and circus arts such as acrobatics and juggling to adults to eliminate shyness and fear, walking on glowing coals in firewalking seminars sponsored by Sundoor throughout the United States to experience a peak state of mind, and swimming with dolphins in the ocean and semi-captive settings of the Dolphin Camp of the Florida Keys to create a sense of playfulness and tap into intuitive potential.

The second part deals with programs that can enhance the way you relate to the people who are significant in your life. These vacations are important because you can't be at your best if your most crucial relationships aren't satisfying. Many of the listings focus on relationships between spouses/partners (such as the National Marriage Encounter offered throughout the United States which helps couples recognize and deal with their strengths and weaknesses or the Art of Conscious Loving seminars in Hawaii which use tantra yoga practices to enhance sexuality). A few address other important relationships, such as the mother-daughter retreats offered by the Center for Exceptional Living in Wisconsin.

Any of the Self-Improvement programs can change your life by altering the way you perceive and relate to yourself and others. The self-knowledge and self-confidence you'll gain maximizes your personal potential in any activity you may undertake. The improved communication and conflict resolution skills in dealing with others can also help you be at your best.

Chapter Five details a variety of learning vacations which teach specific skills such as foreign languages, defensive driving, backpacking, music, art, crafts, writing, homebuilding, and cooking. Any of the listings serve as proof that enjoyable vacations can take place in classrooms and not just on the beach or a sightseeing bus. Examples include the Augusta Heritage Center in West Virginia, with its offerings of Cajun dance, hammered dulcimer, calligraphy, and herb gardening. The skills learned in one of these courses could change your life by giving you a passion to pursue during your leisure time. Some of the programs may transform your career by developing/refining skills such as creative writing (Writers Retreat Workshop in Connecticut), foreign language (learning French in the countryside of Belgium or France through Ceran-Langues), or acting (American Academy of Dramatic Arts in New York or California). You could use these skills to advance your career or even start a new one. Other programs can transform your life by allowing you to build and live in the home of your dreams (Yestermorrow Design/Build School in Vermont) or by becoming a safer driver who avoids accidents and injury (Dodge/Skip Barber Driving School in California or Florida).

The cost of the Programs is provided at the end of each profile and is grouped into three categories:

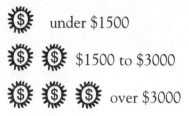

under $1500

$1500 to $3000

over $3000

Unless otherwise noted, prices are inclusive of tuition, programming fees, lodging, and meals. They generally do not include transportation to and from the program.

HOLISTIC VACATIONS

*A*ll of the vacations in this book offer nourishment for the mind, body, and spirit in varying degrees. Those that focus on healing the body and promoting physical health also address the mind and spirit by teaching lifestyle modifications and by developing optimal attitudes. The vacations with a spiritual emphasis don't totally ignore the body, as evidenced by such practices as walking meditation or healthy nutritional practices. But the vacations that follow truly offer equal opportunity for transformation of the mind, body, and spirit.

The first section, Comprehensive Programs, contains both large and small centers which provide all-inclusive programming. All offer activities which promote physical, emotional, social, intellectual, and spiritual well-being. Their approach is as inclusive as their focus; techniques and philosophies are varied and interdisciplinary.

While the focus is just as holistic in the second section, Individual Disciplines Programs, the approach is narrower. Instead of incorporating a variety of disciplines, they concentrate on in-depth learning and experiences in one particular area. The mind, body, and spirit are integrated through a highly specialized approach such as yoga or music therapy.

COMPREHENSIVE PROGRAMS

A weekend or week at any of these programs can result in significant changes in your life. Dedicated to promoting physical, emotional, and spiritual health and to facilitating personal as well as planetary transformation, the holistic centers offer infinite possibilities. There are a multitude of skills to be learned and perspectives to be gained.

Whether the medium is Japanese wooden swordplay or guided imagery, journal writing, or drum building, you can discover something about yourself. You can learn to relax with biofeedback and stress management techniques. Physical fitness can be improved through tennis or yoga. Leisure interests can be developed in areas such as painting or poetry. Your career potential can be enhanced through workshops in management or communication skills. Intimacy can be taken to new heights through sexuality workshops. Spirituality can be discovered through Native American rituals or Tibetan chanting or Judeo-Christian techniques of meditation. Best of all, you don't have to confine yourself to just one area. Many of these programs offer opportunities to participate in myriad activities to truly integrate the mind, body, and spirit.

ALASKA WOMEN OF THE WILDERNESS

"Each day I draw from the sustenance I drank in with you....It runs through my blood and feeds my almost forgotten soul. I have but forgotten my old life, I have shed it. It has fallen away to dust. I weave anew."

—*Alaska Women of the Wilderness participant*

In addition to offering kayaking and hiking trips for women through Alaska's wilderness, Alaska Women of the Wilderness offers a Primal Connections playshop. The whole self is addressed through sound, movement, art, bodywork, and meditation. Participants discover how to bring their bodies toward greater balance and centering through primal African dance, movement therapy, and polarity energy exercises. Art (clay, drawing, and painting) is used to discover individual body images. Bodywork (connective tissue massage, neuromuscular therapy, Reiki, and sound healing) helps release unhealthy patterns and restores the body to balance. Meditation is incorporated throughout the program. By the close of the program, participants have created a ritual of transformation for themselves.

Another playshop, Unleashing Herself: Mask Making, unleashes the creative woman inside each participant. By creating and constructing personalized masks, participants engage in a process of self-exploration. Storytelling, ceremony, music, art, movement, and stillness are also incorporated.

The programs are held over a weekend.

Participants camp out and are provided with meals.

COST:

Alaska Women of the Wilderness
P.O. Box 773556
Eagle River, AK 99577

 (907) 688-2226

BREITENBUSH HOT SPRINGS RETREAT AND CONFERENCE CENTER

Breitenbush is an intentional community whose ethics and interests focus on geothermal and hydroelectric energy, conservation, service, and self-reliance. They welcome visitors year-round for unstructured personal retreats as well as for three-day weekend (and occasional week-long) workshops.

Examples of past offerings include:

- **Expanding Your Inner Light**
  Healing of the body and spirit is accomplished by yoga postures, deep breathing, creative visualizations, meditation, group sharing, positive affirmation, and healing massage.

- **Follow Your Heart**
  Couples enhance their relationship by releasing sexual blocks and experiencing deeper heart bonding. Participants learn Tantric techniques as well as modern clinical sexual knowledge.

- **Changing Woman**
  Participants explore their capacity for creative change through movement, art, sound, ritual, and sharing.

- **On the Way to Sinai**
  The weekend focuses on Jewish spiritual renewal and celebration through prayer, study, song, and dance.

- **Self-Empowerment and Peaceful Relations**
  Native American wisdom, Gestalt therapy, and Zen philosophy are used for exploring dreams and working with anger, grief, fear, and joy.

- **Men's Retreat: Holotropic Breathwork**
  Simple breathing techniques and evocative music expand mystical and creative potential.

Participants stay in shared cabins that accommodate three to five people. Most of the cabins do not have their own bathrooms; toilets and showers are located near the cabin area.

Three vegetarian meals are served daily. Massage services are available. Other facilities include a creek for swimming, hiking trails, hot tubs, natural steam sauna, and hot springs.

Breitenbush is located on the Breitenbush River, two hours south of Portland. It can be reached by car or bus.

COST: $

Breitenbush Hot Springs
P.O. Box 578
Detroit, OR 97342

(503) 854-3314
website: www.breitenbush.com

CHRISTINE CENTER FOR UNITIVE SPIRITUALITY

The Christine Center provides revitalization of the body, mind, and spirit. Embracing the diversity and underlying unity of all spiritual traditions, it offers a variety of workshops with a cross cultural perspective. Programs are both theoretical and experiential, while addressing the emotional, intellectual, and physical components of being a living and spiritual being.

Retreats and workshops generally last three to four days. Held throughout the year on a rotating schedule, they include:

- **Midlife Transitions**
  Women explore the transition of menopause, using meditation, journaling, and sacred dance.

- **Traditional Chinese Medicine**
  The program provides an introduction to Chi-gung (meditation with breath and movement), acupuncture, herbs, and diet.

- **Mystic Christianity**
  The scriptures are used as a guide to the spiritual development and transformation of the Essential Self.

- **Body-Mind Consciousness**
  Massage, movement, and energy work are explored as means of increasing awareness of body patterns and their effect on total wellness.

The staff at the Christine Center view the body as a vehicle for spiritual development. A range of body energetics services are provided so that the energy of the spirit can be refined. These include reflexology (acupressure point work on the feet to stimulate vital organs and relax tension), ofuro (Japanese bath for relaxation), breathwork (using the breath for relaxation and energizing), and Jin Shin Do (acupressure to open and balance energy pathways).

Participants stay in rustic "hermitages," most of which do not have indoor baths. One to three persons stay in a hermitage.

Meals may be prepared in the hermitage's own kitchen or may be taken with the community. Most of the meals served are vegetarian. The Center is located in central Wisconsin. Planes and buses serve Eau Claire (about ninety minutes away). A shuttle service is available.

COST: (barter, work exchange, and scholarships can be considered in lieu of full payment)

 Christine Center for Unitive Spirituality
W8291 Mann Road
Willard, WI 54493

☎ (715) 267-7507
website: www.christinecenter.org/contents.html

CLEARING

In 1935, Jans Jensen, a renowned Danish-American architect and conservationist, started the Clearing. Modeling it after the folk schools of his native Denmark, Jensen developed the Clearing as a place where city people could come to renew their contact with the soil as a basis for life values. Continuing as an adult school of discovery in the arts, nature, and humanities, every summer it offers a variety of weeklong programs for the mind, body, and soul. There are also some weekend programs during the fall. Examples of past offerings include:

- **Spirit of the Land**
  Participants look at the earth and their relationship to it through a Native American perspective. Activities include outdoor experiences, storytelling, dancing, music, solitude, and slide and video presentations.

- **Creative Personal Journal Writing**
  The focus is on developing and using a personal journal to foster inner creativity. Participants are taught journaling techniques of portraits, mapping, dialogues, and sensory acuteness.

- **Visual Arts for Grown-Ups**
  Participants develop ways to access and promote an ongoing artistic consciousness through "user-friendly" art materials and methods which promote spontaneous expression. Collaborative art games, relaxation and sensory awareness activities, collage, drawing, painting, and clay techniques encourage creativity.

- **T'ai Chi/Chi Kung: Opening Our Body's Energy Gates**
  The "internal" martial art of T'ai Chi is learned as a means of stress prevention and reduction. Along with its series of postures and transitional movement performed continuously in a relaxed manner, participants also learn Chi Kung (conditioning exercises for stamina, strengthening, and longevity). Related visualizations and self-massage are taught as well.

- **On Common Ground**
  The focus of the week is the understanding of the sense of harmony within and around us so that community can be built and maintained in the midst of diversity. Participants are involved in music, journal writing, painting, storytelling, sign language, creative dancing, walking, and building dream catchers.

Other courses include wood carving, quilting, watercolor painting, Navajo silversmithing, music appreciation, poetry, storytelling, and photography.

Many of the classes are held outdoors.

Leisure activities include hiking, swimming, fishing, cycling, and storytelling/singing around evening campfires.

Participants are housed in double rooms in historic log and stone cabins (which, like all the buildings in the Clearing, are listed on the National Register of Historic Places). All rooms have private baths. Dining is family-style for daily breakfast, lunch, and dinner.

The Clearing is located in Wisconsin's Door County overlooking the Green Bay waters of Lake Michigan.

COST:

 The Clearing
12183 Garrett Bay Road
P.O. Box 65
Ellison Bay, WI 54210

☎ (920) 854-4088

CREATIVE ENERGY OPTIONS

"...(the experience) has made powerful changes at home and at work. It's helped me make the decision to return to school and walk more strongly into my future."

—*Creative Energy Options participant*

Advertising itself as a center for self-discovery, Creative Energy Options holds a number of workshops, retreats, and tours throughout the year. Many of the programs are geared for persons in healthcare, education, and business, but participation is not limited to professionals in these fields.

A unique four weekend retreat model is offered where the same group returns for all four weekends (about every three months). This allows for subject matter to be pursued in depth and for participants to share their insights and discoveries from the intervening months. Independent study through reading books and articles or listening to audiotapes between retreats enables participants to continue their learning.

Examples of past retreats on the four weekend model have included:

- **Worklife and Health**
  The goal is to design worklife in a healthy, balanced manner while still having a strong bottom line. Participants learn to position themselves and their organizations for success by adjusting leadership styles, developing creative problem-solving, and examining the values, beliefs, and expectations that shape individual and organizational behavior.

- **Creativity and Health**
  The curative power within the creative process is accessed through clay, song, music, journaling, and theater. Participants learn to use the expressive arts for healing.

- **Cross-Cultural Practices and Health**
  Universal themes relating to health, leadership, and relationship dynamics are explored. Participants learn a variety

of cultural perspectives in using myth, ritual, and storytelling to release limiting family patterns, enhance self-esteem, and promote health.

There are occasional single weekend retreats such as Power Couples. Designed for couples who are experiencing problems or those who wish to be proactive and develop an even stronger relationship, the program helps to release invisible loyalties to the past that can damage relationships. Each couple has several private sessions to discuss the blocks in the relationship and also participates in group educational meetings to learn basic rules of conflict resolution. Visualization, meditation, and journaling are included.

Creative Energy Options also sponsors nine-day tours to New Mexico. The "Power of the Southwest" experience includes whitewater rafting, sweat lodges, drumming, vision quests, journal writing, and meditation. The "Leadership in Action" tour is designed for persons in leadership positions (or those aspiring to take on leadership roles). It includes similar experiences to the Power tour, as well as lectures, discussions, and experiential learning in personal presentation, creativity, responsibility, and team building. Participants camp out or reside in double occupancy rooms at hotels and lodges.

Retreats are held at "The Country Place." These fifty acres of woodlands, about two hours from both New York City and Philadelphia, have hiking trails and provide dorm-style accommodations. Three vegetarian meals are provided daily.

COST: (four weekend retreats; couples weekend retreat; nine day tours)

Creative Energy Options
909 Sumneytown Pike, Suite 105
Spring House, PA 19477

 (215) 643-4420

DISNEY INSTITUTE

As the newest addition to Florida's Disney resort, the Disney Institute actually focuses on adults rather than children and stresses participatory learning instead of passive entertainment.

Participants can design their own three, four, or seven day program from over eighty classes and activities. Fitness and sports enthusiasts can attend aerobic training classes, receive personalized golf and tennis instruction, learn optimal cooking and eating guidelines, and participate in new physical challenges such as rock climbing. Participants can visit with Disney architecture, engineering, and gardening experts to learn how to improve their own outdoor and indoor environments. Writers, athletes, chefs, filmmakers, dancers, and musicians hold special workshops to encourage participants' creativity.

Deluxe bungalow or townhouse accommodations house participants. Amenities include a full-service spa, gourmet restaurant, tennis, golf, and swimming pools.

COST:

Walt Disney Travel Company
7100 Municipal Drive
Orlando, FL 32819

 (800) 496-6337
www2.disney.com/DisneyWorld/DisneyInstitute

12

Duck Cove Retreat

Holistic getaways for women are offered May through October. The "On Your Own" option allows participants to design their own stays for a weekend or a week. Up to twenty women can be accommodated for this type of stay. They cook their own meals and plan their daily activities (such as meditation, yoga, swimming, walks along the beach, mountain climbing, and musseling). The "Planned Weekends" held a few times throughout the summer have planned activities led by experienced facilitators. These typically include hiking, biking, meditation, body awareness exercises, and massage instruction.

Duck Cove Retreat is located on the ocean on Mt. Desert Island in Maine (four miles from Acadia National Park).

Participants share communal living quarters in a renovated barn or may camp out in a tent (their own or one loaned by Duck Cove Retreat). Vegetarian meals are served or participants can prepare their own.

COST: 💲 (Partial scholarships are available for those with need.)

(mid-June to mid-September)
Duck Cove Retreat
West Tremont, ME 04690

 (207) 244-9079

(mid-September to mid-June)
Duck Cove Retreat
7A Walnut Avenue
Cambridge, MA 02140

 (617) 864-2372

ELAT CHAYIM

Elat Chayim is a retreat center which helps persons make new, more personal connections to Judaism. Although many of their courses draw from Jewish tradition, persons of any religious beliefs are welcome. The center is committed to incorporating women's experience and spiritual wisdom into their programming. Relevant teachings and practices from other spiritual traditions (such as Zen meditation) are also included.

Program offerings are truly holistic in that they encourage learning and experience in each of the Four Worlds of Kabbalah: the physical world of our bodies and the planet, the emotional world of our feelings and relationships, the intellectual world of our concept of reality, and the spiritual world of striving to be in touch with the underlying unity of everything in the universe.

Examples of recent offerings include:

- **Dancing in the Light of Transformation**
  Traditional Torah study, yoga, meditation, and visualization are used to uncover the hidden light in each participant's body.

- **Get into Your Body for Health and Aliveness**
  The goal is to develop a fuller and healthier life for the body. Activities include hiking, yoga, running, massage, improvisational dancing, breathwork, tennis, basketball, baseball, swimming, and low ropes course work.

- **Healing Your Jewish Self**
  A variety of physical, psychotherapeutic, learning, and spiritual approaches are used to explore the meaning of being Jewish. Participants work towards allowing Judaism to become a greater source of personal strength and joy.

- **Writing Our Own Stories**
  Through short lectures, writing assignments, readings, and visualization, participants learn to capture their life experiences and spiritual journeys on paper.

- **Mourning into Dancing**
  Music, movement, creative writing, and other expressive techniques are used to help participants deal with transition or loss (whether anticipated, recent, or from long ago).

- **Judaic Art: A Journey of Color, Spirit, and Form**
  Jewish texts are used as an inspiration point for work with a variety of art forms to enable participants to express their innermost Jewish selves.

Most programs are for a week, but there are some shorter programs of three to four days (usually over a weekend).

Participants stay in double occupancy rooms. There are a few private baths. Three kosher vegetarian meals are served daily.

The Center is located in the Catskill Mountains two hours north of New York City. Bus service is available. The nearest airport is Newburgh, New York (fifty minutes away).

Amenities include hiking trails, pool, Jacuzzi, volleyball, and tennis courts.

COST: (some financial assistance may be available)

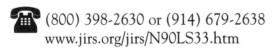 Elat Chayim
P.O. Box 127
Woodstock, NY 12498

(800) 398-2630 or (914) 679-2638
www.jirs.org/jirs/N90LS33.htm

15

Esalen Institute

Since 1962, Esalen has been a leading educational center for work in the humanities and sciences that promotes human values and potentials. It continues to be one of the leading holistic centers in the United States. Numerous workshops are offered throughout the year.

Examples of recent workshops include:

The Arts/Creativity

- **For Adults Who Always Wanted to Play the Violin and Never Have (five days)**
  Movement, music, and rhythm exercises as well as music meditation and visualization allow participants to increase their awareness of how it feels to learn a new skill and to acquire a little musicmaking ability.

- **Living Dance (five days)**
  Participants create dance and movement from their own lives, deepening their life experience through art expression. Both structured practice and spontaneous group interactions are used, along with visualizations, music, and outdoor environments to renew, inspire, teach, and heal.

- **Film and the Remembering of Love (five days)**
  Eight feature films which illustrate the many types of love are viewed and discussed. Participants are assisted in remembering their own loves so that they can integrate these experiences into their present lives.

- **Finding Your Way with Expressive Play: Awakening the Creative Spirit (five days)**
  Through structured exercises and individual and group processes, participants learn about who they are and who they want to become. Included are drawing, writing, storytelling, dance, and movement activities.

BIOFEEDBACK/HYPNOSIS

- **The Awakened Mind: Brainwave Training (three days)**
Techniques for brainwave development and management (such as meditation, visualization, and psychophysiological relaxation) are learned. The focus is on their use for enhanced creativity, mental flexibility, self-healing, problem-solving, and spiritual development.

BUSINESS WORKPLACE

- **Rekindling the Spirit (three days)**
Creative exercises and group sharing enable participants to confront and dissolve major blocks to rewarding work. People who are beginning new careers, thinking about changing careers, or unhappy at work can all benefit from this program.

CHILDREN/FAMILIES/EDUCATION

- **Creating a Workable Stepfamily (five days)**
Gestalt, group process, art, psychodrama, conflict resolution, and communication enhancement activities help create a loving and flexible family structure. While most of the activities are for all family members, a few are for couples/parents only (with concurrent activities for children).

CONTEMPLATIVE/SPIRITUAL & RELIGIOUS STUDIES

- **Living a Spiritual Life in a Practical World (five days)**
Rather than teaching a specific religion or ism, this workshop integrates a variety of spiritual practices such as meditation along with breath and sensory exercises to practice being present and living in the moment. The goal is to restore the natural balance of body, mind, and spirit and realize the aliveness that is our birthright.

- **The Way of the Orisa (five days)**
Ancient African philosophy and rituals focusing on the Orisa (nature) provide followers with practical instructions for improving their everyday lives as well as developing a

17

deep spirituality. The focus is on connecting the energies of the universe with our own personal human energy.

DREAMS

- **Dream Teachings (three days)**
  The workshop incorporates meditation, gestalt, dance, dream recall, dream body awareness, sharing dreams with group members, and drawing dream mandalas. The goal is to show how the true self can be revealed through dreams.

ECOLOGY/SOCIAL RESPONSIBILITY

- **Building in a Sacred Way (three days)**
  The focus is on building and transforming homes and communities from a spiritual base, re-establishing a sense of honor, respect, and value. The modern application of feng-shui (a Chinese philosophy and practice involving the energy actions of people and places) is explored.

HEALTH/HEALING

- **Managing Your Stress, Your Heart, and Your Life (three days)**
  Based on the principles and techniques of Dr. Dean Ornish, this workshop uses many approaches, including diet, exercise, stretching, progressive relaxation, breathing practices, meditation, visualization, and group discussion to help participants transfer optimal health habits into every aspect of everyday life.

- **Spiritual Dimensions of Healing (five days)**
  The workshop teaches both theoretical and practical tools to awaken the healer within. It includes self-healing methods such as opening the energy centers (chakras), communicating with the body, and guided healing imagery, as well as techniques to work with others in a healing capacity (such as laying on hands and psychic healing).

INTEGRAL PRACTICES

- **Experiencing Esalen (three days)**
Designed as an introduction to the practices of Esalen for first-time participants or those who have not attended recently, the workshop's emphasis is on discovering approaches to self-awareness that work best for each individual participant. Exploratory activities include meditation, sensory awareness, gestalt practice, group process, art, movement, and massage.

INTUITIVE DEVELOPMENT

- **Intuition and the Dance of Attention (three days)**
By shifting attention in very precise ways, participants enhance their awareness and reclaim their intuitive powers in all areas of their lives—personal, professional, and spiritual. Techniques to develop intuitive styles include meditation, sensing practices, refined touch, aikido, and Feldenkrais movement activities.

MARTIAL ARTS/YOGA/SPORT

- **Golf in the Kingdom: An Exploration of the Inner Game (five days)**
The game of golf can enhance the journey of self-discovery and reflect issues in other areas of life (such as self-confidence, fear, trust, discipline, and awareness). This workshop applies principles from psychosynthesis and gestalt in a classroom setting as well as allowing participants to practice their new skills and insights on two days of field trips to golf courses on the Monterey Peninsula.

- **The Clean Cut: The Art of Bokken (three days)**
Participants learn to use the Japanese wooden sword or bokken in noncompetitive and noncombative sword work/play. They learn to cut away their own demons (fear, anger, hesitation, and doubt) and bring together mind, body, and spirit.

19

PHILOSOPHICAL INQUIRY/INTELLECTUAL PLAY

- **The Ten Great Questions of Life (three days)**
  Questions such as "Why do we suffer?" "How should we live?" and "What can we hope for?" are explored. Participants learn how great philosophers throughout the ages have responded to these questions and formulate some of their own responses in the search for life's meaning.

PROFESSIONAL GROWTH

- **Healing the Healer: Self-Care for Health Care Professionals (three days)**
  Professional helpers must learn to effectively process fear, sorrow, and resentment in order to remain joyful and healthy. Participants in this workshop share stories from the world of healthcare, in addition to viewing and listening to recorded material as a means of developing or enhancing effective strategies for personal self-care.

PSYCHOLOGICAL/TRANSPERSONAL PROCESS

- **Melting the Frozen Heart (three days)**
  This workshop helps participants take a break from their self-created defense mechanisms and rigid patterns of thinking, feeling, and behaving. Through the use of body awareness, breathing, creative expression, and dyadic exercises, the layers covering hearts and eyes can be gently lifted as participants stop being who they think they have to be and develop the process of who they might become.

- **Accepting Life's Transitions: Letting Go—Moving On (three days)**
  Participants learn how to help complete the past, be open to the present, and create a future. Rather than fearing or avoiding the inevitable changes and transitions in life, participants discover that transitions can be enjoyed and used as growth-promoting opportunities. Intense body work, risk-taking, gestalt imagery, dance, and meditation are explored as supportive measures in times of transition.

- **Courage (five days)**
  Demons such as perfectionism, guilt, avoidance, shame, despair, and failure rob us from experiencing the fullness of life. Participants are given support to help recognize and confront their personal demons through drawing, dance, meditation, gestalt practice, dream work, and bioenergetics.

- **Handwriting Patterns: Possibilities for Healing and Change (five days)**
  This workshop goes beyond conventional handwriting analysis to focus on altering specific writing patterns as a means of restructuring and unlearning old beliefs and imprinting new ones that can expand our potential. Through applied graphotherapy, participants learn to identify both limiting and expansive patterns in their writing and are given personalized stroke or letter changes that reinforce self-esteem and uncover hidden talents and abilities.

RELATIONSHIP/COMMUNICATION

- **A Workshop for Couples: Independence & Intimacy (three days)**
  In a supportive environment offering experiential process drawn from gestalt, Reichian work, dance, imagery, and meditation, couples learn to take risks to improve their communication and intimacy. Ways to begin healing past hurts that create distance and reclaim the unspoken expectations they project on each other are also addressed.

- **Essential Peacemaking: Women and Men (three days)**
  Participants (male and female, couples and individuals) work to heal past and present hurts and miscommunications and learn how to really listen to each other. The goal is to find a common language between the sexes.

- **Relationships: Letting Go—Moving On (five days)**
  All relationships are the focus of this workshop: family, friends, co-workers, lovers, and partners. Participants learn to recognize dysfunctional patterns carried from past relationships into current ones and to create new ways to relate in the moment to themselves, others, and work.

21

RITUAL/SHAMANISM/ANTHROPOLOGY

- **The Medicine Wheel Way (five days)**
  Native American Medicine Wheel ceremonies and teachings are explored as resources for personal growth and healing. Participants embark on a process of self-development and deepen their relationship with the natural world by learning the wheel, making medicine pouches, drumming, rattling, chanting, and using the shamanic journey method for finding power animals and spiritual teachers.

- **The Art of Ceremony (three days)**
  This workshop offers experiential exercises in prayer, meditation, and ceremony as a means of connecting the physical world to the spiritual realms. The focus is on practical approaches to living a life which celebrates Mother Earth spirituality.

SOMATICS

- **Freeing Our Bodies/Our Selves Through Movement: A Feldenkrais Approach (three days)**
  Soft, easy, gentle movements are used to increase body awareness and to improve the ease and ability of movement. Special emphasis is placed on the difficulties of movement that arise from chronic conditions such as lower back and neck pain, tension in the neck and shoulders, and knee injuries.

- **Weekend Massage Intensive (three days)**
  Participants learn basic techniques for giving a full-body massage. Fundamental elements of bodywork, such as breath awareness, grounding, movement, quality of touch, and stress reduction, are also incorporated into the workshop.

- **Reinhabiting Your Body: An Experience in Authentic Movement (three days)**
  Body and psyche are bridged through expressive movement. Each participant's own inner dance is explored as a means of unlocking dysfunctional images of the self which can translate into painful or dissatisfying ways of living.

WILDERNESS

- **Big Sur Wilderness Experience (either three or five days)**
  Participants enjoy hikes of three to ten miles daily through the natural beauty of the Big Sur backcountry while using Esalen as a base camp. Basic outdoor skills such as map reading and minimum impact concepts are taught so that participants can explore the wilderness on their own after these outings.

WOMEN'S/MEN'S STUDIES

- **Women's Wisdom (five days)**
  Through words, silence, drawing, movement, yoga, and ritual, participants learn to reclaim women's wisdom. Legacies handed down from our mothers and grandmothers are explored, as well as images of ancient goddesses.

- **The Myth of Male Power (three days)**
  Participants examine male power and powerlessness as a means of helping the sexes better understand each other. Discussions and role-playing reveal the ways that society molds the other sex's psyche and causes communication barriers.

Work study programs are available for persons who desire a much greater involvement with the Esalen community at a lower expense. Participants work thirty-two hours a week in the kitchen, garden, farm, housekeeping, maintenance, or grounds departments while attending evening and weekend intensive sessions exploring different practices and approaches to personal growth such as dance, music, imagery, meditation, brainwave training, and massage.

Participants stay in shared housing with two or more persons per room. Bathrooms are shared in some cases. Three meals a day are served, with many of the vegetables and herbs from Esalen's organic garden.

Esalen is 300 miles north of Los Angeles and 175 miles south of San Francisco. It is situated directly over the Pacific. Van service from the Monterey Greyhound and Airport (about forty-five miles north of Esalen) is available for a small additional fee.

The property has natural hot springs, as well as a swimming pool and massage area. Swimsuits are optional in all these areas.

COST: (some scholarship assistance is available in exchange for a work commitment—usually in housekeeping)

 Esalen Institute
Highway 1
Big Sur, CA 93920-9616

(408) 667-3000
www.esalen.org

FEATHERED PIPE RANCH

Native Americans consider the Feathered Pipe to symbolize connection with the circle of life and the Great Spirit. The Feathered Pipe Ranch lives up to this meaning by providing programs that promote health, happiness, and positive change. The truths that are found in all traditions are embraced. Intimacy with Nature and Spirit is encouraged by the programming and setting.

Eight day programs are offered in the spring and summer. Recent offerings have included:

- **Your Work as Spiritual Practice**
  Presentation, dialogue, and practical exercises enhance personal possibilities and provide tools to help manifest creativity in the world of work.

- **Rhythm Exploration & Drum Building**
  Participants build their own drums and investigate the potentials of sound and rhythm. They discover their inner rhythms as they connect to each other and with nature.

- **Embracing Yoga**
  Both beginners and advanced practitioners are assisted in connecting the principles of yoga with the process of daily living.

- **Astrology Intensive**
  A psychological approach to astrology helps participants understand *why* things happen rather than just on what will happen.

- **Natural Health, Natural Medicine**
  A physician who exclusively uses natural medicine lectures about vitamins, herbs, exercise, breathing, and visualization.

- **Women's Wisdom**
  Female wisdom and spirituality is explored. By going inward through myth and inner journeying, participants discover the "trusting child with a sense of wonder, the grown woman who is a choicemaker, and the wise woman aware of the sacred dimension of ordinary life."

Similar programs during the winter are available at resorts in San Salvador, Bahamas, and Tulum, Mexico.

Most participants stay in dormitory-style accommodations. A few private or semi-private rooms are available. Camping out in a tepee, tent, or yurt is available. Mostly vegetarian meals are served.

Amenities include hot tubs, saunas, and massage therapy. There are also one day rafting trips down the Montana River or horseback rides into the foothills of the Rocky Mountains.

The Ranch is located in the Northern Rockies of Montana. Van service is available from the airport or bus station in Helena.

COST: (some scholarships are available for those in need of financial assistance)

 The Feathered Pipe Ranch
Box 1682
Helena, MT 59624

☎ (406) 442-8196

FINDHORN FOUNDATION

Findhorn is an intentional community of about 350 persons who study, work, and live together. There is no formal doctrine or creed, but all members of the community are dedicated to planetary transformation. By establishing and enriching a conscious connection with Spirit, each individual contributes to the creation of a new civilization both within the immediate community and throughout the world at large.

Holistic and spiritual education is available to visiting guests as well as members of the community. Most programs are a week in length; a few are offered on the weekends and one lasts twelve weeks.

Before taking part in other workshops and courses, first-time visitors are asked to participate in an Experience Week. Applicants must write a letter describing themselves, their spiritual backgrounds, and reasons for wanting to visit. Those who are accepted spend part of the week by working in the kitchens, gardens, maintenance, and other departments. It is believed that participants can learn spiritual lessons through this work. The rest of the time is spent in activities such as meditation, Sacred Dance, games, and a nature outing.

Once the Experience Week is completed, participants can attend such workshops as:

- **Returning to the Source (one week)**
  Through personal stories, the arts, and meditation, women over the age of thirty-five explore the meaning of aging and connect with their innate creativity.

- **Massage: A Healing Art (two weeks)**
  The course includes basic massage techniques, the use of essential oils in massage, reflexology, and aspects of spiritual healing.

- **The Essentials of Psychosynthesis (one week)**
  As a humanistic psychology, psychosynthesis focuses on

human potential and addresses the value of past experiences. It acknowledges both hopes and dreams as well as difficulties. Techniques and exercises include visualization, meditation, drawing, movement, and individual and group therapy.

- **Essence of Arts in Community (twelve weeks)**
  Participants experience community in depth as they explore a variety of arts such as contemporary dance, creative writing, improvisational drama, mask play, painting, pottery, sacred dance, and singing. Projects are created as a group.

- **The Child Within (one week)**
  Art media and exercises such as guided imagery and role-playing are used to identify the needs and wants that were not met in childhood. Participants learn to take responsibility for fulfilling these needs themselves as adults.

Participants stay in shared accommodations in dormitories or motor homes. Three vegetarian meals are served daily.

Findhorn is located in northeast Scotland. There are planes and trains from London to Inverness (about twenty-five miles away, with available taxi service).

COST: (fees are on a sliding scale depending on ability to pay)

 Findhorn Foundation
The Park, Findhorn
Forres IV36 OTZ
Scotland

(01309) 690311 General Inquiries
(01309) 673655 Accomodations
www.findhorn.org

HEARTWOOD INSTITUTE

Although primarily a vocational school providing training in the healing arts (such as massage therapy, hypnotherapy, and addiction counseling), Heartwood offers a number of intensives for persons who want to enhance their personal growth and spiritual development. Examples of past weekend and weeklong programs include:

- **Loving Touch**
  A weekend for couples to explore the use of massage as a tool to deepen their relationship.

- **Creating Joy in Your Relationships**
  Weekend training examining the barriers that block the joy in relationships and learning how to dissolve these barriers.

- **Healing with Awareness and Whole Foods**
  A six-day retreat which includes dietary healing with raw and organic vegetarian foods, meditation, T'ai Chi movement, and Zen Shiatsu acupressure.

- **Annual Women's Gathering**
  A weekend experience offered by women for women to celebrate life, renew rituals, and worship the Goddess using touch, movement, song, meditation, and prayer.

- **Spirit and Nature**
  A weekend of physical and spiritual purification through Native American prayers and communion with Nature.

Participants who do not wish to enroll in structured programming may develop an individualized wellness retreat. Private sessions may be arranged with any of Heartwood's practitioners in massage, Oriental arts, hypnotherapy, breathwork, nutritional and holistic counseling, and astrology.

Heartwood is 200 miles north of San Francisco. Greyhound buses can take participants to Garberville (about an hour away) where Heartwood staff will pick them up. The campus is set on 240 acres of rolling mountains, meadows, and forests.

The setting is rustic and serene, with moderate temperatures throughout the year.

Participants stay in private or shared guest rooms (with shared bathrooms). Campsites are also available. An outdoor hot tub, sauna, and pool comprise the recreational facilities. The food is primarily organic and vegetarian.

Heartwood's intent of acting as a catalyst for planetary healing through personal transformation enables individuals to enjoy a spiritual pathway to wholeness based on sharing and growing as a community.

COST:  (financial assistance available for individuals who demonstrate need)

 Heartwood Institute
220 Harmony Lane
Garberville, CA 95542

(707) 923-5000
www.heartwoodinstitute.com

HIMALAYAN INSTITUTE

The Himalayan Institute offers a variety of programs through-out the year in holistic health, hatha yoga, meditation, Eastern philosophy, psychology, and self-development. It strives to pro-vide an environment of "gentle inner progress." By combining the best knowledge and practices of the East and West, pro-grams assist participants in physical, mental, and spiritual growth.

Examples of past seminars and workshops include:

- **Self-Mastery: Wisdom Path to Fearlessness**
  Self-knowledge and self-discipline are combined to allow participants to take command of their inner resources. Wisdom from samurai and the great yoga masters assists in learning how to calm personal fears and insecurities.

- **Herbs, Cleansing, and Fasting**
  Herbal preparations from the Ayurvedic, Chinese, and American traditions are presented and discussed. A one-day juice fast is optional.

- **Science of Breath**
  The focus is on the anatomy and physiology of breathing. Ancient breathing exercises (pranayama) enable partici-pants to reduce stress and increase concentration.

- **Transition to Vegetarianism**
  Participants learn the elements of a healthy vegetarian diet. Guidelines for changing one's dietary program are presented.

- **Overcoming Habits and Addictions**
  Participants discover the personality factors, emotional needs, and psychological processes that create and maintain harmful habits. Destructive habits are replaced with those that are more conducive to health and self-expansion.

While there are many weekend courses, there are also medita-tion retreats for seven or ten days, and the monthlong Spiritual Unfoldment and Total Well-Being Residential Program which includes four hours of community service each day, yoga classes, breathing and relaxation sessions, and courses.

The Institute is located in a wooded area of northeastern Pennsylvania within the Pocono Mountains (three to four hours by car from New York City or Philadelphia). There is bus service from the Port Authority in Manhattan to downtown Honesdale (with taxi service available to the Institute).

Recreational activities include hiking, swimming, biking, tennis, skiing, and skating.

Participants stay in single, double, or dormitory rooms. There are no private bathrooms. Vegetarian meals are served.

COST:

 Himalayan Institute
RR1, Box 400
Honesdale, PA 18431

☎ (800) 822-4547 or (717) 253-5551
www.himalayaninstitute.org

HOLLYHOCK HOLISTIC ISLAND RETREAT

Hollyhock offers a number of interesting workshops through-out the spring, summer, and fall. Courses vary in content and length (two to five days), but the central theme is improving one's life through involvement in the arts, enhanced relation-ships, spirituality, and healing of the mind, body, and soul.

Unlike arts and crafts schools which stress artistic achievement and the finished product, Hollyhock arts courses focus on the intrinsic fulfillment of working with the hands and emphasize the process rather than the product. Some of the past arts workshops have included singing, music, basket weaving, pho-tography, creative writing, painting, paper making, wood carv-ing, and sculpture.

Workshops dealing with relationships range from parenting skills to mother-daughter relationships to weekend retreats for couples.

The spiritual workshops can range from Tibetan Buddhism to shamanism (using power objects, animals, and rituals to uncov-er personal myths).

Healing workshops have addressed adult children of alcoholics, dreams, and relaxation through breathing, yoga, meditation, reflexology, "silent communication," creative imagery, affirma-tions, self-esteem, and energy balancing.

All workshops are highly interactive, fully involving the par-ticipants. While there are some lectures, there are also many exercises, games, discussions, and independent study periods, as well as psychodrama, guided imagery, play, storytelling, music, and ritual.

Unstructured retreats are also available where guests can enjoy the amenities of the Hollyhock Holistic Island Retreat without taking a workshop. In-residence artists and health professionals can work with retreat guests in private sessions focusing on health or artistic expression.

Extracurricular activities for all Hollyhock guests include yoga, meditation, massage, reflexology, and acupressure. Hollyhock's naturalist leads morning bird walks, evening owling expeditions, tidal tours, stargazing, cruises, and walks to archaeological sites.

Hollyhock's forty-eight acres of forest, beachfront, gardens, and orchards are located on Cortes Island in British Columbia. This island is known for its rich marine life (including sea lions, otters, and porpoises), more than 220 species of birds, and forests containing fir, cedar, pine, maple, wild berries, mushrooms, and wildflowers.

Guests stay in semi-private dormitory-style accommodations. There are a few private rooms available. Space for tents is also available. Smoking is not allowed in any of the buildings. Vegetarian and seafood cuisine is served buffet-style in the lodge.

The island (which is one hundred miles north of Vancouver) can be reached by car and ferry from Vancouver or by air from Vancouver or Seattle to Campbell River (where a shuttle service goes from the airport to the Cortes Island ferry terminal). There are also float plane services direct to the island from Vancouver and Seattle.

COST:

Hollyhock Holistic Island Retreat
Box 127, Manson's Landing
Cortes Island, BC
Canada VOP 1KO
www.hollyhock.bc.ca

INFINITE POSSIBILITIES SEMINARS

"This week changed my life....I have already seen results of renewed energy and feelings of joy. I feel connected to my life again—not just a passenger on a roller coaster controlled by others."

—*Infinite Possibilities participant*

Optimal health, as described in Dr. Deepak Chopra's books (*Ageless Body, Timeless Mind; Quantum Healing; and Perfect Health: A Complete Mind-Body Guide*) is more than the absence of disease; it is a state of dynamic harmony and balance between mind, body, spirit, and environment. Instead of focusing on specific diseases, the imbalances which are the source of disease are identified and corrected. Meditation, massage, diet, and behavioral changes help to access inner healing potential. Dr. Chopra teaches a number of workshops and seminars that promote this philosophy of well-being.

Primordial Sound Meditation is a two-day course focusing on an ancient method of mantra, or sound, meditation that originated in India. Individually selected primordial sounds are used to create a quiet resonance in the mind for mind/body balance and stress relief.

Journey to the Boundless, a three-day weekend course, shows participants that their true nature is boundless rather than bounded. It uses meditation, yoga, and education about natural solutions to weight control, chronic fatigue, and insomnia. Current Western scientific principles are merged with Ayurvedic (ancient Indian science of healing) techniques. Participants develop strategies for enhancing spirituality, conquering stress, and improving health, strength, and energy.

The Seduction of Spirit program, at seven days, provides a foundation for understanding how connection with the Spirit is the basis of mind/body balance. To access the deepest level of being and promote the flow of energy, primordial sound meditation is used, along with subtle body cleansing exercises to identify and eliminate emotional pain and blockages. Advanced psychophysiological techniques (Sutra meditation) and pranayama (yogic breathing) activate the expansive qualities of the heart, mind, and spirit. Tantra (the ancient system which seeks to find spirituality in every aspect of life) is included so that participants can explore the bridge between sexuality and spirituality. Daily and seasonal Ayurvedic routines are explained and suggestions given for diet, massage, exercise, and lifestyle changes.

The courses are given in hotels throughout the country. Participants are responsible for making their own accommodations and for most meals.

COST:

Infinite Possibilities Seminars
P.O. Box 1088
Sudbury, MA 01776

 (800) 757-8897

INTERFACE

As a holistic education center, Interface has presented a wide range of courses, workshops, and conferences since 1975. Their mission is "to explore those trends in health, personal growth, science, and religion which excite and encourage us to seek new ways of living, expand personal horizons, and join with others to help create a better world."

Interface offers programs throughout the year. Among the recent offerings of one to three day courses (usually over the weekend) are:

BODY

- **Dance of Tennis (two days)**
  Participants learn a new way of playing tennis—one that transforms the "opponent" into a dance partner as the game becomes a celebration of life rather than intense competition. Techniques are used from gestalt, psychosynthesis, self-hypnosis, neurolinguistic programming, creative dance, hatha yoga, and t'ai chi.

- **Running Whole and Healthy (one day)**
  Personal attention is provided by a movement therapist and coach/trainer to enable participants to run with an improved sense of balance, alignment, and posture.

- **TMJ: A Feldenkrais Approach (two days)**
  Participants learn Feldenkrais movement exercises to repattern the muscular tension associated with temperomandibular joint syndrome and decrease facial, jaw, and tooth pain, headaches, and stiffness in neck and shoulders.

CREATIVE ARTS

- **The Artist's Way: Breaking Through Creative Blocks (two days)**
  The workshop enables participants to move beyond pain and creative constriction and assists in the process of creative recovery and discovery. Participants learn ways to dissolve

fear, remove emotional scar tissue, and strengthen their spirituality as a means of moving into a richer and more creative life.

- **Drawing: The Art of Seeing (three days)**
  The exercises in this workshop teach how to shift perception to the spatially-oriented right hemisphere of the brain, as well as seeing and drawing contour, shape, negative space, proportion, perspective, shadow/light, texture, and composition. Self-expression is facilitated through the teaching.

- **Journal Writing as a Spiritual Quest (one day)**
  Intended for both new and experienced journal writers, this workshop focuses on writing as a spiritual practice. Lecture, group discussion, meditation, and private writing time are incorporated.

COMPLEMENTARY MEDICINES

- **Sacred Medicines: Healing Words, Rituals, and Spiritual Optimism (three days)**
  Experiential exercises (including meditation, guided visualization, and individual/group prayer) are used to demonstrate the connection between health, healing, and the human spirit.

- **Cancer and Healing (two days)**
  Topics include self-hypnosis and guided imagery, the doctor/patient relationship, the effect of psychotherapy and lifestyle changes on the outcome of cancer, and a survivor's panel discussion.

- **How Food Affects Your Mood (two days)**
  The focus is on the relationship between food and health/healing. Participants learn how to use diet to promote optimal health, balance moods, and heal ailments such as headaches, fevers, colds, skin problems, and digestive disorders.

RELATIONSHIPS

- **Healthy Boundaries (two days)**
  Participants learn how to have healthy boundaries and set

personal limits which enhance the sense of self. Optimal external and internal boundaries (rather than having no boundaries at all or having a rigid system of walls) can improve relationships and prevents victim/offender issues.

- **Healing the Heart (two days)**
  This workshop shows how to mend wounded feelings that may be carried from past relationships and become more receptive to current relationships. When the heart is healed and opened, relationships can become more intimate and satisfying.

- **Sexuality and Intimacy for Couples (one day)**
  Couples learn how to communicate more freely about their feelings and needs while discovering new ways to experience sexuality and sexual energy. Methods of integrating touching, music, play, and fantasy into sexuality are discussed.

SPIRITUAL INQUIRY AND PRACTICE

- **A Course in Miracles (one day)**
  This workshop introduces participants to the self-study collection of spiritual teachings which uses Christian terminology but expresses universal truths. Meditation, instruction, discussion, and experiential exercises inspire participants to look within, acknowledge and celebrate their selves, extend love and forgiveness, and let go of fear, anger, and guilt.

- **Chado: The Way of Tea (one day)**
  Participants learn and experience the Japanese tea ceremony as a contemplative and centering art form. The four principles of Tea (Harmony, Respect, Purity, and Tranquility) are taught, along with meditation and haiku writing.

- **A Day of Lovingkindness (one day)**
  The Buddhist practice of Metta (lovingkindness) promotes a loving, compassionate, joyful, and balanced relationship with the self and others. Instruction, discussion, and sitting/walking meditation deepens the feeling of connectedness with the world and reduces any sense of separation.

PSYCHOLOGY/PERSONAL GROWTH

- **Doing What You Love, Loving What You Do (two days)**
  Visioning exercises, meditation, and action planning techniques are used to help participants identify and see personal dreams. Practical action plans can then be developed for connecting with the jobs and organizations that will support these life goals and plans.

- **The High Ropes Course (one day)**
  As participants climb the series of ropes, nets, bridges, and ladders built thirty feet or more above the ground (while attached at all times to a safety line), they acknowledge both fear and strength. The lesson learned is that it's possible to let go of self-imposed fears of being weak or stuck in life.

- **The Inner Child Workshop (one day)**
  Guided exercises, visualizations, drawing, and dyadic work enable participants to develop a relationship with the internalized version of the children they once were. They learn to stop repeating those patterns of behavior learned while growing up which limit full enjoyment of adult life.

WOMEN'S PROGRAMS

- **The Body Language of the Goddess (one day)**
  This workshop redefines women's beauty and strength by immersing participants in ancient Goddess images and finding her body in their own through movement, life-size body drawings, and sharing.

- **Women and Self-Esteem (two days)**
  The focus is on the "three A's" of self-esteem: awareness (ending internal censoring and trusting one's perceptions, needs, and feelings), acceptance (befriending oneself), and assertion (living with a congruence between inner responses and outer actions).

Interface also offers professional development courses for nurses, social workers, and other healers. These range from The

Healing Power of Anger to Responding to the Bereaved to Today's Time Management.

There is no lodging available at Interface, but the staff can recommend nearby bed and breakfasts and guest houses.

Interface is located in Cambridge, Massachusetts. It can be reached by car, train, or bus from Boston or other Massachusetts locations.

COST: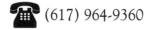

 Interface
55 Wheeler Street
Cambridge, MA 02138-1168

☎ (617) 964-9360

KIRKRIDGE RETREAT AND STUDY CENTER

Although founded by a Presbyterian minister, Kirkridge is a nondenominational center for personal and social transformation. Through presentations, small group sharing, reflection, silence, morning and evening prayers, and hiking, participants can gain nourishment and direction for their personal journeys. Kirkridge extends a special welcome for "outsiders" (with nonconventional choices, lifestyles, or circumstances).

Recent examples of the many year-round retreats, workshops, seminars, and conferences include:

- **A Celebration for Bi-racial/Inter-Ethnic Couples**
  Participants network, vent, and celebrate while learning to insulate their relationships from the interference of others.

- **For the Unemployed**
  The retreat is designed for persons who recently have lost their jobs. It provides the time and space to reflect on the feelings, fears, and hopes that accompany unemployment.

- **Therapeutic Touch: An Experience in Self-Healing**
  This contemporary version of "laying on of hands" facilitates healing in ourselves and others. Participants learn to use it to alleviate pain, reduce anxiety, hasten wound healing, and bring balance to bodily function.

- **A Gathering of Men: Moving Out of Isolation and Into Wholeness**
  Through presentations, storytelling, poetry, meditation, and small group sharing, men are drawn into healing and wholeness.

- **Walking by Faith, Living in Hope: A Retreat for Persons Affected By the HIV/AIDS Crisis**
  Persons with HIV/AIDS, their care-partners, relatives, and friends provide mutual support while sharing joys and sorrows.

- **Examining the Mother/Son Connection**
  Individual participants or mother/adult son pairs explore the

dynamics of the mother-son relationship. Healing and friendship between mothers and sons is promoted.

Most programs are three to four days in length and are held both on weekends and during the week.

Participants share double rooms in lodges and houses on the property. Meals are served buffet style three times a day. Red meat is not served, but fish and fowl are, as well as grains, vegetables, fruits, and low-fat dairy products.

Hiking opportunities on the Appalachian Trail as well as smaller paths and roads are available.

Kirkridge is forty-five minutes away from the nearest airport (ABE serving Allentown, Bethlehem, and Easton, Pennsylvania). There is bus service from Philadelphia and New York City into the nearby town of Stroudsburg (where a taxi can be called).

COST: (some financial assistance may be available)

 Kirkridge Retreat and Study Center
2495 Fox Gap Road
Bangor, PA 18013-6028

☎ (610) 588-1793
www.kirkridge.org

LIVING WATERS

Living Waters is a unique spiritual health spa based on ancient Kabbalistic teachings. Kabbalah (Hebrew for "to receive") is the name given to ancient wisdom teachings that have been received over the centuries by enlightened intellectuals, philosophers, spiritual teachers, and visionaries. It honors a way of thinking, feeling, and being that is totally connected with the Divine in all things. Although Kabbalistic teachings are in the Jewish tradition, Living Waters is open to people of all faiths. The two rabbis who lead the weekends draw from both Eastern and Western traditions.

The weekend includes ancient ceremonies, new rituals, relaxation techniques, and skills for healthful living. Some of the activities are meditation, storytelling, sunrise walks, yoga stretches on the beach, music worship, health talks, meals with guided conscious eating instruction, water aerobics, breathing techniques, and a co-ed mikvah (ritualistic cleansing bath in the ocean).

Participants stay at a beachfront resort hotel in double occupancy rooms in Jupiter Beach, Florida. Vegetarian meals are served.

Weekends are held four to six times throughout the year. Expanded programs of a week in length are sometimes available.

Designed to stimulate the body, heal the mind, and liberate the soul, the weekend enables participants to return home with a greater sense of peace and spirituality. Jewish participants may rediscover their origins while non-Jewish participants may discover truths and practices of another faith which can benefit their own lives.

COST:

 Temple Adath Or/Living Waters
11450 SW 16 Street
Davie, FL 33325

 (954) 476-7466

Mount Madonna Center

Although the Mount Madonna Center is sponsored by a fellowship of yoga enthusiasts, its offerings go far beyond basic yoga courses. The Center offers a wide variety of programs throughout the year. These programs focus on the creative arts and health sciences within a context of spiritual growth. Past programming has included:

- **Healing the Child Within: Recovery and Celebration (weekend)**
  Guided imagery, music, metaphor, dialogue with the historical child, and presentations show participants how to move through and beyond childhood traumas to befriend the child within and live more fully in the present.

- **Couples Renewal Weekend**
  Couples can heal and enhance their relationship through couples meditations, yoga, presentations, and discussions.

- **Summer Retreat for Mothers (weekend)**
  This retreat gives mothers a break in their routines while learning about healthy discipline, maintaining cooperation with fathers and other co-parents, and blending motherhood with womanhood.

- **For Young At Heart Seniors: Yoga and Community (five days)**
  Older participants learn ashtanga yoga (including precepts for daily conduct, postures, and breathing practices) while participating in the 100-member multigenerational residential community at Mount Madonna (including finances, decision making, and personal relations).

- **Touching Spirit (seven days)**
  Participants master self-healing skills while learning how to work with others through the laying on of hands to open the flow of healing energy for enhanced physical, emotional, and mental health.

The Center is located on 355 mountaintop acres of redwood forest overlooking the Monterey Bay in California. Recreational facilities include hiking trails, volleyball, tennis, and basketball courts, gymnasium, swimming lake, and hot tub. Oil massages and steam baths are available at a nominal charge.

Bus service is available from either the San Jose or San Francisco Airports (one to two hours away, respectively). Taxi and limo services will deliver participants directly to the Center.

Participants may camp out in their own tent or van or reside in indoor rooms. There are a few private rooms, but accommodations are for two to seven persons. Vegetarian meals are served cafeteria style.

COST:

Mount Madonna Center
445 Summit Road
Watsonville, CA 95076

(408) 847-0406
www.mountmadonna.org

NAROPA INSTITUTE

As a private liberal arts college offering undergraduate and graduate degrees in the arts, social sciences, and humanities, Naropa emphasizes "contemplative education" which combines intellect and intuition along with training in awareness which integrates mind, body, and spirit. Although founded by a Buddhist scholar, Naropa explores and celebrates teaching from all faiths and disciplines.

During the summer, a variety of intensives, retreats, and seminars are offered to non-degree students. These generally range from three days to two weeks. Recent examples have included:

- **Tibetan Language Seminar (two weeks)**
  Buddhist wisdom can be best understood by hearing and reading it in its language of transmission. The seminar teaches understanding of the Tibetan language and traditions through scriptural study and translation, communication and comprehension skills, and liturgical chanting practice.

- **Honoring the Spiritual Nature of the Child (two days)**
  Participants learn to recognize and assist the unfolding of the spirit of the child through lectures and discussions.

- **Coming Home: Deep Ecology and Native American Perspectives (four days)**
  Natural history, ecopsychology, the systems approach to environmental problems, sociocultural systems, bases for land-use decisions, environmental justice, and place-centered solutions to problems are discussed.

- **The Soul's Theater (five days)**
  Theater games, guided fantasy, free writing, storytelling, and vocal/physical exploration locate the stories, dreams, memories, and voices of each participant, allowing innate creativity and expression to flourish.

- **Sound Sculpture (three days)**
  The healing properties of working with clay are explored as participants create instruments such as drums, flutes, and whistles.

- **Ordinary Leadership: Working Genuinely with Others (three days)**
  Through lecture, discussion, team activities, and meditation, participants learn Eastern perspectives as well as contemporary Western management methods so that they can work more effectively with others.

- **Our Bodies: Myths and Metaphors (five days)**
  Individual and group movement, breath activities, and creative arts exploration enable participants to learn to discriminate between essential messages from their bodies and their body stories (things believed about the physical self that have been inherited from families, cultures, and religions).

Naropa does not have housing accommodations on campus, but there are local hostels, motels, bed and breakfasts, sublet apartments, and camping facilities in Boulder.

COST: 💲

Naropa Institute
2130 Arapahoe Avenue
Boulder, CO 80302

☎ (303) 444-0202
www.naropa.edu

NATURE AWARENESS SCHOOL

Most of us who grew up in urban or suburban settings don't know as much as we would like about nature. We would like to feel more comfortable and connected with the natural world, but are intimidated by our lack of experience and education in outdoor living. To remedy this situation, consider a crash course at the Nature Awareness School.

Participation in Nature Awareness programs teaches students how to live simply and in harmony with the natural environment. Confidence in outdoor living enables students to enjoy the gifts provided by nature and allows escape from the worries of modern life. In addition to technical skills, inner awareness and insight are developed.

The Nature Awareness Week provides mostly hands-on experiential education in the following areas:

- **Survival Skills**
  Students learn how to survive in the outdoors with no food, water, shelter, or fire by constructing emergency and long-term shelters, discovering and using safe drinking water and wild edible and medicinal plants, and constructing tools and utilitarian items.

- **Nature Observation and Awareness**
  Students learn to see, hear, feel, and observe nature on a deep level. The emphasis is on silent stalking to enable close-up observation of animals.

- **Tracking**
  This segment focuses on identifying, "reading," and following animal tracks.

- **Native American Philosophies**
  Native American philosophies and ceremonies such as the Sweat Lodge and the Sacred Medicine Pipe further students' appreciation of nature.

An abbreviated weekend of the Nature Awareness week is available, as are specialized courses in tracking, earth philosophy, edible wild plants, tanning (deer skins into cured leather), winter awareness, and advanced nature awareness.

The school is located on three hundred acres in the Blue Ridge Mountains of Virginia.

Beginners and experienced outdoor persons can be accommodated.

Students sleep on fresh straw inside Native American-style shelters or in a heated sleeping loft. Meals (including a vegetarian option) are provided.

COST:

 Nature Awareness School
P.O. Box 219
Lyndhurst, VA 22952

☎ (540) 377-6068
www.smartsubmit.com/nature/nac2.html

NEW YORK OPEN CENTER

Unlike most of the holistic centers which are located in rural areas, the Open Center is in a very urban environment: lower Manhattan. It addresses the inner and outer—intellectual and the physical—aspects of life just like the others, but with the added excitement of New York City. For over ten years, they've offered alternative learning experiences in psychology, ecology, the arts, science, medicine, bodywork, and contemplation.

Courses focusing on the body include bodywork and movement, Chinese health and martial practices, holistic health, nutrition and herbs, and yoga. Representative one day and weekend workshops include:

- **Beyond Basketball (weekend)**
  Through both half-court and full-court games, lectures, and videos, male and female participants learn to play better hoops.

- **Massage for Couples (one day)**
  Lectures and hands-on practice enable participants to learn a variety of massage techniques for pleasure and healing.

- **Wherever You Go, There You Are (one day)**
  Group discussion, lectures, and practice enable participants to learn mindful meditation to help with chronic pain and stress-related disorders.

- **Essential Oils for Emotional and Physical Health (one day)**
  This hands-on workshop shows how to use the fragrances of natural essential oils from flowers, roots, herbs, and seeds to enhance and balance physical, emotional, and intellectual well-being.

- **Love and Heal Yourself (weekend)**
  Participants learn to reveal the light within, heal wounds, and discover their creative nature through conscious breathing and other healing techniques.

The psychological courses tackle issues of creativity, self-expression, self-development, relationships, gay and lesbian being, sexuality, and female concerns. Past courses have included:

- **Getting Through the Day (one day)**
  Adults who were hurt as children (by growing up in homes that were chaotic, neglectful, addictive, or abusive) learn to manage their feelings in effective, non-destructive ways.

- **Winter and Renewal (one day)**
  Deep process work, guided imagery, expressive release, and dialogue enable participants to understand and accept our connection to nature's cycles, appreciate winter's lessons of barrenness and loss, and prepare for spring's renewal.

- **Intensive Journal Method (weekend)**
  Participants deepen their connection to their inner selves through contemplative writing and systematic introspection.

- **Overcoming Eating Obsessions (weekend)**
  Inner-child work to reclaim the self, guided imagery, group discussions, and exercises enable men and women with eating disorders (anorexia, bulimia, compulsive eating, and obesity) to see the relationship between shame, self-abuse, and eating issues, and establish a framework for healing.

- **A Couple's Retreat (weekend)**
  All couples (married or unmarried, recent or long-term, heterosexual, gay, or lesbian) can increase the fun, romance, communication, and compassion of their relationship by attending this retreat in upstate New York.

- **Menopause: A Turning Point and a Liberation (one day)**
  Women can learn how menopause affects physical, spiritual, mental, emotional, and psychosexual health and learn how to deal with these changes most effectively.

Courses for the spirit include:

- **A Course in Miracles Intensive (one day)**
  This spiritual psychotherapy helps to relinquish fear and to accept love and joy. Most of the concepts are expressed in

Christian terms, but the course is nondenominational and embraces wisdom from all the world's religions.

- **Meditation Retreat Weekend**
  The emphasis is on practicing specific meditative techniques to enhance the powers of concentration and living in the moment in accordance with Buddhist teachings.

- **The Art of Dying, for the Sake of Living (one day)**
  Participants focus on the process of dying (either facing one's own death or helping another with that transition) while gaining a new perspective on the meaning of life.

Courses in the arts have included:

- **Zen and the Art of Harmonica (one day)**
  Nonmusicians can learn a set of meditational tools that can benefit them in learning to play blues, rock, and classical music on the harmonica.

- **Freeing the Voice—Freeing the Self (weekend)**
  To awaken the pleasure of the voice and liberate our natural eloquence, the workshop uses exercises dealing with physical awareness, relaxation, breathing, the discovery of sound within the body, the connection of emotion to the vibrations of sound, and the circulation of language and experience in open relationship with others.

- **Painting, Drawing, and Meditation (weekend)**
  Even nonartists can be empowered to bring their inner visions (such as dreams, mystical experiences, and fantasy visions) to outer form through exercises to access their creativity.

- **Proprioceptive Writing: Writing From Within the Self (weekend)**
  Practiced to music in twenty-five minute sessions under relaxed and stress-free conditions either in groups or alone, Proprioceptive Writing enables writers, thinkers, and growth-seekers to deepen and expand their abilities of expression and reflection.

Participants are responsible for locating their own housing, as well as recreational activities for the off-hours.

There are also some off-campus programs occasionally offered by the Center. Past examples include weekend and midweek escapes in the Connecticut Berkshires, five-day sailing adventures in Hawaii, seven-day Vision Quests (with a three-day solo fast) in Wyoming and five-day herbal intensives on a farm in upstate New York.

COST: 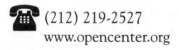 (full or partial scholarships are available for most programs and are awarded on the basis of need)

 New York Open Center, Inc.
83 Spring Street
New York, NY 10012

(212) 219-2527
www.opencenter.org

Oasis Center

Oasis is a holistic educational institution dedicated to exploring the most effective ways of unlocking the dormant human potential in each of us. A variety of workshops and programs are offered throughout the year. Most provide group experiences designed to heighten self-awareness, increase understanding of the ways that others see us, and develop more effective ways of dealing with each other.

Subject areas include health and healing, spirituality and meditation, myth and archetypes, exploration through the arts, personal growth and change, ritual and shamanism, relationship/partnership communication, massage, psychodrama, business, hypnosis and trance, and male/female issues. There are also training programs for professionals in the helping and healing fields.

Examples of past programs include:

- **It's About Time: Restoring a Healthy Relationship to Time (two days)**
  This workshop shows how to understand and strengthen individual natural timing while connecting gracefully to the timing and rhythm of others.

- **Physicians of the Soul (two days)**
  Participants learn how to search for the Self in accordance with the central spiritual teachings of the world: Taoism, Judaism, Christianity, Buddhism, Hinduism, and Islam.

- **Experiencing the Dark Side (one day)**
  Lecture, music, humor, movement, sound, visualization, meditation, and energy awareness exercises enable participants to become aware, appreciate, and embrace their "shadow sides" which are as much a part of their spiritual selves as love, light, and harmony. Participants learn to deal with death, loss, disillusion, and despair.

- **How Scribbles Mean (two days)**
  Through scribbling and drawing with simple materials, par-

ticipants become better acquainted with the messages from their hearts and develop paths for the soul's emergencies.

- **Intensive Journal—Life Experience Workshop**
  Rather than using a passive recording instrument such as a diary or other unstructured methods, the Intensive Journal workbook provides exercises and techniques which enable reconstructing major phases of each participant's life in a non-judgmental way. Insights are developed regarding rela-tionships with key people, career, special interests, and important events and situations. Inner symbolic experiences such as dreams and images are also tapped into as a means of clarifying life meaning.

The Oasis Center can be reached by Chicago rapid transit or bus. Out of town participants are furnished with information about local hotels.

COST: 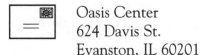 (partial scholarships are available on a limited basis)

Oasis Center
624 Davis St.
Evanston, IL 60201

 (847) 475-7303
www.oasis-center.org

OJAI FOUNDATION

As an educational retreat center, the Ojai Foundation offers both structured groups and individualized experiences to enable personal transformation and growth. The Ojai staff views their land as encouraging "simplicity, silence, creation of sacred space, personal reflection, deep connection with the natural land, and self-renewal."

Scheduled programs focus on ecology and spirituality. Most are held over a weekend or week, while a few last a month. Past programs have included:

- **Meeting the Shadow**
  Led by a clinical psychologist, this weekend program helped participants to examine their shadow side (so-called negative feelings and actions, such as rage, jealousy, lust, lying, blaming, and greed) and defuse these negative emotions, heal relationships, and achieve genuine self-acceptance.

- **Stonepeople Lodge**
  This traditional Native American practice of ceremonial purification enabled participants to cleanse body, mind, and spirit over a weekend and reconnect with the natural world.

- **Singing the World Alive**
  Participants in this week-long workshop investigate the meaning, significance, and performance of story in our lives. The interdisciplinary faculty (storyteller, writer, teacher, anthropologist, and mythologist) helped weave participants' personal stories in a way which enables better understanding of what it means to be human and interdependent with all of nature.

- **Earth As Home—Creation in Balance**
  As a month-long retreat taught by an anthropologist and potter, ample opportunities were provided for exploring personal relationships with the environment and individual creativity.

In addition to structured programs, individuals are allowed to come to the Foundation for up to thirty days of alone time for personal reflection, rest, and meditation. The Ojai staff also offers personalized Vision Quest experiences typically lasting one to five days. Fasting, solitude, meditation, chanting, silence, drumming, medicine wheel teachings, and sweatlodge may be incorporated into the Vision Quest.

The Ojai Foundation is located between Santa Barbara and Ventura (about an hour away from Los Angeles) in a heavily forested area.

The facilities are rustic and simple. Participants bring their own camping gear or can rent a tent. Toilet facilities, hot showers, sinks, and a food preparation area are available. Participants who don't wish to camp out in the semi-wilderness setting may stay in a motel in the town.

COST: ⚙$

Ojai Foundation
P.O. Box 1620
Ojai, CA 93024

 (805) 646-8343
www.ojaifoundatioin.org

OMEGA INSTITUTE FOR HOLISTIC STUDIES

Omega is more than just a retreat center. It's more than just a facility for continued education. It's a new kind of learning community that provides a unique combination of education and vacation. More than ten thousand participants attend workshops and conferences at Omega each year to learn, socialize, and celebrate together.

More than two hundred workshops and conferences are offered each summer and fall at Omega's campus in the countryside of Rhinebeck, New York. The courses are as diverse as the nationally and internationally known faculty who are truly experts in their subject areas. Although some of the workshops are so eclectic that they're hard to classify, they tend to fall into five major areas:

PERSONAL HEALTH AND DEVELOPMENT

- Holistic health courses such as Light and Color Therapy, Food and Healing, Time and Health, Psychology of Illness, Stress Reduction, Breast Cancer Retreat, HIV/AIDS Retreat, and Indian Vegetarian Cooking

- Practitioner training such as Holistic Nursing and Psychotherapy and Meditative Practice; Body-Centered Approaches such as Couples Massage and Body-Mind Centering

- Psychological development courses including Spiritual Advantages of a Painful Childhood, Sexual Fantasies, Reclaiming the Disowned Self, and Midlife Passage

- Recovery workshops such as Advanced Healing for Adult Children of Alcoholics, When Money Is the Drug, Eating Disorders, and Women, Sex and Addiction

- Intuitive Development such as Out-of-Body Experiences and Dreams and Personal Mythology

- Martial Arts and Yoga including Self-Defense Through Martial Arts and Hatha Yoga

GENDER, RELATIONSHIPS, AND FAMILY

- Relationships courses such as Couples Retreat, Mothers and Daughters, Fathers and Daughters, Workshop for Singles, and Men and Their Mothers, Lovers, and Wives
- Parenting workshops including Coparenting After Divorce and Teens and Parents
- Women-only courses such as Self-Esteem for Women, Women and Power, Joy of Self-Loving, Lesbian Retreat, and Women's Rites of Passage
- Men-only courses such as Art As Awareness for Gay Men and Exploring Manhood Through Yoga

ARTS, CREATIVITY, AND SPORTS

- Music workshops including Healing with Great Music, Free Your Singing Voice, and Songwriting Intensive
- Dance/Movement workshops including Modern Dance, African Dance, and Tango
- Theater and Storytelling including Soul of Acting, Healing Power of Theater, and Telling Life Stories
- Fine Arts including Photography, Clay, and Drawing on the Right Side of the Brain
- Writing and Language including Workshop for Poets, Writing the Natural Way, and Immersion Spanish
- Play and Creativity such as Origins of Creativity and Playful Community
- Sports and Fitness including Fly Fishing, Dance of Tennis, Bicycling, Women's Baseball, Basketball, and Tao of Boxing

NATURE AND SOCIETY

- Caring for the Earth including Garden As a Healing Space, Becoming One with Nature, and Hiking
- Society courses such as Diversity Training for Professionals, Healing Racism, and Holistic Education

60

- Work, Business, and Leadership including Art of Empowerment, Workshop for Lawyers, Spirit of Work, and Zen of Business

SPIRITUAL UNDERSTANDING

- Myth and Shamanism including Communicating with the Dead, Inca Medicine Wheel, and Celtic Shamanism
- Spiritual Retreat such as Hindu Tantrism, Heartfulness, Practice of Mindful Living, Meditation for Beginners, and Ancient African Wisdom

Workshops are either two days (weekends) or five days (weekdays).

Winter workshops are held at retreat and conference centers in Virginia, Connecticut, and St. John, U.S. Virgin Islands.

Omega also offers special conferences in New York and other major U.S. cities. Topics may range from A Revolution of Hope (Changing the World From the Inside Out) to Conscious Aging: A Creative and Spiritual Journey.

There are also Omega Journeys which range from a six-day wilderness encounter in the Catskills to twelve days in Thailand.

The Rhinebeck campus is located in New York's Hudson River Valley on eighty acres of woodlands. The grounds feature a Zen meditation garden, flower and organic vegetable garden, and sculptures. Tennis, basketball, and volleyball courts provide recreation, as do the walking and jogging paths and the lake (where participants can canoe, boat, swim, or laze on the beach).

Omega charters its own bus from New York City (about a three hour trip). Participants may drive, take a train, or take a commercial bus, or fly to nearby Stewart (and the take the shuttle to the campus).

61

Housing ranges from campsites to dormitories to cabins with shared or private bath. Natural foods are served (mostly vegetarian, with some fresh fish).

COST: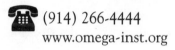

 Omega Institute
260 Lake Drive
Rhinebeck, NY 12572-3121

☎ (914) 266-4444
www.omega-inst.org

REMEMBER THE MAGIC CONFERENCE

"There is a healing quality about these conferences...I may be dealing with my usual struggles, but there is a difference in me, and I think I shall not unchange."

—Remember the Magic participant

For seven days every August, the International Women's Writing Guild holds its "Remember the Magic" summer conference. Although the focus is on writing, the conference is not strictly a writer's workshop as are those included in Chapter 5, *Learning Vacations*. Many of the workshops deal with the nuts and bolts of writing, but there are also a large number that focus on the arts, the body, non-linear knowledge, and personal transformation. The goal of the conference is to create an atmosphere where participants can stretch not just as writers, but as women and people as well.

Every day fifty separate workshops are offered. Examples of recent options in the arts and the body category are:

- Sounding Out Your Feelings: Using Your Own Voice as a Tool for Wellness & Creativity
- Fill Your Body with the Energy of Your Spirit
- Pathway to Freedom: Music and Sound
- Letting the Magic In: 3-Ball Juggling for Writers
- Women Lead the Dance: Waltz, Foxtrot, Swing and Tango
- A Naturalist's Sketchbook: Taking Nature As Your Subject with a #2 Pencil

Offerings in the mythology and non-linear knowledge category have included:

- Drawing on the Spirit: Psychic Exercises for Empowerment
- In the Silence Is Your Source
- The Language of Sacred Symbol
- Living (and Writing) with the Angels

63

Transformation workshops have included:

- A Continuing Journey Toward Spirituality through Writing
- The Sacredness of Self: Writing from Your Heartland
- Li(v)es of Girls and Women
- Women's Journals, Women's Lives
- Writing the Autobiography in Your Own Words: Mothers, Daughters, Grandmothers

There are always numerous workshops on the techniques and business of writing, such as self publishing, finding an agent, poetry, and writing for children.

There are no admissions requirements. The conference is open to all women regardless of professional portfolio.

The conference is held at Skidmore College in Saratoga Springs (three hours north of New York City). Accommodations are in single or double occupancy dormitories. Meals are served cafeteria style. Flights are available into Albany (with taxis available from the airport which is thirty miles away from the college). A scenic train ride from New York City to Saratoga Springs is another option.

Leisure activities on campus include swimming, racquetball, handball, and tennis. The town of Saratoga Springs has mineral springs baths, horse racing, and arts performances.

COST:

 The International Women's Writing Guild
Box 810, Gracie Station
New York, NY 10028

 (212) 737-7536
www.iwwg.com

ROWE CAMP AND CONFERENCE CENTER

"At Rowe, I was able to gather in and free up and let go. This magical place has changed my life."

—Rowe participant

Rowe is loosely affiliated with the Unitarian Universalist religious denomination, but persons of all religious affiliations are welcome. Since 1924, Rowe has been at the forefront of providing holistic educational and spiritual experiences. It provides a nurturing and supportive environment where participants feel free to express their individuality while enjoying being part of a dynamic community. It enables participants to connect with nature, to begin to believe in themselves, to allow laughter to get beyond the usual everyday cares, to experience the "AHA!" of genuine insight, and to discover a purpose in life that is greater than one's personal concerns.

Rowe offers two camps for adults. Their weeklong Liberation Camp allows single adults, couples, and families with children eight years and older to form a lively intergenerational community. In addition to workshops which address emotional, spiritual, physical, and political well-being, there are unlimited opportunities for silliness and spontaneous fun. Special emphasis is placed on understanding and valuing differences (of gender, personality type, sexual orientation, age, race, and ethnic background).

There is programming for children during the day; at night they join the adults. Each year's Liberation Camp is spontaneous and different than any which preceded it, but traditional activities include walking in the woods, swimming, singing, canoeing, telling stories around a campfire, dancing, discussions, and participating in a talent show.

The weeklong Recovery Camp empowers participants with the ability to move forward in their lives and gain the physical, emotional, and spiritual health that may have been missing in

65

the past. Those persons who grew up in dysfunctional families which did not provide a loving and accepting environment can learn new methods of relating to themselves and others. Criteria for participation is the willingness to exchange pain for love and the desire to grow. The loving community is in itself healing, as are the workshops which deal with creativity, self-expression, relationships, spiritual exploration, and body awareness/acceptance. Activities include 12-step meetings, hiking, canoeing, swimming, dancing, and art projects.

Workshops, retreats, and conferences can range from three days to a week throughout the year. Examples of past offerings include:

- **WomenCircles (seven days)**
  Women's spirit is honored, nurtured, and celebrated through workshops on such topics as yoga, African dance, story-telling, dreamwork, aging, healing, applied ritual, herbs, magic, Goddess archeology, and sweat lodges. Ceremonial circles allow participants to give voice to hopes and visions and to feel connected with other women, regardless of lifestyle, sexual orientation, age, and spiritual paths.

- **Men's Wisdom Council (six days)**
  Men learn to revitalize their sense of masculinity by devel-oping meaningful relationships with the other participants and getting in touch with their inner lives. Activities include exploration of male archetypal energies, breathwork, meditation, guided soul journeys, sweat lodges, dreamwork, shamanic practices, connecting with nature, music, drum-ming, laughing and crying together, chanting, and rituals.

- **Annual Labor Day Retreat for Gay Men (four days)**
  Sexuality is integrated with spirituality as gay men celebrate their gayness and enjoy a loving, safe community. Workshop topics include intimacy, meditation, spiritual practice, body-work, anger, living with AIDS, music, and consciousness.

- **Wild Hearts Dancing (three days)**
  Participants explore the expressive arts (singing, dancing,

writing, and painting) as vehicles of healing and the expression of authentic Self. The atmosphere enables joyful, spontaneous expressions similar to what children are able to enjoy without adult inhibitions.

- **Cherokee Teachings of Renewal: Spirituality in Everyday Life (three days)**
  Native American spiritual wisdom teaches how to restore balance and harmony to all living beings on earth. Participants learn to release creative energy through chanting, dance, breathing, moving, song, visualization, drumming, and meditation.

- **Writing for Your Life: A Writing Retreat (three days)**
  Through a series of exercises to open the imagination, participants learn to discover and tell their life's story. Finding the meaning in these stories helps to heal past hurts and develop new directions for the future.

- **Managing with Heart (five days)**
  This workshop is designed for managers, supervisors, and others who want to improve their organization's consciousness and business practices. Participants learn to give organizations a heart and develop "corporate soul" through quality circles, teamwork, and win-win ethics.

- **Love & Anger: Daring to Feel (three days)**
  Participants practice a full range of emotional expression. The focus is on loving ourselves, fighting fairly, expressing anger at work and home, and the connections between repression of emotion and life-threatening illness.

Rowe is located in the mountains of Massachusetts. It can be reached by car or by bus from Boston or New York city. Rowe staff will pick up participants at the towns of Williamstown or Greenfield (about forty minutes away) for a small fee. They will also attempt to arrange car pools.

Participants usually stay in dorm-style housing, with single and bunk beds in winterized cabins and a farmhouse. Some single and double occupancy private rooms are available (all with shared bedrooms) in the guesthouses. Participants may also bring their own tents for camping or may stay in a nearby inn or motel. Three gourmet vegetarian meals are served a day (with fish and chicken served occasionally).

COST: ⊛ (cost of programs depends on each participant's gross income; bartering is possible)

Rowe Camp and Conference Center
Kings Highway Road
Rowe, MA 01367

☎ (413) 339-4954
www.rowecenter.org

SAGAMORE INSTITUTE

Sagamore offers year-round environmental, Adirondack arts and crafts, and personal empowerment programs. One of its most unique programs is a five-day grandparents' and grand-children's camp held every summer. (Four separate sessions in July and August are usually available.) Created by the Foundation for Grandparenting and Sagamore, the program is designed as a bonding experience for the two generations. Any ages are welcome, but most activities are geared for children aged five to twelve. Intergenerational activities include storytelling around a campfire, hiking, canoeing, and creating art with natural materials. There are also separate activities for children and grandparents each afternoon. Lifetime memories and closer relationships develop as a result of these five days.

Another noteworthy program is the annual Magic of Humor and Creativity: A Personal and Professional Skillshop. During these five days in July, participants discover the humor, creativity, and magic in themselves and others. Topics include comic vision, spontaneity, the art of laughing at yourself, magic tricks for evoking laughter and imagination, skills for nurturing creativity and humor in others, and creative problem-solving. The focus is on practical uses of humor and creativity for managers, health care and helping professionals, educators, and parents to prevent burnout, to motivate, to promote health, to manage conflicts, to enhance self-esteem, and to build relationships.

Other programs throughout the year include a variety of outdoor and environmental programs (cross-country skiing, llama trekking, kayaking, mountain biking, canoeing, fly fishing, and women in the wilderness), Adirondack history courses, and crafts and arts (woodcarving, winter photography, fly tying, basketry, rustic furniture, storytelling, and mountain music and dance).

Recreational opportunities include hiking or skiing on twenty miles of trails, canoeing, fishing, and swimming on the lake, croquet, tennis, volleyball, and bowling.

Sagamore is located in the heart of the Adirondacks in upstate New York (two and one-half hours from Albany). The buildings are rustic and date back to the turn of the century. As a National Historic Site, it does not provide the services of a resort; instead, it offers the experience of an incomparable historical and natural setting.

Participants may stay in a variety of rooms at the lodge. None has television, phones, or locks on the doors. Bathrooms are shared and electrical outlets are scarce. Smoking is not allowed in any of the buildings. Three meals a day are served buffet style in the dining hall. Very little red meat is served.

COST:

 Sagamore Historic Adirondack Great Camp
P.O. Box 146
Raquette Lake, NY 13436

☎ (315) 354-5311
www.sagamore.org

Serenity by the Sea

"Each time I'm here, my life is enriched and I return home with a storehouse of strength and tranquility and nourishing memories and feel I am one step closer to that wholeness I long for."

—Serenity by the Sea participant

Serenity by the Sea provides holistic programming to reduce stress and to promote creativity and self-discovery. Although it is a small center, it offers a variety of three- and four-day workshops during the spring, summer, and fall, as well as unstructured retreats throughout the year.

Workshops include:

- **The Next Step**
  Through life evaluation and right-brain work, participants rediscover their passion and purpose. Decision-making for the immediate and distant future is facilitated.

- **The Playfulness of Painting**
  Participants learn by doing as they paint their dreams and inner-being.

- **Finding Your Source**
  A 24-hour Spirit Quest and other activities put participants back in touch with nature and life.

- **Wise Ones and Masks**
  Participants discover their Creative Self, Higher Self, Inner Male, and Inner Female, and create a mask of power to embrace them all.

- **Have Journal, Will Paddle**
  While kayaking, participants engage in discovery journaling to develop and record new personal insights and harmony.

- **Design Your Dream Home**
  Participants tour area homes, as well as discuss and draw possibilities that can make their homes responsive to their personal needs and desires.

71

Leisure activities include hiking, kayaking, hot tubbing, and just enjoying the island pleasures of forest and waterfront. Available services include massage, breathwork, energy balancing, and creative release work using color and dialogue to resolve personal issues.

Participants shared a private cabin or a room in a house. Three vegetarian meals are provided each day.

Serenity is located in the Canadian Gulf Islands, accessible via a fifty minute ferry cruise from Vancouver.

COST:

 Serenity by the Sea
225 Serenity Lane
Galiano Island
B.C. Canada VON 1PO

☎ (800) 944-2655

SKYROS

"Whatever you come expecting to find, you're sure to go home a different person. The change may be subtle, but it's there."

—*Skyros participant*

Skyros provides participants with a spectacular Greek island setting, but its offerings go way beyond scenery. Its three centers are ideal for persons who want to rediscover nature, people, and themselves. A variety of two-week programs are available.

Atsitsa is a holistic center which provides a wide range of courses each week. Aimed at relaxing and revitalizing the whole person, these programs may include yoga (asatanga/kundalini/hatha), dance, movement, fitness, T'ai Chi, voice work, singing, music, art, art therapy, outdoor adventures, windsurfing, juggling, theater, mime, writing, storytelling, massage, shiatsu, reflexology, Alexander/body-mind work, dreamwork, imagework, visualization, relationships, self-awareness, healing, rituals, and myths.

Classes and activities are suitable for beginners as well as those who have more advanced skills or experience in the specific areas. Participants may do as much or as little as they like of the approximately five hours of structured programming. (Generally, three courses are chosen from the fifteen that are usually offered each week.) Atsitsa is located right by the sea. Participants live in shared accommodations in the stone lodge or in bamboo huts. Three meals are served a day, with both vegetarian and nonvegetarian options. Recreational activities include sunbathing, swimming, parties, walks through the pine forest, and cabaret shows.

Skyros Centre is located ten minutes from the sea. It offers personal development courses for persons who wish to reconsider the form and direction of their lives. Participants are generally facing important career, relationship, or lifestyle decisions or in need of healing after painful life events (broken relationships, career setbacks, bereavement, etc.). Courses run for three hours a day, five days a week. Facilitators (who are professional therapists) use a variety of approaches (gestalt, psychodrama, voice

73

dialogue, dance, movement, massage, and yoga). Some courses address general personal development, whereas others focus on a specific theme such as honoring the child within, the alchemy of happiness, or the family origins of adult patterns.

The Skyros Institute (also ten minutes from the sea) provides training courses in personal development, holistic health, and painting for anyone with a personal or professional interest in the area. Courses are both theoretical and experiential, held four hours a day, five days a week. They include painting, massage, imagework, psychodrama, sacred sexuality, shamanism, and astrology.

At both Skyros Centre and Skyros Institute, participants share rooms in the homes of neighboring villagers. Breakfast and lunch are provided by the Centre. Vegetarians are always provided for. Dinner is usually eaten at local tavernas. Recreational activities include swimming, sightseeing, boat trips, hiking, snorkeling, windsurfing, theater performances, parties, and discos.

At all three centers, there is some built in time for rest and relaxation, as well as two hours of community affairs programming where participants meet as a group to voice practical or emotional concerns and make daily decisions together. Participants also make a contribution to the community by helping with food preparation and minor cleaning for up to an hour each day.

Participants fly from Athens to the island of Skyros (and are taken by taxi to Atsitsa or the Skyros complex).

COST:

Skyros
92 Prince of Wales Road
London NW5 3NE, Great Britain
+44(0) 171 267 4424/284 3065
www.skyros.com

WHOLISTIC LIFE CENTER

The purpose of the Wholistic Life Center is "to help each individual integrate all aspects of his or her total awareness and reality...to be rejuvenated into the natural flow of life." To this end, a variety of weekend workshops are offered to provide learning or re-learning experiences that can eliminate myths and correct misunderstandings about physical, emotional, or spiritual health. In a supportive and loving atmosphere, participants can expand their concept of themselves and realize their own true potential.

Regularly held weekend workshops include:

- **Quit Smoking Workshop**
  Classes and discussions reveal the true reasons for smoking and help find healthy substitutes for the physical and emotional lure of smoking.

- **Wholistic Gourmet Workshop**
  Fresh ingredients are used in gourmet preparations that can enhance health.

- **Executive Workshop**
  Time and stress management skills are stressed. Participants learn to integrate all the other aspects of their lives (family, leisure, health) with their careers.

- **Relationship Workshop**
  Dealing with all aspects of communication, the workshop details the contrast between personal intentions and how actions and words are perceived by others. The goal is to deeply connect with others.

- **Creativity Workshop**
  Classes and exercises focus on the healing qualities of color, sound, and movement, the emotional root of blocked creative flow, and the impact of the right side of the brain on imagination. Participants are encouraged to release the artist within them by producing and presenting a work of art (painting, musical piece, short story, etc.).

- **Child-Within Workshop**
  The focus is on the impact childhood associations and experiences have on adult life, self-esteem, and emotional/physical health. Through classes, exercises, and discussions, participants learn to discard any restrictions that prevent full expression of innate talents.

- **Inner Beauty and Rejuvenation Workshop**
  Years of accumulated toxins and emotional stress are discarded to alleviate premature aging and to revitalize the body from the inside out. Classes are offered in nutrition, digestion, exercise, relaxation, massage, and basic natural skin cleansing.

Leisure activities include hiking, basketball, tennis, ping pong, volleyball, singing, and dancing. Exercise and movement classes are available, along with massage and hot tubbing.

Participants stay in semi-private cabins. Three vegetarian meals are served each day, with emphasis on fresh fruits, vegetable juices, and salads.

The Center is located in the Ozark countryside. The closest air transportation is in Fayetteville, Arkansas.

COST:

 Wholistic Life Center
Route 1, Box 1783
Washburn, MO 65772

☎ (417) 435-2212

WISE WOMAN CENTER

"I observed my body filled with intense and subtle energy...I felt empowered and connected to the earth as never before."

—Wise Woman participant

Susun Weed, the founder of the Wise Woman Center, is a green witch who uses herbs and weeds for healing. Her center provides teaching in the Wise Woman Tradition and the arts of spirit healing, herbal medicine, women's spirituality, and meditation. Some of the two- to four-day intensives are open to men, while others are for women only. Examples of offerings include:

- **Sacred Sex**
  Tantric, Taoist, and Native American techniques are used to activate sexual energy as a vehicle for enlightenment.

- **Spirit Healing Intensive**
  Participants experience auras, chakras, color therapy, and chant/tone/sound for healing. They set up their own sacred space and call their personal spirit helpers.

- **Herbal Intensive**
  The general goal is to connect with the earth and the deeper self. Specific activities include weed walks, making tonics, and learning to recognize, harvest, and use local medicinal weeds.

- **Transformational Healing**
  To open the heart and mind, tarot, astrology, drumming, trance, meditation, chanting, discussion, and physical hands-on healing are used. Pains of the past are released while possibilities and potential are celebrated.

- **Awaken the Wise Woman and Wizard Within**
  Participants learn who they are and what their mission is through a movement meditation, study of the Cycles of Truth, constructing a wisdom wheel, and hearing the teachings of Native American women.

Leisure activities include hiking, swimming, and visiting with the many goats on the property.

Participants use sleeping bags or tents indoors and outside. Vegetarian meals are provided.

The Center is located between Woodstock and Saugerties in upstate New York. It's accessible by car, bus, and airplane (from Albany).

COST: 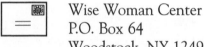 (sliding scale depending on personal finances. Work exchange and barter are available)

Wise Woman Center
P.O. Box 64
Woodstock, NY 12498

☎ (914) 246-8081

INDIVIDUAL DISCIPLINE PROGRAMS

Just as the preceding programs can change your life by helping you grow as a whole person, so can a vacation at any of the Individual Discipline Programs. The difference is that these programs provide in-depth learning in one specific area such as yoga, bodywork, life force energy, or ancient Hawaiian arts. You are the best judge of whether you prefer to focus exclusively on a particular subject or practice or prefer exposure to a variety of experiences and philosophies. If you choose the more singular approach, you can be assured of acquiring the knowledge and skills in that particular area which will promote your physical, mental, and spiritual integration and well-being.

Dances of Universal Peace

"Dance enhances our response to life. It makes us more living, which is to say, more spiritual. What life gives may be expressed with body, heart and soul to the glory of God and the elevation of humanity, leading therein to ecstasy and self-realization."
—*Samuel L. Lewis, originator of the Dances of Universal Peace*

"Your workshop truly opened the door to my heart in a way I have not experienced before. It's one of those experiences I'll treasure and profit [from] for a long time."
—*Dances of Universal Peace participant*

Sacred movement, song, and story have brought people together since the beginning of time. These traditions were used to celebrate the seasons, mark life passages, and provide daily renewal and meditation. Samuel L. Lewis, a Sufi teacher and Zen master (who also studied deeply in the mystical traditions of Hinduism, Judaism, and Christianity), revived many of these ancient dances and created the Dances of Universal Peace as a method to promote "peace through the arts." He felt that the use of sacred phrases, chants, and movements from many traditions could promote unity and harmony within individuals and groups. Since its beginnings in the early seventies, the collection of dances has grown from around fifty to more than five-hundred encompassing Hinduism, Buddhism, Zoroastrianism, Sikhism, Judaism, Christianity, Islam, Celtic, Native American, Native African, and the Great Goddess traditions.

There are numerous workshops, meetings, and programs of the Dances throughout the United States and the world. The coordinating body, the International Center for the Dances of Universal Peace, sponsors weeklong camps which teach the dances and provide an environment for personal, interpersonal, and global growth and transformation. There are also some weekend retreats. Events are held throughout the year. Recent locations included Michigan, New Mexico, Washington, Connecticut, Utah, California, Canada, Poland, New Zealand, England, and Russia.

Dance camps have a practical and spiritual focus on work with breath, sound, use of the voice, contemplation, and meditation as they relate to the dances. All dances and activities are fully taught; no prior experience is necessary. Participants don't have to be especially coordinated or physically fit. Most of the dances and walks are at a moderate pace and don't demand physical prowess.

Depending on the facilities at the specific location, participants stay in double or dorm-style indoor rooms, cabins, tents, and teepees. Bathroom facilities are usually shared. Vegetarian meals are provided.

Most of the camps are held at rustic sites which offer forests, ponds, trails, and lakes for swimming and boating. Yoga sessions are also available. A few sites have saunas and hot tubs.

The Dance Camp experience offers a week of learning, rest, rejuvenation, reflection, and renewal. It is felt that the Dances can really change lives as they touch the spiritual essence of ourselves and others. The Center notes that "participants may grow in openness, honesty, insight, love, flexibility, accountability, and compassion."

COST: (partial scholarships are available)

International Center for the Dances of
    Universal Peace
444 NE Ravenna Blvd., Suite 306
Seattle, WA 98115-6467

 (206) 522-4353

HAWAIIAN PATHWAYS

Pre-missionary Hawaiians had a highly advanced spirituality. The Kahunas (priests and priestesses) developed and refined religious activities such as meditation, dance, chant, and sacred massage.

Westerners have not had much opportunity to be exposed to these ancient teachings and practices, but Hawaiian Pathways is a program which offers experiential training in an authentic Hawaiian setting. Ten-day Ho'okele (the "navigator") courses enable participants to learn the necessary skills to "navigate" their canoes (themselves) through the waters of their lives.

Daily instruction is provided in the arts of No-ono'o (Hawaiian meditation), Oli (chant), Hula Kahiko (ancient dance), and Lomi Ha'a Mauli Ola (sacred Hawaiian massage). Participants meet and learn from Hawaiian elders and experience living in a nurturing and supportive Ohana (family environment).

Recreational activities include swimming in tropical pools, outrigger canoe rides, sightseeing to ancient temples, and traditional luaus (parties).

The Hawaiian Pathways trainings take place on Maui in a secluded retreat center. Accommodations are in a lodge (two to four to a room). Three meals a day (both vegetarian and non-vegetarian) are provided. Locally grown food is featured and is prepared the old way in an imu (in-ground oven).

A video describing the training is available.

The expanded awareness and self-mastery gained through this experience doesn't end in Hawaii, but can be continued in settings that aren't quite as close to paradise.

COST:

 Hawaiian Pathways
P.O. Box 520
Suite 232
Paia, HI 96779

☎ (808) 243-0929

HELLERWORK TRAINING

"The body stores the trauma of our lives in muscular rigidity, thereby keeping us stuck in the past. When we release the tension in the body and align ourselves with gravity, we take a new stand in life. This allows us to be at ease with ourselves and in harmony in our relationship to others and to our planet."

—*Joseph Heller, founder*

"The Hellerwork Training opened a new world for me...by teaching me how to live and move my body in an entirely new and exciting way."

—*Hellerwork Training participant*

The Hellerwork system relates physical structure to human function in the context of a healing relationship. The guiding principle is "that by balancing the body's structure, and freeing natural movement and expression, the individual's innate wholeness is revealed." Balance is not viewed as a static state, but as a constant process of seeking wholeness and ease.

The process consists of:

- **Bodywork**
  A hands-on process which releases chronic tension and rigidity in the body. (Unlike classic Swedish massage which manipulates the muscles, or chiropractic which works on the vertebrae and other bones, this massage component focuses on connective tissue, or fascia, which envelopes the muscles and links them to bones.)

- **Movement education**
  Training to become aware of set movement patterns and assist in bringing balance and alignment to movement so that tension is prevented from returning.

- **Dialogue**
  Verbal exercises to recognize the ongoing attitudinal patterns which contribute to body tension and to assist in discovering new ways of dealing with life stresses.

The training uses lectures, demonstrations, movement, music, video, and personal process. Those who wish to become certified to practice Hellerwork as a career need to take a 1,250 hour course. Persons who wish to learn the process for their own personal revitalization can take eleven sessions with Joseph Heller. The program lasts for five to six days, with two sessions per day.

There are no residential facilities at the Heller offices, but there are a variety of lodging possibilities in Mount Shasta. Hellerwork furnishes a brochure detailing motels, chalets, cabins, bed and breakfasts, camping, and RV parks.

Local recreational opportunities include fishing, hiking, swimming, skiing (downhill and cross country), golf, whitewater rafting, boating, and sightseeing. Mount Shasta is 295 miles north of San Francisco and 245 miles north of Sacramento.

Joseph Heller also gives workshops and intensives nationwide.

Hellerwork is said to increase energy and fitness, improve posture, enhance body awareness, reduce pain, add flexibility and ease to movement, develop consciousness, and release buried memories of past physical and emotional traumas.

COST:

Hellerwork, Inc.
406 Berry Street
Mt. Shasta, CA 96067

 (916) 926-2500

Hotel Nabalam Yoga Retreats

Several times throughout the year, weeklong yoga retreats are offered at this Mexican hotel. As with most yoga workshops, there are two sessions each day dealing with the postures and exercises. What's unique about these retreats is that the instructor specializes in "musicosophy" (a conscious method of listening to music which leads to spiritual growth).

The hotel is located on the Isla Mujeres (reachable from Cancun's international airport). In addition to enjoying swimming in the Caribbean and sunning on the white coral sand beaches, participants can snorkel and explore Mayan ruins.

Accommodations are air-conditioned and oceanfront. Rooms are shared. Three vegetarian meals and a fish entree are offered each day.

COST:

Hotel NaBalam
Calle Zazil-Ha No. 118
Playa Norte
Isla Mujeres, Q. Roo
Mexico

www.mundacatravel.com/islamujeres/hotels/
nabalam.htm

INSTITUTE OF HEARTMATH

"I feel I have control over my life now. I don't react to things as I did before. It's quite dramatic how it works, and it work fast."
—*HeartMath participant*

A scientific laboratory may not sound appealing as a vacation setting, but this institute is located in a redwood forest in California's Santa Cruz Mountains. While the natural beauty of the site is conducive to relaxation, it's the techniques taught at the Institute that really make it a life-changing experience.

HeartMath engages in research as well as providing training for the general public. Extensive studies have formulated some simple techniques that have been scientifically validated. Their scientists have discovered that meditation and visualization are centered in the head. The focus here is on the heart and bringing the two branches of the autonomic nervous system into balance.

Freeze Frame® is one of the cornerstone tools. Stressful feelings are recognized and then dealt with by "freeze-framing it" and taking time out while pretending to breathe through the heart. A positive feeling recalled from some other life experience is re-experienced so that the heart can guide its owner to a more efficient response.

In the Cut-Thru® exercise, emotional distortion is replaced so that a feeling of peace can be entertained. Feelings of worry and insecurity are replaced with "balanced care." Participants learn to read their own "emotional weather reports."

The Heart Empowerment® is the flagship personal development retreat. Participants learn to master their thoughts and understand the heart/body/mind dynamic. They learn and use the latest biomedical research on the heart's influence over higher intelligence and better health.

Quantum Empowerment™ Retreats enable participants to master their feelings by retraining emotional and mental circuitry. Blocks that restrict life goals and desires are eliminated.

There are also retreats specifically for women, parents, educators, and health professionals.

All retreats are held over three days.

Once participants learn to stop damaging themselves with negative thoughts and feelings, the body's physiology changes. Levels of DHEA (the anti-aging hormone) increase dramatically, improving vitality and decreasing fatigue, depression, and anxiety. Cortisol (a stress hormone that can damage brain cells and accelerate aging) levels decrease. When the endocrine system is working optimally, a heightened state of well-being is experienced. Participants feel happier and healthier.

Many patients with diabetes, heart disease, chronic fatigue syndrome, obesity, and immune disorders have been referred by their physicians to the HeartMath program. The military and corporations have sent scores of employees to the training and believe that it has reduced absenteeism and increased communication, creativity, and productivity.

Studies have shown that, a year after the training, the majority of participants are still using the techniques to dissolve negativity and change their heart rhythms by focusing in the heart with feelings of love and appreciation.

The site consists of one hundred acres in the mountains on the coast. Participants stay in private guest facilities. Gourmet food and nightly entertainment is provided. Hiking trails are plentiful.

COST: 💲

Institute of HeartMath
14700 West Park Ave.
Boulder Creek, CA 95006

 (800) 450-9111 or (408) 338-8700
www.heartmath.org

International Center for Reiki Training

Reiki is an ancient Japanese healing technique. Loosely defined, it means "life force energy" that is spiritually guided. This energy is channeled through the hands to heal others as well as the self.

It can be used to revitalize and restore the balance of an individual's physical and emotional being. As a non-invasive, completely benign technique, it is believed to break up and wash away any negative thoughts or feelings lodged in the unconscious mind/body. Eliminating negative thoughts and feelings enables health to be maintained or increased. Proponents note that it can help individuals to stop smoking or drinking, to lose or gain weight, or recover from serious illness. It also enhances emotional peace and well-being.

Weekend training intensives allow participants to learn the Reiki hand positions, give a complete Reiki treatment, use Reiki for specific conditions, heal unwanted habits through Reiki, administer a self-treatment, and send Reiki to others at a distance.

Reiki classes are taught all over the United States as well as in other countries. The Center for Reiki Training can provide specific information about upcoming locations.

Beginners start with a weekend intensive combining Reiki I and II. Advanced Reiki training, Reiki III, and master classes can be pursued after taking this introductory course.

Proponents of Reiki feel that this technique enables individuals to use negative and positive experiences to heal and grow. By assuming that everyone has the resources (or the ability to develop them) to solve any problem that may be encountered, participants assume personal responsibility for their own lives. Trust in the Higher Power (regardless of what name it may be called) is maintained through the spiritual elements of the practice.

89

COST:

 International Center for Reiki Training
21421 Hilltop #28
Southfield, MI 48034

 (248) 948-8112 or (800) 332-8112
www.reidi.org

KRIPALU CENTER FOR YOGA AND HEALTH

"Kripalu offers the opportunity to discover who you really are. It is only through this experience that you can find true and lasting satisfaction in life."

—Gurudev, yoga master at Kripalu

"I came to Kripalu feeling out of touch with myself — dead on the inside. Now I feel totally alive...ready to dance, play, sing, love, and feel the pain in my life...what a glorious feeling."

—Kripalu participant

Kripalu offers a variety of yoga programs, but it is much more than a yoga ashram. It's a holistic center for physical, mental, emotional, and spiritual health. It offers programs, workshops, and retreats which enable participants to awaken to their true inborn potentials. Every program incorporates yoga twice a day as a clearing process to release physical, emotional, and mental blocks.

Offerings at Kripalu include:

- **Gentle Yoga (three days)**
  An introductory program, with focus on warm-ups, stretches, and simple postures.

- **Women and Yoga (six days)**
  Yoga postures specifically beneficial for women, enabling a sense of personal empowerment and hormonal activity to be balanced in changing cycles.

- **Men and Yoga (six days)**
  Yoga practiced with self-awareness activities to allow men to transcend social conditioning and become more compassionate and sensitive with themselves and others.

- **Enlivening the Chakra System (fourteen days)**
  An indepth program to awaken the seven chakras (energy centers) in the body through yoga postures, pranayama (yogic breathing), meditation, visualizations, chanting, self-reflection, silence, group sharings, and an optional one day fast.

91

- **Self-Esteem (six days)**
  A liberation from the unconscious beliefs that have created self-doubts insecurity, enabling the true self (loving, wise, and unafraid) to be uncovered.

- **Opening to Life After Fifty (seven days)**
  Yoga, meditation, breathing techniques, conscious eating, self-reflection, and sharing with others to become aware of attitudes and choices which may be sabotaging life goals.

- **Raw Juice Fasting (seven days)**
  Purification of the body/mind through raw fruit and vegetable juices, as well as instruction on fasting and detoxification, journaling, self-exploration, stretching, relaxing, and walking.

- **Transformation Through Transition (seven days)**
  Dialogue, journaling, deep relaxation, creative movement, and yoga to enable participants to tackle the challenges of such life experiences as marriage, divorce, illness, job change, and so on.

Special bodywork services are available for an added cost (including shiatsu therapy and energy balancing, footcare/ reflexology, meditative massage, and skin care.)

Participants stay in dormitory rooms which accommodate ten to twenty-four people, semi-private rooms with shared or private baths, or private rooms with shared or private baths. Vegetarian meals are served. Meals are eaten in silence to create a contemplative atmosphere.

COST: (partial scholarships are available)

Kripalu Center for Yoga and Health
Box 793
Lenox, MA 01240

 (800) 967-3577
www.redienergy.com/dripaly.htm

Shoshoni Yoga Retreat

"When I came to the intensive I wasn't sure what I was looking for. I only knew I felt something lacking in my life. What I got was much more than I imagined. I could feel my heart open to a degree that was fathomless...my mind became still and quiet. I felt a warmth spread across my chest like a great joy. I felt like crying with happiness. I felt like a child again safe in my mother's arms. I had no fears. My true nature, my Inner Self was such a tangible presence."

—Shoshoni participant

Shoshoni offers yoga and meditation retreats and renewals year-round "to become new all through." The founder of Shoshoni Yoga Retreat, Sri Shmambhavananda, endeavors to provide a nurturing environment for rest and revitalization so that participants can discover the beauty and love within themselves. Years of tightness and tension are quickly stripped away through the Shoshoni experience.

Unlike some of the other yoga retreats and ashrams, Shoshoni is geared towards beginners.

Daily classes include:

- **Hatha yoga** to release physical tension and gently stretch tight muscles.

- **Pranayama** for recharging through the natural energy of the breathflow.

- **Meditation** for quieting the mind and witnessing thoughts.

Other healing arts and facilities are available, including massage, herbal body scrubs, aromatherapy facials, saunas, and hot tubs.

Guests are welcome at any time for as short or long a period as they wish. There are some special weekend intensives offered throughout the year where participants may study under Sri Shmambhavananda.

Shoshoni is located about thirty-five minutes from Boulder, Colorado. A pickup service is available from the Denver airport or downtown Boulder: Spectacular Colorado alpine scenery is part of the experience. Hiking through the aspen groves, valleys, and mountains supplements the yoga and meditation activities. Evening activities include reading, relaxing, socializing, and training (such as deep relaxation sessions).

Housing is usually in a log cabin. Tent camping is available. Three vegetarian meals are served daily.

COST:

 Shoshoni Yoga Retreat
P.O. Box 410
Rollinsville, CO 80474

☎ (303) 642-0116
shell.vmi.net/~shoui/

Sivananda Ashram Yoga Camps and Retreats

"Mysterious is this peace. If you enjoy this peace, you will be contributing peace to the whole world. Realize the peace that passeth all understanding and be free."
—*Swami Sivananda, yoga master and inspiration for Sivananda Yoga Vedanta Centres*

Followers of Swami Vishni-devananda (the founder/director of the International Sivananda Yoga Vedenta Centres) believe that radiant health and inner peace can be obtained through proper exercise (yoga asanas), proper breathing (pranayama), proper relaxation (savasan), proper diet (vegetarian), and positive thinking and meditation (Vedanta philosophy and dhyana).

There are five ashrams. The ones in the United States are in New York and California. In addition to the ashram in India, there are two other notable ones outside the United States: one in Quebec (Canada) and one in Nassau (Bahamas).

Participants at the Canadian ashram follow the daily schedule of waking up at 5:30 A.M. and engaging in yoga, asana (postures), pranayama (breathing exercises), and meditation until the 10 A.M. breakfast. Between breakfast and the 6 P.M. dinner, there is more yoga and breathing exercises as well as time for silent nature walks, hiking, swimming, and sauna. Following two hours of silent meditation, lights are out at 10 P.M.

There are special programs throughout the year, such as Yoga and Stress Management, Golden Yoga Week for older persons, Mantra Yoga (sound vibrations which tune into the mind), and Raja Yoga (eight-step system to control the mind). Participants are also welcome to drop in for a visit of any length.

The ashram is located in the Laurentian Mountains one hour north of Montreal. It can be reached by car or bus from Montreal.

95

Participants may camp out in their own tents, stay in a dormitory, or have a single or double room with a bath. Two vegetarian meals are served each day.

COST:

 Sivananda Ashram Yoga Camp
8th Avenue
Val Morin, Quebec, Canada JOT 2RO

 (819) 322-3226
www.sivananda.org

(international headquarters for the centers can provide information about the other ashrams)

The routine is similar in the Bahamas. Recreational activities such as snorkeling and swimming may be pursued between the 10 A.M. brunch and the second asana session at 4 P.M. At 8 P.M., there is a bonfire meditation and evening lectures on the concepts and applications of yoga (including exercise, breathing, relaxation, diet, positive thinking, meditation, karma, and reincarnation).

There are no private bathrooms, but there is a range of housing accommodations: single or semi-private rooms (many with an ocean view), dorm rooms, cabins, or tents. Two vegetarian meals are served each day.

COST:

 Sivananda Ashram Yoga Retreat
P.O. Box N-7550 Paradise Island
Nassau, Bahamas

 (242) 363-2902

T'AI CHI IN PARADISE RETREATS

"As a result of this week I have found an inner strength I was unaware of. I feel more centered, more at peace with myself and others. Overall, I feel wonderful."

—*T'ai Chi in Paradise participant*

The ancient Chinese discipline of T'ai Chi is believed to produce a balanced unification of body, mind, and spirit while stretching and toning the body's muscles. Chi (internal healing energy) is released and circulated throughout the body, producing a relaxed yet alert state with increased focus. This form of meditation in motion coordinates dance-like movements with breathing as practitioners move arms and legs away from the body's center.

Every summer a nationally known T'ai Chi teacher conducts a five-day retreat program (including T'ai Chi philosophy, forms, and energetics) in an idyllic location. No previous T'ai Chi experience is needed. The retreats are open to all styles and levels, beginners through advanced. The slow and gentle movements of T'ai Chi can be performed by anyone of any age; participants do not have to be in excellent physical shape.

The retreats have been held at retreat centers in Volcanoes National Park, Hawaii (in an oceanfront jungle setting); Puerto Viejo, Costa Rica (in a rainforest lodge); and Stewart Hot Springs, California. Saunas and hot tubs enable relaxation between classes.

Participants stay in double occupancy rooms and are served three meals a day.

There are also "Ski T'ai Chi" programs available in the winter. Participants spend five days in a first-class hotel in Lake Tahoe learning to integrate T'ai Chi principles into their skiing. By applying the principles of relaxing and centering, new levels of skiing enjoyment and performance can be achieved. The double-occupancy fees are $885 for the five days.

97

Once the powerful life tool of T'ai Chi is learned and lived, participants are better able to create balance in all of life's situations. Even in the midst of challenges and change, a life of harmony, power, and joy can be enjoyed. Physical benefits include improved posture, muscle control, and flexibility.

COST:

 Pacific School of T'ai Chi/T'ai Chi in Paradise
P.O. Box 962
Solana Beach, California 92075

☎ (619) 259-1396

T'AI CHI SCHOOL OF PHILOSOPHY AND ART

"It is not possible to save a minute; it is possible to save energy. Practice T'ai Chi to save energy, to transform your body/mind. You'll be healthy, happy, and spiritual, even at a mature age of one hundred."

—T.Y. Pang, T'ai Chi master/retreat leader

T.Y. Pang conducts retreats and summer camps around the world. Ranging in length from two to seven days, these programs offer classes, lectures, and discussions throughout the day. T'ai Chi is the focus, but other Chinese forms of meditation are incorporated as well.

All programs can accommodate beginners through experienced students of T'ai Chi.

Many programs are held on Orcas Island, Washington, but there are also some in Hawaii, Oregon, Montana, Utah, and California.

Accommodations and costs vary according to the site. All locations are in natural, wooded settings at retreat centers or state parks. Cabins are shared. Vegetarian meals are served. Extracurricular activities usually include hiking in the forest and swimming in lakes.

COST:

 T'ai Chi School of Philosophy and Art
Box 2424
Bellingham, WA 98227

 (800) 442-2380

99

THYMEWAYS

Thymeways derives its name from its grounds which are covered with thyme, and its focus on living time (in each present internal moment) rather than clock time. It's a small operation run by a husband and wife who are a physician and yoga teacher, respectively. Yoga workshops are offered in the spring, summer, and fall. Most of these workshops also incorporate breathing, meditation, nutritional awareness, music, drumming, haiku poetry, and art appreciation.

Workshops can range from two to seven days. They use the Iyengar Method and can accommodate beginners through advanced students. The learning emphasis is on yoga asanas (postures) and pranayama (breathing practice), but the focus is on using yoga to enrich daily life bodily, mentally, and spiritually.

A special three-day workshop is offered for maturing women (menopausal and beyond). Participants learn to deal with the changes they're experiencing and to promote their self-development.

Thymeways is in a rural setting on Galiano Island in British Columbia. The setting includes many trees, rocks, mountains, inland sea, and birds such as swallows and eagles. Participants arrive from Vancouver or Victoria by ferry (which can accommodate vehicles). Transportation from the ferry landing is available.

Accommodations include a modern cottage, rooms in the main house, a sleeping loft, a cabin, and tents. Three meals are served daily.

All workshops are limited to twenty participants or less. This size provides a congenial atmosphere where participants and instructors can get to know each other.

COST:

 Thymeways
790 Devina Drive, RR 2
Galiano Island, British Columbia
Canada VON 1P0

☎ (604) 539-5071

YASODHARA ASHRAM

"...(the experience) gave me the tools and awakened the will for personal change."

—Participant at Yasodhara Ashram

There are numerous yoga ashrams throughout the world, but the Yasodhara Ashram is unique in that its founder (Swami Sivananda Radha) focuses on interpreting Eastern teachings for the Western mind. Consequently, the offerings are very accessible and practical.

As with any ashram, there are numerous courses and workshops. Many different yogas and spiritual disciplines originating from the ancient system of Kundalini Yoga are represented. There are five- and ten-day courses which provide an introduction to Swami Radhi's essential teachings. The Yoga Development Course, an intensive three-month program, includes courses on Kundalini Yoga (investigating the nature of mind and consciousness), Hatha Yoga and prayer dance (cultivating the body as a spiritual tool), Mantra Yoga (chanting words of power), and dream interpretation (studying symbols and their meaning). Special growth workshops include Life Seals (where participants create symbolic drawings of their lives and arranging the pictures into a whole to discover obstacles, strengths, and potentials) and Spiritualizing Your Life (learning to bring spiritual ideals into your work, home, and social environments).

Individuals who don't wish to take a course may stay at the Ashram for a self-directed retreat. They can chant, perform yoga, and attend Satsang (evening worship with meditation and inspirational readings).

Participants stay in semiprivate rooms in the lodge. Meals are mostly vegetarian, with meat, fish, and poultry dishes available a few times a week. Silence is observed during the meals.

The Ashram is located in the southeast corner of British Columbia, Canada, on the shores of a lake surrounded by mountains. Bus service is available from Vancouver or Calgary.

COST:

 Yasodhara Ashram
Box 9
Kootenay Bay, British Columbia
VOB 1X0 Canada

(250) 227-9224
www.yasodhara.org

*G*oing away somewhere and just relaxing can restore your spirit. A week at the beach or in the mountains can counteract the effects of accumulated stress and renew your zest for life. But unfortunately, the spiritual restoration is very short-lived. Within a few days of returning to work and resuming regular routines, the benefits of the getaway are lost. It's back to business as usual where you become so involved with the details of everyday living that you forget the deeper meaning and experiences of life.

The vacations profiled in this chapter focus on long-lasting spiritual benefits. By participating in one of these programs, you can be confident that you'll acquire a new or renewed spiritual focus that can greatly enhance your life. The programs are varied in their approach. Some are Buddhist, others Christian or Jewish, and still others are Sufi or New Age. Some use silence and meditation, whereas others focus on service work within the spiritual community or the broader world. All will assist you in developing a more active spirituality in your life that continues long after the vacation is over.

The first section, Spiritual Discovery and Renewal Programs, includes centers and retreats that have a primary emphasis on spiritual concerns. Many of the programs provide structured training in specific approaches such as meditation, Quaker prayer, or spiritual healing through the laying on of hands. Others provide the environment to work on personal spirituality in an unstructured, individualized way (such as an isolated retreat experience conducted in silence or a pilgrimage to sacred natural sites).

The second section, Social Action and Service Programs, contains some possibilities for living your faith and putting your spirituality into action.

SPIRITUAL DISCOVERY AND RENEWAL PROGRAMS

Most children are exposed to formal religious training and experience through their parents' churches and synagogues. Some of us continue this religious practice throughout our lives. Others seek alternative spirituality that meets individual needs. Some don't actively seek spiritual experiences because time or energy seems too limited to incorporate them into schedules that are already too full. A number of us don't know where to begin to look for meaningful spiritual teaching and practice.

If you're happy with your current spirituality, you don't need to read further. But if you, like so many of us, feel that there is something lacking in your life, you just may find a vacation that can give you a lasting spiritual focus.

(Chapter 1, Holistic Vacations, also provides information about spiritual programs.)

ABODE OF THE MESSAGE

"...You have the ability to bring forth all that is in you and more; you can really innovate and find new ways of being a special person."
— *Pir Vilayat Khan, head of Sufi Order in the West/founder of Abode of the Message Community*

"This place has a strong vibration that has helped me, in these few days, to do some deep healing."
— *Abode of the Message visiting participant*

The Abode is a Sufi residential community which offers retreats and educational programs to visitors. Sufism, as neither a religion nor a doctrine, allows individual perspectives in looking at the world and living in the world. Rather than requiring a withdrawal from the world, it practices immersion in life. Its messages are the spirit of brotherhood, tolerance for all religions and cultures, thoughtfulness and consideration, service, and usefulness. Community life in the Sufi tradition is regarded as a spiritual practice itself, teaching lessons of mastery, generosity, kindness, and harmony.

Aegis is the educational component of Abode. It offers a variety of two- and three-day programs with a spiritual focus. Recent examples have included:

- **Polishing the Mirror of the Heart**
  Participants work towards finding the courage and energy to clear the obstacles between themselves and the Highest Truth, the Greatest Love. Music, poetry, and movement are used to inspire and touch various levels of being.

- **Breath of Life and Light**
  Through Sufi breathing practices (as well as meditation, sharing, and discussion), participants open their connection to their own inner being, health, happiness, and higher states of consciousness while discovering a personal relationship to the universe.

107

- **Awakening the Inner Teacher**
  Meditation and stories from the sacred traditions (ranging from Buddhism to mystical Judaism) help to make the ever-present teacher within each of us conscious. This inner guide can point to the next stage of spiritual development.

Guest housing during the fall, winter, and spring is in single or shared rooms with shared baths. From June to September, accommodations are in rustic huts, log cabins, or tents; bathroom facilities consist of separate outhouses and showerhouses. Three vegetarian meals are served a day.

The Sufi Retreat Center offers guided individual retreats at the Abode of the Message throughout the year. A trained, certified guide structures each retreat to meet individual needs and goals.

Retreat participants stay in a private hut. Three vegetarian meals are served each day.

The Abode is located in the pastures and wooded mountains of the Berkshires. State parks, lakes, and forests offer a number of recreational possibilities. Nearby Tanglewood offers some cultural opportunities. It's about forty miles north of New York City and 140 miles west of Boston. Shuttle service is available to meet the bus, train, or plane from Albany, New York, or Pitsfield, Massachusetts.

COST:

Aegis/Abode Sufi Retreat Center
RD 1, Box 1030D
New Lebanon, NY 12125

☎ (518) 794-8095
www.theabode.net

BEN LOMOND QUAKER CENTER

A variety of retreats and conferences are offered throughout the year by the Religious Society of Friends. The focus is on spiritual and personal growth. While some programs may be of limited interest to non-Quakers, most are of general interest and all are open to the public. Programs are held mostly on the weekends, but some weeklong conferences are offered as well.

Examples of recent programs include:

- **Coming Home to the Core**
  Participants learn how to seek their deepest center.

- **Art and the Spirit**
  Personal exploration is facilitated through creative activities.

- **The Silent Retreat**
  Participants experience Quaker worship.

- **Sacred Clowns, Holy Fools: A Weekend for Women**
  Women explore the spiritual aspects of laughter and foolishness.

Individuals who don't wish to participate in a program can come for a private retreat.

In addition to hiking opportunities, the Center offers a volleyball court and potter's wheels for ceramics.

Participants stay in a lodge with semiprivate rooms. Vegetarian meals are served. Participants share kitchen chores.

The Center is located in northern California (approximately thirty miles from the San Jose airport).

COST:

Quaker Center
Box 686
Ben Lomond, CA 95005

 (408) 336-8333
www.geocities.com/WestHollywood/2473/blqc.html

109

CREATIVE HARMONICS INSTITUTE (CHI)

"CHI has offered me the opportunity to work through and explore visions and ideals that have long been part of my awareness."

—*Creative Harmonics Institute participant*

Creative Harmonics uses "color, sound, movement, and form exercises to open up the channels of energy and harmonic patterns that bring creativity through imagination." The Institute facilitates harmonious relationships between humans and nature through research, the arts, and teaching. Participants in CHI summer workshops and year-round retreats experience the patterns of color, sound, movement, and form that are inherent in nature and learn how to transfer them into relationships with the self, other people, to the Earth, and the entire universe. They live CHI with an awareness of the sacredness of everything in the cosmos.

Previous summer workshops have included:

- **Sacred Ground to Sacred Space (week-long intensive)**
  Energy and light are worked with so that participants can experience resonance with the Earth. They find symbols, colors, and forms that harmonize with their souls and then create altars in sacred places on CHI land. Musical instruments, chant and song, postures, and dances are also used to invoke the spirits of a particular site that resonate with one's own soul.

- **Watercolor Painting Raft Journey (four days)**
  Participants renew themselves through water as they raft down the Main Klamath River practicing the Zen and Taoist way of pure moment-to-moment attention. Novices to both painting and rafting can participate and create impressionistic paintings each day while they open up a capacity to clearly see and appreciate the nuances of nature.

- **Gaia Matrix Oracle Week Intensive**
  The Gaia Matrix Oracle, a deck of 108 cards with a book of readings, contains symbols that provide insight as to the relationship of the sacred and profane aspects of life. Art and theater techniques are also used to help participants better understand their personal stories and destinies and determine their alignment with their world. They learn to create their own rituals for transformation into new ways of being.

Flexible, personalized retreats for a month or longer may also be developed by each participant and Rowena Pattee Kryder (founder of CHI). Participants can consult with Rowena on a weekly basis while studying and reading on their own. Areas of concentration can include world myths and symbols, sacred art, dream work, perennial wisdom literature, and creative harmonics. Applicants must write a proposal stating the intent, areas of interest, and purpose of the stay, as well as submit a brief biography and astrology chart.

Workshop participants camp in leveled campsites and have access to indoor restrooms. Retreat residents stay in the Retreat House. Vegetarian meals are provided.

The Institute is located in the Mount Shasta foothills of California (with views of Oregon mountains).

COST: (all-inclusive fees for the workshops are on a sliding scale. Half the fee can be exchanged for working at CHI performing such tasks as massage, editing, secretarial work, gardening, carpentry, and maintenance)

Creative Harmonics Institute
Box 940
Mount Shasta, CA 96067

 (916) 938-2142
www.creative-harmonics.org

DAYSPRING RETREAT CENTER

Dayspring offers a number of silent retreats on most weekends throughout the year. Its founders believe that the world provides too little time and space for listening to God. The retreats provide both a time and a place for prayer, meditation, and contemplation.

Most of the retreats could be classified as nondenominational Christian, but persons of any spiritual/religious orientation are welcome. Some of the retreats do not have a specific Christian orientation but instead deal with universal themes.

Examples of offerings throughout the past years include:

- **Meditation**
  Christian, Buddhist, and Native American meditation methods are practiced, as well as working with clay, walking mindfulness, and storytelling, all layered with silence.

- **The Life of the Holy Family**
  The course looks at the forces that influenced the childhood and youth of Jesus and provides parallels in the formation of participants' psychology and religion.

- **Finding the Center of Life by Entering the Cave of the Heart**
  By opening a path to the Divine, the depths of the heart can be opened. Participants work towards finding a balance between God's grace and individual human efforts.

There are occasional ten-day intensive retreats which include three sittings of Centering Prayer, in addition to meditative walks, periods of silence, and private time. Some retreats are leaderless and allow participants to engage in self-guided silence.

Participants stay in shared accommodations in a lodge. Simple, mostly vegetarian meals are served (although some participants prefer to fast to heighten their spiritual awareness).

Dayspring is located in a wooded Maryland suburb of Washington, D.C.

COST:

 Dayspring Retreat Center
11301 Neelsville Church Road
Germantown, MD 20876

☎ (301) 428-9348

THE EXPANDING LIGHT

"The Meditation Training Program helped me see that meditation is much more than calming the mind; it is truly a way of
life. I'm glad that we also covered so many aspects of the spiritual path — attitudes, relationships, etc. Now I see how all
aspects of my life are related."

—Expanding Light participant

The Expanding Light offers a variety of retreat and workshop
options. Their programs are based on the teachings of
Paramhansa Yoganda, a great Indian spiritual master. The
retreat experience includes classes in spirituality, meditation
instruction, group discussions, and private spiritual counseling.
Retreats can be tailored to individual needs, goals, and available time. There are special workshops on meditation, yoga,
spirituality, life-work planning, and marriage. Workshops can
range from two to five days.

Meditation training is at the core of all Expanding Light offerings. Beginning through advanced meditators can learn both
the art and science of meditation (from the basics of breathing
and posture to the creative application of meditation practices
in personal lifestyles). Experiential activities to enhance meditation include nature outings, walking meditations, healing
prayers, and devotional singing. Free time can be spent relaxing, reading, walking, bicycling, jogging, or hiking. Healing
services such as massage therapy, yoga therapy, medical and
chiropractic care, and hot tubs are also available.

Special weekend and five-day programs have included:

- **Couples Retreat**
  Participants learn to develop deeper, more conscious communication and problem-solving, as well as how to love in
  good and difficult times.

- **The Art of Running**
  Yogic principles of energy control and flexibility are applied to any level of running to enhance enjoyment and conditioning.

- **The Dynamics of Healing**
  Participants learn to use affirmations as a healing tool and techniques to strengthen the human aura. Methods of sending healing energy to the self and others (even at a distance) are also included.

Retreats are available year-round since the winters are so mild.

The Expanding Light is part of Ananda Village (cooperative spiritual community). The Village has over 350 residents on more than 750 acres and includes a school, market, and medical clinic. It's located ninety minutes northeast of Sacramento and two hours west of Reno Nevada in northern California's Sierra Nevada Mountains. Popular sightseeing spots are the Yuba River, mining towns, old covered bridges, and historic parks.

Participants who do not drive to the Expanding Light can use a shuttle service from the airport, train, and bus stations in Sacramento.

Indoor accommodations in a house or cabin are available. Bathrooms are shared, but there are some private rooms available. Tents or recreational vehicles provide other housing possibilities. Vegetarian meals are served.

The Expanding Light views meditation as the key to transcending the normal state of consciousness and entering into the realm of the soul. Through optimal meditation practices, participants develop qualities of the heart (love and devotion) and mind (willpower, concentration, and clarity). Even a few days at the Expanding Light can give participants the tools to maintain the sense of peace and joy that is realized through meditation and expanded spiritual awareness.

COST: (work programs enable participants to reduce the costs by performing cleaning, landscaping, painting, and other tasks)

 The Expanding Light
14618 Tyler Foote Road
Nevada City, CA 95959

☎ (800) 346-5350
(916) 478-7518
www.expandinglight.org

HEART SEED RETREAT CENTER

Heart Seed offers a variety of week-long retreats throughout the year. All are designed to facilitate discovery and renewal of spirituality.

The Mystery Teachings retreats introduce participants to the mystery teachings of Western and Eastern traditions including Hermetic, Alchemical, Rosicrucian, Theosophical, Vedic, and Esoteric Christian traditions.

Earth Energies and Power Points retreats offer instruction in earth energies such as leys and energy lines. Participants learn to use dowsing and deep sensing to explore the known power points and sacred natural sites on the property and nearby lands. They develop intuitive abilities to work with and understand these energies.

The Soul's Journey provides guidance in deepening each participant's relationship with his or her inner teacher or guide. There is also instruction in working with the earth energies on the property. An optional sweat lodge ceremony and an overnight spiritual quest is held at the end of the week.

Two silent retreats are held each year. The Holy Days Meditation Retreat is held during the week between Christmas and New Year's. Each day begins with T'ai Chi and group meditation. The remainder of the day is spent in silence in activities such as meditation and journaling. Each evening a class is held in the esoteric meaning of the season and is followed with group meditation. The Easter Week retreat is similar to the Holy Days Retreat but explores the esoteric teachings of the Easter, Passover, and Equinox seasons.

Basic retreats furnish the opportunity for participants to plan a personalized week of activities. Possibilities include meditation, guided mountain hikes, mountain biking, reading, hot tubbing, star gazing, and spa treatments such as massage, polarity, cranial-sacred therapy, herbal wraps, and aromatherapy.

Pilgrimages to sacred sites are also offered. These include a week-long experience by land and water around the Southwest and a three-week program in India.

Heart Seed is located in the Ortiz Mountains of New Mexico. It's located on one hundred acres twenty-five miles from Santa Fe and one hour from the Albuquerque airport.

Breakfasts are provided. Each room (shared or private) has its own kitchenette so that participants may prepare meals.

COST:  (retreats and Southwest pilgrimage)

 (India pilgrimage)

    Heart Seed Bed and Breakfast and Spa
P.O. Box 6019
Santa Fe, NM 87502

(505) 471-7026
www.nets.com/heartseed/

INSTITUTE OF NOETIC SCIENCES TRAVEL PROGRAM

"There are no unnatural or supernatural phenomena, only very large gaps in our knowledge of what is natural...We should strive to fill those gaps of ignorance."
—*Edgar Mitchell, Founder, Institute of Noetic Sciences*

In 1973, astronaut Edgar Mitchell founded the Institute of Noetic Sciences, a nonprofit education, membership, and research group. The word "noetic" is derived from "nous" — the Greek word for mind, intelligence, and transcendental knowing. Noetic sciences focus on the scientific study of human potential and conscientiousness. The Institute's brochures note its quest as "the discovery of vision for humanity which integrates science and spirituality, and in so doing, reminds us of our wholeness and connectedness, not only to each other and to the Earth, but to the inner self most particularly."

Although the Institute's travel programs offer a wide range of trips all over the world, they all share a common element: all are geared for seekers on journeys of both inner and outer exploration. Regardless of the exact nature of the travel, all participants gain insight into diverse cultures and belief systems while becoming more knowledgeable global citizens. Exposure to other expressions of spirituality, celebration, and worship can open up new possibilities for spiritual exploration and growth that can be continued at home once the trip has ended.

Recent examples of these travel experiences include:

- **Exotic Bali (14 nights)**
  Participants talk with locals about the Balinese traditional health and healing practices and their religion and spirituality while enjoying Balinese music and dance. They can learn how the Balinese have been able to move into the modern

world without losing their sense of balance with the earth.

- **The Desert Vision Quest (9 nights)**
  After four days of preparation with the group, participants have three days of solo time in the Northern California desert. Fasting is part of the experience. Participants learn to honor the sacred dimension by paying attention to the small things of life while exploring their own interiors.

- **European Study Tour: Christian Mysticism and Inner Healing (8 nights)**
  In addition to sightseeing in German medieval towns, participants are guided in the exploration of the roots of Western mysticism and mythologies, the native wisdoms of Europe, Christian meditation, and workshops in imagery for inner healing and wellness enhancement.

- **Touch the Earth (6 nights)**
  Participants live on an American Indian (Gros Ventre and Assiniboine tribes) reservation in northern Montana. Activities include hiking, horseback riding, and learning about tribal art, medicine, and ceremonies.

- **Shaman of Ecuador (8 nights)**
  In addition to experiencing the earth's largest tropical rainforest, participants work and study with the shamans of Ecuador. Learning focuses on environmental stewardship, healing techniques, and shamanic journeying into sacred worlds.

- **Nepal and Tibet (14 nights)**
  Participants explore Eastern consciousness by meeting and studying with Tibetan Buddhist nuns and monks and worshipping with Hindu followers. The emphasis is on looking at the way in which the sense of place affects human consciousness and elevates it to commune with the cosmos.

Participants generally stay in a hotel with shared accommodations and a private bath, except on those trips which offer more unique arrangements such as camping out in the desert, living in a teepee on the Indian reservation, or sleeping in a lodge in an Ecuadorian village.

COST:

(airfare from the United States included in many programs)

 Institute of Noetic Sciences Travel Program
P.O. Box 1369
Sausalito, CA 94965

☎ (800) 353-2276
(415) 332-4366
www.noetic.org

JOURNEY INTO WHOLENESS

"I came feeling burned out. I leave healed, refreshed, energized, and guided in new directions. This conference and this community were soul-renewing for me!"

—Journey into Wholeness participant

Journey into Wholeness provides a bridge between Christian spirituality and the psychology of Carl Jung. Their retreats and seminars are both secular and spiritual. The intellect is stimulated as the emotions are challenged. Art, drama, bodywork, and lectures are used to explore the relationship of Jung's depth psychology to Christ's message of spiritual/psychological healing and wholeness.

Whereas the majority of psychologists and psychiatrists downplayed or denied humankind's religious nature, Jung stressed its importance. His psychology nurtures openness to the Divine. To this end, Journey into Wholeness programs enable participants to discover their true natures as well as the Christ within.

Typical offerings are:

- **Journey into Wholeness**
  Each five-day conference is different, but each consists of lectures in the mornings and evenings with experiential workshops in the afternoons. Subjects include dreams, mandalas, Jung's Psychological types, expressive therapy, and meditation. Specific workshops have included: Jungian Sychronicity in Astrological Signs and Ages, Leading a Symbolic Life, Healing Aspects of Stories and Myths, owning One's Shadow, Dreams, Depression: The Rejected Feminine, Angels and Archangels: Archetypal Energies of the Unconscious, and the Soul in the Body.

- **The Way of the Dream**
  In this six-day program, a documentary series of twenty half-hour films are shown. Each film describes a variety of dreams by the persons who dreamt them. Jungian analysts lead the

small group discussions of the films. Participants also work creatively with their own material stimulated by the films' dream motifs using various art mediums such as paint and clay.

- **A Time of Sisters**
  Lectures, rituals, and activities help women learn to cherish themselves so that they can cherish others.

- **A Time of Brothers**
  Men learn to trust themselves and each other through this healing experience.

- **Vision Quest**
  There are other Vision Quests offered by a number of companies, but the only one that includes Jungian analysts is Journey into Wholeness. They believe that time alone in the wilderness should be more than just a survival experience. To ensure that it is truly an encounter with the Self and a connection with personal spirituality, trained analysts lead dream groups before and after the four days in the wilderness to prepare participants for their time apart and then better understand the experience when it's over. The total experience is nine days.

- **Aren't We a Pair?**
  This three-day couples seminar uses Jung's theory of personality types to identify similarities and differences. Couples explore ways to understand and encourage each partner on his or her unique path.

- **Individuation and Recovery**
  The psychology of Carl Jung is applied to the recovery movement and Twelve-Steps philosophy.

The three-day pre-conference seminar entitled "Introduction to Jung" explores basic concepts and terminology for participants who are new to the psychology of Carl Jung or need a refresher course.

Most of the programs are offered at retreat centers in North Carolina's Blue Ridge Mountains. A few are offered in coastal Georgia. The Vision Quest is on Lake Temagami in Ontario, Canada.

Except for camping in the Vision Quests, participants stay in single or double rooms in lodges. Three meals are provided daily.

COST:

 Journey into Wholeness, Inc.
P.O. Box 169
Balsam Grove, NC 28708

(704) 877-4809

LAMA FOUNDATION

The Lama Foundation is an intentional community that teaches the oneness of all paths by presenting a diversity of practices from spiritual traditions. The goal is the awakening of consciousness through the Hindu, Sufi, Buddhist, Islam, Christian, and Jewish faiths.

During the summer, Lama welcomes visitors for retreats of one to two weeks. Examples of past retreats have included:

- **Community Camp (thirteen days)**
  Participants share practices such as meditation, Dances of Universal Peace, Shabbat, Hindu chanting, and Japanese tea ceremony. They also assist with community work projects such as laying utility lines and gardening.

- **Sitting in the Wild Heart (seven days)**
  Participants move from periods of meditation which deepen the inner world to wild and free expression of the creative spirit through painting, dance, poetry, and song.

- **Animas Vision Quest (ten days)**
  Group and individual ceremonies are used to renew participants' relationships to Self, Earth, and Spirit. After three days of preparation with dreamwork, meditation, deep imagery journeys, ceremonial drumming and dance, sweat lodge, and other ritual practices, participants dwell for seven days in the mountain wilderness (three days and nights of which are spent alone, fasting, gazing into the mirror of nature, and crying for a vision).

Participants provide their own tents in the camping area or a sleeping bag for the dorm. Vegetarian meals are served.

All participants are asked to give at least an hour a day in service as karma yoga. This can range from repairing a truck to baking bread.

The Lama Foundation is located in the Sangre de Cristo Mountains of northern New Mexico, twenty miles north of Taos.

COST: (scholarships are available for those in need)

 Lama Foundation
Box 240
San Cristobal, NM 87564

(505) 586-1269
www.taosnet.com/lama

Linwood Spiritual Center

In addition to serving as a residence for retired nuns, Linwood provides year-round programs for spiritual renewal. Most have a Christian focus, but persons of any denomination are welcome and should feel comfortable participating. Many programs combine pastoral and psychological insight to enhance spirituality and human development.

Weekend programs have included:

- **Bio-Spiritual Focusing**
  By listening to and following the wisdom of the body, participants become physically and mentally available to their personal realities and to God.

- **Dance as Prayer: Moving with the Spirit Toward Wholeness**
  No dance ability is needed since this is an experience of prayer, not performance. The focus is on movement activities which allow the healing power of Jesus to touch personal joy and pain.

- **Simplify Your Life: The Spirituality of Clearing Clutter and Living Free**
  Participants examine the mental and physical issues that keep them stuck in the clutter of too many material things. They learn how to simplify their lives so that they can concentrate on more important, fulfilling things.

- **People on a Spiritual Path: The Celtic Way**
  Celtic spirituality from the pre-Christian and early Christian era is explored. Images, stories, and rituals are used to enable participants to retrieve some of the nature-centered soul of the ancient past.

Special guided retreats are available for women.

Twelve-step spirituality retreats for men and women recovering in Alcoholics Anonymous are offered each month.

127

Most programs are held on the weekends. A few are a week in length.

Hiking, tennis, and swimming are the main recreational activities.

Linwood is located on the Hudson River two hours north of New York City. Center staff will pick up participants at the local train or bus stations.

Most of the rooms are singles, but bathrooms are shared. Meals are served buffet-style.

COST:

 Linwood Spiritual Center
139 South Mill Road
Rhinebeck, NY 12572

☎ (914) 876-4178

THE MYSTIC JOURNEY RETREAT CENTER

Other centers provide opportunities for silent meditation, but only The Mystic Journey Retreat Center provides a retreat with this amount of individualized flexibility and solitude. The Center accepts only one person at a time for a retreat. There is no fixed schedule. Participants are asked to follow a regimen of sitting and walking meditation practice. They listen to individually selected Sacred Space Music, watch talks on videotape, and meet with a retreat guide/teacher each day. The retreat is silent for the most part.

The Mystic Journey is defined as "the only truly significant journey we ever make...the interior journey, the journey into the center of our own being." It is suggested that participants do not enter into the retreat with pre-planned goals or expectations. Instead, they should attempt to keep their hearts open. In the silence, each participant learns the truths that he or she has always known but did not realize was known.

Although the Center's founder, Father John Groff, is an Episcopal priest, the Center is completely nonsectarian. Persons of any (or no) religious tradition are welcome.

Applicants must submit a statement about themselves, including their physical/emotional health, formal religious and spiritual backgrounds, and meditation experience.

Participants stay in a private room. They purchase and prepare their own food as a way to deepen spiritual practice.

The Center is accessible from Huntsville and Birmingham via major air and bus lines.

The length of stay is flexible. Five to fourteen days is generally recommended.

COST: ⚙$ (scholarships are available to those in need)

The Mystic Journey Retreat Center
P.O. Box 1021
Guntersville, AL 35796

 (256) 582-5745

PENDLE HILL

"I still feel, after twelve years gone by, that Pendle Hill touched my life and made a difference. My time at Pendle Hill stands out as one of the most important events of my life. I may spend the rest of my lifetime exploring the strands of spiritual growth begun there."

—Pendle Hill participant

Although this adult center for study and contemplation is run by Quakers and reflects their social and spiritual values, it provides a nurturing and enlightening environment for people of all faiths. Transformational experiences are available through conferences, retreats, and sojourns.

The personal transformation which can take place at Pendle Hill serves as preparation for taking part in the transformation of society and the world. The spiritual basis of life and work deepens as new sources of inward guidance, peace, and power are discovered. Non-Quakers can still find the four basic Quaker testimonies to be valuable:

Equality of opportunity and respect for individuals.
Simplicity of the educational and material environment.
Harmony of inward and outward actions.
Community in daily life and in the seeking of the Spirit.

A variety of conferences and retreats are held during the fall, winter, and spring. Most are held over a weekend, but a few last for a week. Past examples have included:

- **Awakening to the Present**
  Examines how to be truly present in each moment with gratitude and happiness, including slowing down and becoming more aware.

- **"Oh Wow" Experiences**
  Seeks the Divine in everyone and everything by evoking the sense of wonder in nature, in ritual, in play, and in ordinary places and occasions.

131

- **Healing from Lifewounds**
  Participants experience the healing arts of the body or heart through music, massage, ideas, and stories.

- **Writing a Spiritual Autobiography**
  Participants expand their spiritual self-awareness through reading the classics of spiritual autobiography and understanding/writing their own.

- **Parents and Teens**
  Parents and teens learn to love together through reflection, sharing, worship, and play.

- **Song, Silence and Spirituality**
  Explores the links between musical sound and transcendent experience in our lives through such varied types as Gregorian chants, Hindu/Buddhist mantras, Jewish cantorial liturgy, and bamboo-tube playing of the Malaysian rain forest dwellers.

Sojourning at Pendle Hill enables participants to live in the community for short stays lasting anywhere from one day to three weeks. During the resident terms (October to June), sojourners have the opportunity to share in the life of the community as much or as little as they wish. They may take classes in Quakerism, the Bible, religious thought, literature and the arts, social concerns, and crafts. They may also participate in the daily meeting for worship held in the Quaker tradition (which includes long periods of silence), share in meal-time preparation and fellowship, and pursue individual study and personal spiritual development. Sojourners may avail themselves of the space and time for silent reflection, libraries, crafts facilities, and the organic gardens and grounds.

In the summer months there are no courses or community activities scheduled, but sojourners may use the facilities at Pendle Hill for individual retreats, research, writing projects, or relaxation.

Participants stay in private, simply furnished bedrooms. Three meals a day (with a vegetarian option always available) are provided.

Pendle Hill is located about twelve miles southwest of Philadelphia in a suburban area with easy access to public transportation (train or taxi from the airport). Pendle Hill staff will pick up participants at the train station in the nearby town of Media. The center is set on twenty-three acres of trees and gardens. Recreational activities include singing, volleyball, ping-pong, folk dancing, and walking. Nearby Philadelphia offers museums, gardens, parks, and theaters.

COST: (some scholarship aid available)

Pendle Hill
338 Plush Mill Road
Wallingford, PA 19086-6099

 (800) 742-3150
(610) 566-4507
www.quaker.org/pendle-hill/

POWER PLACES TOURS

"The whole trip—starting with the pyramid and journeying onward—was a very powerful experience...the changes/transformation I can only begin to understand for I know my life will be different because I chose this experience."

—Power Places Tours participant

As the largest Transformational Travel tour and conference organization in the world, Power Places Tours provides travel experiences which are truly out of the ordinary. Each tour and conference incorporates spiritual elements that set them apart from other travel programs.

The tours and conferences are conducted in mystical places with intense energy and power. Past tours have included dolphin swims in the Red Sea, pyramid exploration in Egypt, mountain climbs in Tibet and Nepal, and hiking through the Brazilian rain forest. Conference settings have included the Tantric temples and Taj Mahal in India, the Great Pyramid in Egypt, the unspoiled Hawaiian island of Moloka'i, and Stonehenge, England. All the sites are chosen for their magical abilities to help transform lives through their inherent spiritual forces. Scenic as these places are, the purpose of the trip is not to obtain souvenir photographs; the goal is to experience the magic of the ancient structures or natural settings in a way which enables personal growth.

The tours sometimes include optional workshops on a variety of metaphysical subjects. The conference themes have ranged from channeling to angels, nature spirits to sexuality, and spirituality to healing and rejuvenation. Some of the content is presented in a lecture format, but there are also many experiential activities (such as personal healing sessions with world-class healers or discovering how to communicate with a personal guardian angel).

Most tours and conferences last about a week.

134

At the end of the week, conference participants take home enhanced knowledge, skills, and emotional and physical well-being.

COST:  to

(breakfast is the only meal included in the price; airfare is included on some of the tours)

 Power Places Tours
24532 Del Prado
Dana Point, CA 92629

(800) 234-8687
(714) 487-3450 in California
www.powerplaces.com

THE RAINBOW EXPERIENCE

"I had a truly life-affirming experience! I cannot believe how my life has shifted, and my energy level."

—Rainbow Experience participant

Life Spectrums, as an international organization of spiritually-minded individuals who provide opportunities for exploration and growth to other persons seeking enhanced awareness, holds an annual event every July focusing on heightened consciousness. This Rainbow Experience offers a variety of workshops throughout the week. All are taught by prominent spiritual educators, speakers, and writers. No single philosophy or religious doctrine is advocated; the goal is individual enlightenment.

The presenters and topics change from year to year. The general focus is on the inter-connectedness of all life, human potential, connecting to the Divine, and visions for the future. Past examples of the two-hour long workshops have included:

- **Close Encounters of an Angelic Kind**
  Combining lecture, slide presentations, meditation, inner expansion exercises, and healing techniques, this workshop shows how to walk, talk, laugh, and cry with the angels.

- **Sacred Art**
  Participants get in touch with the sacred artist hidden within each of them by producing art inspired by spirit.

- **Opening the Sacred View**
  By combining elements from T'ai Chi, Zen, yoga, Tibetan Buddhism, Taoism, and Native American traditions, participants learn to connect inner nature with outer nature, with the goal of human awakening and the preservation of Planet Earth.

- **Death and Enlightenment**
  The focus is on the biology, psychology, and metaphysics of death so that participants may understand the meaning of

their own death. Through meditation, guided imagery, and other exercises, the fear of death can be diminished so that life can be fully lived in the present.

In addition to the workshops, there are less structured activities such as group drumming, creating a medicine wheel, impromptu musical concerts, and other social gatherings. There is also yoga, morning meditations, and massages.

The Rainbow Experience is held at Kutztown University in the Pennsylvania Dutch countryside (a ninety-minute drive from Philadelphia). Recreational possibilities in the area include antique and flea markets, craft shops, and historic sites such as covered bridges. Participants who do not drive to the campus may arrive by bus or by Rainbow shuttle from the ABE Airport in Allentown.

Participants stay in a double-occupancy dormitory room on campus. Off-campus housing can be arranged for those who wish private rooms. Vegetarian meals are served.

COST:

 Life Spectrums
P.O. Box 373
Harrisburg, PA 17108

☎ (800) 360-5683

137

ROSE MOUNTAIN RETREAT CENTER

Rose Mountain provides a number of six-day programs during the summer and fall. All workshops and retreats have a spiritual component and encompass a variety of spiritual/religious traditions. Typical of recent programming are:

- **The Unfolding of Emotion**
  Mindfulness, dance, personal analysis, and group sharing are used to explore each participant's unique relationship to fear, anger, sadness, joy, and compassion. Emotions are cultivated as allies for spiritual development and maturity.

- **Spirituality Beyond Structure**
  Islamic Sufism is explored in a context of gender egalitarianism and inclusivity. The focus is on intimate spiritual truth.

- **Silence is Praise**
  Complementary practices of the Jewish and Buddhist faiths are combined so that participants gain expanded awareness and a greater appreciation for each moment. Silence, mindfulness, and chanting provide indepth devotional experiences.

- **Deep Listening Retreat**
  Participants learn to maximize many forms of listening as meditative practices. The training includes inventing instruments, using voices and found sounds, keeping a sound journal, and creative movement meditation practices based on T'ai Chi and Taoist breathing techniques.

Participants generally camp out, although private indoor accommodations are available. Vegetarian meals are served.

The Center is located in the southern Rockies of New Mexico bordering the Santa Fe National Forest.

COST:

Rose Mountain Retreat Center
P.O. Box 355
Las Vegas, NM 87701

 (505) 425-5728

SACRED JOURNEYS

"Our old patterns, personally and globally, are being shattered to herald in the New Dawn. As we look around our world, we see the old forms crumbling, our belief systems being challenged and new forms beckoning to be born. The robot within us who blindly repeats the old ways is dying, and the angel with its global brain is heralding our Rebirth and fullest Potentials."
—*Helene A. Shik, Director of Purple Mountain Tours*

Purple Mountain Tours offers several Sacred Journeys throughout the year to the power centers of Europe, the Americas, Egypt, and Asia Minor. Going far beyond routine sightseeing, these trips incorporate rites, ceremonies, and teachings of the ancient Mystery Traditions. Local healers, teachers, and experts in archaeology and mythology provide a unique learning experience for participants who desire to heal themselves as well as the planet.

Examples of Sacred Journeys include:

- **Pilgrimage to Egypt and Mount Sinai (14 days)**
  The energies of the ancient Egyptians are considered to still be available today, with the Nile at the center. Participants also explore temples, tombs, pyramids, and Mount Sinai. They learn how to balance the masculine and feminine energies in each of us, use the power of compassion rather than strength through force, celebrate the miracle of personal rebirth, and meditate and pray for world peace.

- **Initiation into the Earth Mysteries of the British Isles (13 days)**
  Participants explore the Celtic Mystery Traditions while following the oath of the Holy Grail. They visit a number of springs and holy wells, bathing in healing waters and experiencing the life force that flows from this water. Ancient rites of purification are combined with meditation, examination of each participant's own sacred journey, and opening up to the energy of ancient labyrinths and temples like Stonehenge.

139

- **Mythical Journey to the Gods and Goddesses of Greece (12 days)**

  This pilgrimage to the ancient temples, land, and sea of Greece enables participants to learn to blend matter and spirit, and human and God selves. They learn the wisdom of the many gods and goddesses while exploring archaeological and natural sites. Participants connect with the gods and goddesses to develop personal relationships with them just as the ancient Greeks experienced.

Other journeys have gone to France (on the path of the Black Madonna), Peru (travelling the path of the Incas), and Turkey (exploring the Sumerian, Babylonian, Persian, Roman, and Byzantine civilizations).

Participants stay in double-occupancy rooms at deluxe hotels.

COST: 💲💲 to 💲💲💲

(includes airfare from a designated U.S. city to the destination and back)

Purple Mountain Tours
RD 2, Box 1314
Putney, VT 05346

☎ (802) 387-4753

School of Spiritual Healing and Prophecy

"This training has opened up latent talents within me, expanded my confidence, and raised me to a higher level of spirituality. It has helped me to stretch, while giving a strong support system for my faith, my work, and new techniques which accelerate growth."

—*School of Spiritual Healing and Prophecy participant*

The weekend retreats offered by this unique school combine modern, accelerated learning methods with age old spiritual development approaches. Each Spiritual Insight Training program focuses on three areas:

- **Meditation**
  Deep levels of meditative practice are emphasized.

- **Spiritual healing**
  Tools such as hands-on healing, dowsing, labyrinths, crystals, color and sound, and gemstones are used to open the heart to love and healing.

- **Spiritual insight development**
  Participants learn to enhance their psychic and intuitive faculties.

Interviews with the school director are generally required prior to admission.

Weekend sessions are held at a retreat center in western New York State. Rooms are double occupancy. Three vegetarian meals are served daily.

The school feels that its training enables participants to reach the same levels of spiritual healing and prophecy that can take a year or more in standard metaphysical training programs. The retreat formats allow participants to temporarily step away from their everyday life demands and devote themselves to inner reflection. By the end of the training, there is a sense of inner

peace, creativity, wonder, and joy. Participants develop a deter-
mination to live spiritual truths on a daily, practical basis, and
a commitment to lifelong spiritual discovery is made.

COST: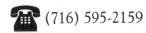

 Fellowships of the Spirit/School of Spiritual
    Healing and Prophecy
P.O. Box 252
Lily Dale, NY 14752

☎ (716) 595-2159

SUNDOOR

> "It's in the mountains that your heart gets pure. The peaks, the clouds, the water natural from a stream, it purifies you. Walking, your mind gets quiet. That's when your spirit wakes up."
>
> —*Richard Aguayo, Sundoor guide*

Sundoor offers two- to three-week trips to Peru that combine physical and spiritual adventure. The focus is on the mystical aspects of the Andes and the Amazon. The highlight of the trip is the ritual ceremonies at the Temple of the Sun at Machu Picchu (a setting believed to have special power drawn from the juxtaposition of the mountains and constellations). The ancient Incas cherished the sunrise at Machu Picchu. Participants in Sundoor trips can enjoy the same opportunity to feel the renewal of life and refresh their spirituality. In addition, there are many opportunities to interact with the shamans and natives of the region.

Participants trek through the Andes for much of the trip. Other activities include exploration of ruins, participation in cleansing and healing ceremonies, sunrise meditation, canoeing, and soaking in hot mineral baths.

Guides set up tents for sleeping while on the trail. Hotels are used for the couple of days spent in cities before and after the trek. Every dietary need can be accommodated.

COST: 🌞$ 🌞$ 🌞$ (includes round-trip airfare between Miami and Peru)

 Sundoor Foundation for Transpersonal Education
P.O. Box 669
Twain Harte, CA 95383

 (800) 755-1701
www.sundoor.com

TARA SINGH RETREATS

"My life will never be the same. Everything seems to have a different meaning, a different light, a different value. I am grateful for the space you have given me, and at the same time, the space that I have been able to find within myself. As a consequence of having been here this week, now I have the chance to live life from service and satisfaction."

—Tara Singh Retreat participant

Tara Singh has been following a spiritual path since he was eighteen, exploring the Eastern religions and then moving beyond conventional religion to other activities facilitating the search for Truth (such as silent meditation and yoga). In 1976, he came into contact with A Course in Miracles, the self-study collection of spiritual teachings which uses Christian terminology but expresses universal truths. Meditation, instruction, discussion, and experiential exercises inspire participants to look within, acknowledge and celebrate their selves, extend love and forgiveness, and let go of fear, anger, and guilt.

Every year, Mr. Singh conducts two seven-day retreats on A Course in Miracles, one on the West Coast at Eastertime and one on the East Coast during Yom Kippur. The great spiritual teachings and religions of the world are incorporated as well.

Tara Singh also teaches some weekend workshops throughout the year. Past topics have included For What You are Grateful You Will Never Be Denied, The Light of Goodness Is In You, and It Is Heaven In You That Supports The Earth and Provides the Food.

The workshops and retreats are held at hotels, resorts, and inns throughout the country. Accommodations can be either single- or double-occupancy.

COST:

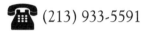 Foundation for Life Action
P.O. Box 48932
Los Angeles, CA 90048

☎ (213) 933-5591

TASSAJARA

As a Zen monastery in a remote part of California's Ventana wilderness, Tassajara provides spiritual refreshment through summer workshops and retreats. All programs enable Zen practice to be integrated within the context of personal relationships—with ourselves, with others, and with the environment. Examples of past programs include:

- **Invitation to Zen Buddhism**
  Activities include meditation, lectures, discussions, hiking, group projects with clay, and evening tea.

- **Cooking As Spiritual Practice**
  Opportunities to experience generosity, kindness, careful effort, patience, concentration, and awareness give a spiritual element to cooking.

- **Living with Pain**
  Buddhism teaches that suffering can be dealt with only when it is fully understood and acknowledged. Activities to help learn how to do this include sitting and walking meditation, lecture and discussion, gentle movements, ritual, and mindfulness practices.

There is no direct public transportation to Tassajara. It can only be reached by car (two hours from Monterey or Carmel, or five hours from San Francisco). The center will pick participants up in Jamesburg (about 40 minutes away). The last 14 miles of Tassajara Road can be very scenic but dangerous as the dirt road has a steep and narrow descent.

The resort has natural hot springs, a creek, hiking trails, and a swimming pool.

Rooms are shared or private (with a private bath). Three vegetarian meals are served daily.

COST: (work-study programs at greatly reduced rates are available in which participants follow the daily resident schedule of meditation and work, such as meal preparation and serving, dishwashing, cabin cleaning, and gardening)

Tassajara
300 Page Street
San Francisco, CA 94102

(415) 431-3771
bodhi.zendo.com/~sfzc/pages/tassajara_controls/zmc.html

147

ZEN MOUNTAIN MONASTERY

"By giving our awareness to the moment we can reclaim our lives. Without that awareness, we eat without tasting, love without feeling, die without having fully lived."

—*Zen Master John Daido Loori*

Zen Buddhism is a twenty-five hundred-year-old spiritual system that allows its disciples to discover the peace, wisdom, and compassion within themselves through zazen (a simple yet profound form of meditation). The Zen Mountain Monastery provides training to both clerical and lay persons in a discipline which merges traditional practices with American methods. Unlike other retreat centers which offer weekend or weeklong retreats and conferences whose sole focus is the specific topic, this center integrates monastic Zen training with all other activities.

Participants are asked to attend all scheduled activities. They include walking meditation, chanting and bowing during services, working together during the period of silent "caretaking" or work practice, and participating in the sessions pertaining to the retreat's topic. Each day begins before dawn and ends at 9:30 P.M. with zazen.

Examples of past retreats include:

- **Introduction to Zen Training Weekend**
  Introduces the basics of self-realization, spiritual training, and integrating Zen practice into daily life.

- **Sesshin**
  Teaches silent meditation in weeklong intensives or weekends.

- **Deep Listening Weekend**
  Participants engage in breathing training, listening as an ensemble, keeping a sound journal, and inventing instruments.

148

- **The Perfection of Giving Weekend**
  Featuring training in both giving and receiving, this retreat includes a community service project such as preparing and serving a holiday meal to the homeless, abused children, and the elderly.

Other retreat activities have included Ikebana (Japanese flower arranging), birdwatching, haiku poetry, rock climbing, landscape painting, and T'ai Chi.

In addition to the scheduled weekend retreats, a one-month monastic training experience can be arranged. The intensity of round-the-clock practicing of Zen can be best experienced through this unique experience under the tutelage of Zen teachers and monks. Meditation, classes, and work activities are the main focus.

The monastery is located ninety-seven miles north of New York City on 230 acres of mountains and rivers in a state forest preserve. It can be reached by bus from New York. Dormitory-style accommodations are available for short-term stays; private accommodations are available for residents of one month or more. Meals are primarily vegetarian.

After a challenging and intense weekend at the Zen Mountain Monastery, participants are able to continue their spiritual journey in their home environment. The sense of peace and increased wisdom about the self and the outside world can be used in every facet of daily life.

COST:

Zen Mountain Monastery
P.O. Box 197PC, South Plank Road
Mount Tremper, NY 12457

 (914) 688-2228
www.zen-mtn.org/zmm/mro.shtml

149

Social Action and Service Programs

None of the following experiences will be the most relaxing vacation you've ever taken. Whether it's learning more about poverty in less developed nations, building a home for a family who could not otherwise afford one, walking for peace, cleaning up the environment, tracking timber wolves, or teaching English and other subjects to children in other countries, some physical and mental exertion is required.

But for a week or more, you can be involved in something that helps people, animals, the environment, or scientific and social knowledge. By making a difference in the world, you can make a difference in your own life. You can return to your daily schedule with a renewed faith in your ability to contribute to the well-being of humans or to nature. Your vacation can give you the vision and commitment to continue working for those causes you believe in. The experience can help you determine what's really important to you. The frustrations and stresses in your personal and professional life may not seem so bothersome once you apply your time and energy to something beyond yourself.

APPALACHIAN MOUNTAIN CLUB TRAIL PROGRAMS

"The experience was more than I had anticipated. I feel a very strong need to preserve our wilderness areas, so I felt a great sense of accomplishment both from the physical point of view and also by donating my time to a worthy cause."

—Appalachian Mountain Club Trail Programs participant

The Appalachian Mountain Club uses over one thousand volunteers every year in its trail building and maintenance efforts. They work in partnership with the U.S. Forest Service, National Park Service, nonprofit organizations, and state natural resource agencies to conserve natural resources, maximize access, and minimize harmful environmental impacts of hiking and camping.

No special skills are needed. Participants just need to have the stamina for physically demanding work such as cutting new trails or installing step stones.

Some volunteer opportunities are for a week, whereas others are for a weekend or even a day.

Most of the programs are in the Northeast: the White Mountains of New Hampshire, Acadia National Park in Maine, the Berkshires in Massachusetts, and Catskills in New York. There are also opportunities in Idaho, Wyoming, Iceland, and England.

Participants generally camp out or stay in a lodge.

COST: (tools, training, lodging, and meals are provided; a small program fee is charged)

Appalachian Mountain Club
P.O. Box 298
Gorham, NH 03581

 (603) 466-2721
www.volunteers.com/mtnclub.html

Center for Global Education

"I have begun to make conclusions more slowly about individuals and their situations because I am better aware that they have very different cultures and frames of reference from mine. I am not as quick to judge conduct or attitudes because I understand more fully how culture has had a profound impact on behavior, thinking, and learning. I (now) have new ways of thinking about politics, theology, and daily life."

—Center for Global Education participant

As the largest of the "reality tour" operators, the Center for Global Education at Augsburg College specializes in seven- to twenty-one-day travel seminars throughout Central America and in Mexico, South Africa and Namibia, the Middle East, and Southeast Asia. They coordinate more than thirty educational immersion programs each year. Rather than simply taking tourists to exotic places, the Center brings participants into direct contact with real people who are struggling for justice, freedom, and human dignity. Participants also meet with decision makers from government, business, and church for exposure to a variety of viewpoints and perspectives.

Examples of past travel opportunities have ranged from a ten-day trip to El Salvador to observe the election process to two weeks exploring the social issues and needs of Thailand and Laos to eight days in Mexico focusing on poverty and hunger.

By the conclusion of the tour, participants have sharpened their thinking about global issues and find themselves in a better position to work toward a more just world.

Participants stay in various types of lodging, ranging from private residences to dormitories to hotels.

Interested persons can borrow a videotape from the Center which shows actual footage of travel seminars and explains the kinds of experiences participants have on "reality tours."

COST: 🌞 to 🌞 🌞 🌞

> (depending on destination and length; airfare from and to a U.S. city included)

Center for Global Education
Augsburg College
2211 Riverside Avenue
Minneapolis, MN 55454

☎ (612) 330-1159
aug3.augsburg.edu/global/index/html

CLOSE UP FOUNDATION

"...gives the 'chronologically gifted' citizens an understanding of the way public policy affects their lives."

—Close Up Foundation participant

Washington, D.C., is a popular vacation spot for many tourists. Our cosmopolitan capital offers a wealth of things to do and see. But all too often, tourists don't gain a real understanding of how the government functions. That's why Close Up Foundation came into being in 1971. This nonprofit, nonpartisan civic education organization's mission is to "help citizens better understand the important role they play in democracy."

With a Close Up week in Washington, visitors gain firsthand knowledge of the nation and the democratic process. By witnessing legislative proceedings on the House floor, attending a Capitol Hill committee hearing, and meeting with senators, representatives, and aides, participants get a behind-the-scenes look at government in action. Seminars on a variety of issues and topics are provided by members of the administration, policy analysts, media representatives, and other Washington experts. There are also small-group discussion sessions and a visit to a foreign embassy or international organization.

But the week is not all work and no play. To the contrary, each day includes a visit to a historical or cultural site. Scheduled trips may include the Smithsonian museums, monuments and memorials, botanical gardens, as well as an evening at the theater. Meals are arranged at well-known restaurants around the metro area.

Special programs include the National Leadership Issues Forum in collaboration with major national aging organizations (an intense week of seminars, briefings, workshops, and study issues for aging advocates), The American Presidency (five days in Washington and three in Charlottesville, Virginia learning about the highest office in the land and the men who have filled it), Close Up Washington and the World (a week in Washington focusing on world politics and the interaction of domestic and international policy), and Close Up Washington and Williamsburg (five nights with the Close Up activities in Washington and two nights exploring Colonial Williamsburg).

At the end of the week's learning adventure, participants come away with a better understanding of how things work in Washington. The perspectives gained about current issues, government, and politics makes reading the paper or watching the evening news much more rewarding. Participants may feel compelled to become involved in the political process and explore opportunities on a volunteer or paid basis.

Most of the programs are offered in the spring. A few are offered during fall.

The program is designed especially for (but is not limited to) adults age fifty and over. The pace is comfortable for older adults and addresses many of the public policies that affect their lives.

Participants share rooms in quality hotels. All meals during the program are provided.

COST: (transportation to and from Washington, D.C., not included)

 Close Up Foundation
44 Canal Center Plaza
Alexandria, VA 22314

(703) 706-3668
www.closeup.org

EARTHWATCH

"Earthwatch alone offers individuals the opportunity to act, not just send money or change a vote, but to engage the mind and talent in solving fascinating problems."

—*Brian Rosborough, Earthwatch President*

Most of us care about the planet but generally feel at a loss when attempting to acquire knowledge about and truly understand the important environmental issues. Reading up on the issues could help to some extent, but much of the available material is either highly technical or overly simplistic. Reference materials just aren't as engrossing or enlightening as hands-on study and experience.

Earthwatch provides opportunities for volunteers to assist scientists on two-week environmental research expeditions throughout the world. Since 1972, the nonprofit organization's mission has been "to sustain the world's environment, monitor global change, conserve endangered species and habitats, explore the heritage of the earth's people, and foster world health and international cooperation." Each year more than four thousand volunteers are assigned to one of the 165 projects. Past projects have included excavating and cataloging fossils in Uganda, measuring and recording volcanic debris in Russia, collecting rare plants in Mexico, collecting insects inside caves in Oregon, birdwatching in Australia, tracking timber wolves in Minnesota, interviewing local people in Ireland to document ancient Celtic cultural and religious symbolism, photographing coral reefs in Fiji and surveying women's health in Bolivia.

Volunteers are not required to have any scientific training or skills; all that's required is a willingness to work and learn. A few projects do require specialized skills such as scuba diving. Some projects are more rigorous than others, demanding that participants be in excellent shape (for hiking through the Himalayas, for instance). Anyone age sixteen or older is eligible to apply. Depending on the location of the project, lodging can range from tents to cabins to dormitories to bed-and-breakfasts to hotels. Earthwatch volunteers feel that their experiences in the EarthCorps enrich their professional and personal lives. More than forty-five hundred volunteers have returned throughout the years to work on subsequent projects. Making a difference by assisting with scientific expeditions can be very satisfying. Volunteers return with enhanced knowledge and self-confidence which can be used for continued learning and action.

Volunteers help fund the expedition they join by making a tax-deductible contribution to cover food, lodging, support, and equipment.

COST:

(not inclusive of airfare; grants are available to teachers, high-school students, and artists)

 Earthwatch
680 Mount Auburn Street
P.O. Box 403
Watertown, MA 02272-9924

(800) 776-0188
(617) 926-8200
www.earthwatch.org

FOUNDATION FOR FIELD RESEARCH

Like Earthwatch, the Foundation for Field Research is a non-profit organization which coordinates research expeditions. Since 1982, the Foundation has met the needs of scientists conducting research by furnishing them with volunteers who contribute both physical and financial assistance.

Project areas include prehistoric archaeology, historic archaeology, marine archaeology, folklore, paleontology, sea turtle conservation, ornithology, primatology, entomology, and forest conservation. The projects take place all over the world. Australia, New Guinea, Liberia, French Polynesia, Mexico, Canada, United States, Italy, France, Germany, Spain, Peru, and Costa Rica are only a few of the countries which have hosted scientific projects. Examples of past projects have included:

- Monitoring the behavior of Mona monkeys on Grenada Island.

- Diving to record shipwrecks off the West African coast.

- Tracing and mapping a volcano that erupted in Texas thirty-two million years ago.

- Making architectural drawings of historic buildings in Mexico.

- Canoeing down the Missouri River in Montana to study prairie dog colonies.

Lengths of stay can vary from two days to one month. Most projects are from one to two months.

There is no upper age limit for volunteers. Generally, they must be fourteen or older.

Volunteers work on a team ranging from five to twenty-five persons.

As both a labor force and funding source, volunteers pay a share-of-cost contribution covering meals, lodging, ground transportation, and the researcher's expenses, including equipment and supplies. The costs to travel to the project site are tax deductible.

Accommodations vary according to the location. Most are dorm-style in a house, but camping is occasionally done.

In addition to helping with scientific research, participants must occasionally help with other tasks such as cleaning and cooking.

Because living and working conditions may be very different than what participants typically experience (and there are some hazards relating to weather, disease, and wildlife), it is important that volunteers have adaptability and perseverance.

COST:

 Foundation for Field Research
680 Mount Auburn Street
P.O. Box 403
Watertown, MA 02272-9924

GLOBAL AWARENESS THROUGH EXPERIENCE (GATE)

"This short immersion with the poor will enable each of us to simplify our lives, to experience conversion to the Jesus we have met on our travels, and further bond us as we work for justice and the building of the kingdom in our world."

—*Global Awareness Through Experience participant*

Standard packaged tours usually highlight only the most photogenic and famous places. Tourists seldom gain a real perception of what life is actually like for the residents of other countries. Meaningful interaction with the locals is very limited.

For an international immersion experience that goes far beyond the norm, GATE is worth exploring. Participants visit third-world communities and attend lectures by social and political analysts, theologians, and economists. People-to-people connections are emphasized.

There is an ecumenical focus to the program. The local spiritual and religious traditions are investigated. Dialogue with representatives of the faith community is emphasized. GATE believes that it is carrying forward the call of the Christian church to recognize and help the poor.

By the end of the ten- to fourteen-day experience, participants have an enhanced understanding of the culture, the faith, the struggles, and the dreams of the people. The end result is enhanced motivation for helping less fortunate people around the world, as well as practical knowledge of what needs to be done. Participants also note an increased appreciation for what they personally have, along with a desire to simplify their lives and deemphasize the material things.

Participants may choose Mexico, Guatemala, El Salvador, Eastern Europe (eastern Germany, the Czech Republic, and Slovakia), and Zimbabwe. Activities include neighborhood visits, conversations with local leaders, trips to social service programs such as schools and clinics, and conferences with human rights leaders. While there may be a few short excursions that are similar to those on typical tours (such as a coffee plantation, agricultural cooperative, or church), the focus is not on photographing these spots for souvenirs and then climbing back on the tour bus. Instead, the goal is to familiarize participants with the struggles of the local people.

Lodging is not in deluxe hotels. Creature comforts are limited, but the essentials are provided for in local inns, hostels, monasteries, and local homes. Guides and interpreters are provided.

COST: to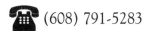

    (depending on length and destination; airfare to and from the destination is extra)

GATE
912 Market Street
La Crosse, WI 54601-8800

(608) 791-5283

GLOBAL VOLUNTEERS

"I started out thinking we were going to other countries to help other people, but frankly, after three years I think I'm getting the most help."

—Global Volunteers participant

Global Volunteers is an international service organization like the Peace Corps, but participants serve two to three weeks (rather than years) and there's none of the bureaucratic red tape found in federal programs. Their work projects vary widely in location and type of volunteer assistance since each reflects the priorities of the host community. Recent projects included teaching the basics of capitalism to potential entrepreneurs in Russia, building a preschool in Costa Rica, and teaching English in Poland, Vietnam, or Indonesia.

Volunteers typically do not need any specialized skills. Attitude is more important than education or experience. Participants must be willing to learn with and relate to the local people. They can't bring any rigid expectations to the project; instead, they must be open to the conditions and customs they find.

Global Volunteers function as a team. No volunteer is entirely on his or her own; there is always support and assistance available from peers.

Most trips are two to three weeks, but there are some service projects in the Mississippi Delta that last only a week.

Accommodations depend on the locale. They can include dormitories, hotels, campsites, guest houses, and homestays with local families.

COST: to

(airfare extra; fees are tax-deductible)

Global Volunteers
375 East Little Canada Road
St. Paul, MN 55117-1628

(800) 487-1074
www.globalvolunteers.org

HABITAT FOR HUMANITY

Originally founded as a Christian housing ministry which focused on replacing the tarpaper shacks in rural Georgia, Habitat for Humanity is on its way to becoming one of the largest builders of homes in the United States. Volunteers of all faiths and ages work in thirty-eight countries to build simple, decent shelter that is sold to people in need at no profit with no-interest loans. Potential home owners are required to invest five hundred hours of sweat equity alongside the volunteer builders.

Most of the volunteers are not in the building trades; their qualifications are simply a willingness to pick up a hammer or paintbrush. Former President Jimmy Carter, for example, is an enthusiastic participant each year. Some office duties are also available.

Participants treasure the opportunity to express their spirituality and love for humanity by taking direct action to help solve one of the most pressing problems of our time: the lack of decent, affordable housing.

Although Habitat is a Christian organization, volunteers are not required to be members of a Christian church.

Interested persons can join one of the four hundred-plus affiliate projects in the United States and Canada and work on local projects. For those who enjoy travel, a work camp may be a more appealing way to spend a week or more.

Volunteers pay for transportation to and from the work camp. Housing is available in some areas for volunteers; in others, volunteers must find their own housing.

COST:

 Habitat for Humanity
121 Habitat Street
Americus, GA 31709-3498

 (912) 924-6935
www.habitat.org

164

THE LISLE FELLOWSHIP

"Lisle played a crucial role in my search for maturity. It encouraged me to risk myself in new relationships, and gave me the opportunity to test myself in new situations. Lisle was the place where I experienced the reality of a multicultural world, and became forever dissatisfied with a more limited point of view."

—Lisle Fellowship participant

Since 1936 Lisle has demonstrated and symbolized the world's interdependence. There is no economic or political agenda. Instead, their trademarks have been inclusion, evaluation, and reconciliation. The Fellowship Method presumes that no one has a monopoly on the truth. People throughout the world all have something to teach their neighbors.

The Lisle Fellowship opens minds to other cultures, creating the possibility for world peace and survival through understanding. Its experiential approach to global education enables participants to enhance their communication skills, discover the value of diverse ideas, learn to effectively resolve conflict, build community, increase self-knowledge, and gain greater respect for all life.

One to three weeks with Lisle enables participants to experience the reality of a multicultural world and become forever dissatisfied with a more limited view. Instead of lectures in a classroom by a professor, Lisle emphasizes small group experiences which enable hands-on exposure to other ways of life. Participants are engaged physically and emotionally as well as intellectually.

Recent experiences have included two weeks in Oklahoma focusing on Native Americans; three weeks on the Indonesian isle of Bali observing spiritual and cultural conflicts arising from increasing modernization, tourism, and trade; two weeks on the Hawaiian island of Kaua'i learning about local culture,

165

spiritual beliefs, and political concerns while helping community groups rebuild their island from the devastation of a hurricane through projects such as trail building, native tree planting, and cleanup of sacred sites; six days at Ohio's University of Toledo exploring the diverse religions, customs, and traditions of its many foreign students; three weeks in New Delhi, India, in cooperation with the Gandhi Peace Foundation increasing understanding of the global issues involved in air and water resource management; and three weeks in Uganda, Africa, expanding knowledge of this part of Africa and working with social service agencies.

Participants stay in local hotels, private homes, and unusual settings such as a yoga ashram or tepees on an Indian reservation. Meals are provided.

Most programs are scheduled during the summer.

COST:  to
(depending on destination and length; airfare extra)

 Dr. Mark B. Kinney
The Lisle Fellowship, Inc.
433 West Sterns Road
Temperance, MI 48182-9509

☎ (800) 477-1538
(734) 847-7126
www.lisle.utoledo.edu

PLOWSHARES INSTITUTE

"The trip is still influencing my life...I have the strong feeling that my faith and my purpose has been validated."

—Plowshares Institute participant

Plowshares describes its purpose as "education, research, and dialogue toward a more just, sustainable, and peaceful world community." The focus of their activities is cross-cultural experiences which can initiate new levels of global understanding. Immersion seminars in Africa, Asia, Latin America, and Eastern Europe provide a unique opportunity to learn and live outside of North America.

These traveling seminars allow participants to experience the many issues (social, economic, environmental, political, cultural) of other countries. They feature direct contact with religious, business, academic, government, and grassroots leaders, in addition to individual home visits with host families.

No special training or education is required of participants, but they are expected to prepare for the experience through advance reading, live "safely and simply" in the style of their host, and share and interpret their experiences when they return.

Regardless of the destination of their trip, participants return with enhanced awareness of the ways in which North American government, business, religious, and academic policies impact the rest of the world. They retain the perspective of our common humanity and interdependence with the rest of the world.

Representative traveling seminars include a two-week trip to South Africa (as a society in transition) and two weeks in

Brazil (focusing on the ecological crisis of the global community as especially reflected in this country).

COST:  (includes airfare from and to major
U.S. cities)

 Plowshares Institute
P.O. Box 243
809 Hopmeadow Street
Simsbury, CT 06070

☎ (860) 651-4304

Service Civil International

Awarded the title of "Messenger of Peace" by the United Nations, Service Civil International promotes international understanding and peace through community service. Volunteers may select the country and project which interests them the most. Recent projects included running a daycare project in Northern Ireland, educating Russians about pollution, repairing fences at a wolf sanctuary in Colorado, or renovating a women's shelter in Germany. Each workcamp has a local sponsor (such as an environmental group or a community with persons with disabilities). A typical camp has between eight to fifteen volunteers and lasts two to three weeks. Most take place between June and October, but some are available during the winter.

Anyone can volunteer, as long as they're sixteen or older for U.S. camps or eighteen and older for overseas camps. Students, professionals, working people, and retirees are all welcome.

Participants must be willing to share cooking and cleaning duties in addition to the physical, intellectual, and emotional labor they expend on the project.

While Service Civil International covers room and board, participants pay their own way to and from the workcamp site, cover pocket expenses, and also pay a registration fee.

COST:

 Service Civil International
Route 2, Box 506
Crozet, VA 22932

 (804) 823-1826

WORLD FELLOWSHIP CENTER

"Probably not a week passes without our thoughts returning to World Fellowship—such an invaluable learning and growing place it was for me."

—*World Fellowship participant*

Billing itself as a "camp with a conscience," World Fellowship Center offers weeklong series of discussions and lectures throughout the summer. Programs address a variety of social issues and global concerns, such as:

- **Multi-Racial and Multi-Cultural Families**
  A sharing especially, but not exclusively, for those with a multi-ethnic heritage and culture.

- **Chile and Mexico**
  Explores recent political developments in these countries.

- **Education**
  Participants examine changes in the public and private educational systems.

- **Middle East and the United Nations**
  Addresses politics, economics, and the potential for peace in this region.

- **The Politics of Health Issues**
  Participants discuss the politics of women's health concerns, including breast cancer and AIDS.

- **Jewish Culture and History**
  Programs explore Jewish history, music, culture, and Christian-Jewish dialogue.

Participants leave with a better understanding of the important issues of today. The international, interracial, multicultural, and intergenerational aspects of the experience help to renew respect and appreciation for human value and the worth of all individuals. An increased commitment to work for world peace and social justice can result.

Participants have a number of recreational options to enjoy between the morning and evening events. These include swimming, sunbathing, canoeing, rowboating, fishing, basketball, volleyball, and blueberry picking. Nature walks, musical entertainment, and body movement classes are also offered.

Programs are offered from the middle of June to the beginning of September and last three to ten days.

The Center is located in New Hampshire's White Mountains in a rustic setting among the pine trees. Buses or trains from Boston have a drop-off point in Chororua (four miles away); Center staff will pick participants up from there for a small charge. Driving time is 2.5 hours from Boston and 6.5 hours from New York City.

Lodging is available in single or double rooms in the lodges. Campsites are also available for those who wish to bring their own tents. Meals (three a day) are served family-style and are mostly vegetarian, with a turkey dinner every Sunday.

COST:

 (September through May)
World Fellowship Center
46 Ash Street
North Conway, NH 03860

 (603) 356-5208

 (June through August)
P.O. Box 2280
Conway, NH 03818

 (603) 447-2280

www.worldfellowship.org

171

WORLDTEACH

"WorldTeach volunteers are making a difference for thousands of schoolchildren around the world...but I think I've learned and received even more than I've given."

—*WorldTeach participant*

WorldTeach volunteers work in developing countries such as China, Costa Rica, Ecuador, Namibia, Poland, Russia, South Africa, and Thailand. They teach English, math, science, and physical education. While the majority of the teaching positions are in elementary and high schools, there are also some opportunities to teach in universities, nonprofit organizations, and public enterprises such as state-run oil companies or fisheries. The locations can range from rural villages to big cities.

There are many rewards from participating in this program. Volunteers have the satisfaction of making a real impact on their students and the community. They know that they have made a difference in a number of lives by providing instruction in crucial skills and knowledge. The deeper understanding of another country, teaching experience, and foreign language skills that develop will be a source of personal and professional growth that could provide an edge in the work world.

Most of the teaching commitments are for a year, but there are some summer positions as well.

WorldTeach volunteers must have a bachelor's degree in any subject. Prior to starting to teach, they must take a course in teaching English as a second language or spend twenty-five hours teaching or tutoring English. Volunteers do not have to know another language, although it's strongly recommended that they begin to learn the language before they depart. They must furnish a resume and recommendations. Successful applicants are interviewed in their local areas.

Orientation and some support are available.

WorldTeach participants live in dormitories, apartments, hostels, or with host families. Housing is provided and financed by WorldTeach.

Volunteers must pay a fee to cover the cost of travel, health insurance, placement, orientation, field support, and program administration. Costs are highly variable depending on the assignment.

COST: to

(some financial aid is available and WorldTeach can provide guidance on fundraising)

WorldTeach
Harvard Institute for International Development
One Eliot Street
Cambridge, MA 02138

☎ (617) 495-5527

www.igc.org/worldteach

*A*nyone who is experiencing discomfort or pain (whether physical or psychic) can benefit from a vacation. Just getting away from the usual routine and surroundings alleviates stress, promotes relaxation, and establishes more positive attitudes. Unfortunately, the effects are almost always very temporary. The vacation ends, but the same problems are still there. Nothing has changed. No new behavioral strategies, spiritual insights, or lifestyle modifications occurred. The weekend or week was only a temporary escape.

But the following vacations can dramatically change your life. Although they can't undo the physical or emotional suffering you may have experienced in the past, they can give you the knowledge and skills to deal more effectively with your problems in the present. You can learn to live life in a more comfortable and healthier manner.

You don't have to be currently undergoing a major medical or psychological crisis to benefit from these vacations. Some are geared for persons who have survived significant trauma or illness, but others are appropriate for any individual who wants to improve his or her well-being through personal growth, exercise, or nutrition.

The first section, Mind/Spirit Programs, focuses on vacations which primarily promote emotional healing.

The second section, Body Programs, contains vacations which assist in healing the physical self and in promoting optimal health.

The two sections are not mutually exclusive. Programs for the mind and spirit incorporate physical practices such as breathwork. Some of the programs address the emotional impact of physical illness. Similarly, programs for the body utilize mental and spiritual practices such as meditation. The Mind/Spirit Programs affect the body, and the Body Programs influence the mind and spirit. But for the purposes of organization, vacations are classified as to their primary focus.

MIND/SPIRIT PROGRAMS

The listings in this section focus on healing psychic pain resulting from abuse, trauma, personal and family problems, substance abuse, and physical illness. Techniques include lectures, arts activities (drama, writing, sculpture), group therapy, individual counseling, twelve-step programming, and alcohol-free cruises for those in recovery.

A number of the Comprehensive Programs in the Holistic Vacations chapter also offer programming directed at healing the mind and body, as do some of the Spiritual Discovery and Renewal Programs under the Spiritual Vacations chapter.

AESCULAPIA WILDERNESS HEALING RETREAT

"It nourished my body, mind, and soul when all was disintegrating. I now face life and my fears with new resources."

—*Aesculapia participant*

Aesculapia uses its own Creative Consciousness Process through techniques from Eastern and Western psychologies, imagination, visionary processes, and the ancient Greek schools of dream healing. Believing that dreams are just another way of seeing our realities and our selves, Aesculapia's consciousness guides help participants find the healing powers within the dream itself. The sensory nature of the dream is used to go beyond the dream's surface and its symbols. Through the dream-healing process, participants can "transform trapped disease energy vortices into creative life flows."

The small number of participants at any given time ensures highly personalized attention from the consciousness guides. Retreats are not structured but instead are flexible and individualized to the needs of each individual. The Creative Consciousness Process promotes self-healing so that participants can reach new levels of awareness, confidence, and self-esteem during the retreat and then continue the process at home.

Aesculapia also offers a Wilderness River Quest. The experience begins with four days of mental and physical preparation at Aesculapia. Activities include sweat lodges, meditation, drumming, dream and consciousness journeys, as well as learning about and preparing the equipment during shorter trips in milder waters. Participants then experience a six-day life-changing quest navigating the white waters of the Rogue River. Dreams and visions are discussed and worked with during dreamshare mornings and evening campfires. The quest ends back at Aesculapia with four days of preparation to reenter the world that was left behind.

Participants stay in shared accommodations in a retreat house or rustic cabins, or may camp out. Vegetarian meals are served (or may be prepared by participants if desired). Hiking trails and a sauna are available.

Aesculapia is located on eighty acres of secluded forest in the Siskiyou Mountains of southwest Oregon. Air and bus service is available to Medford, Oregon (about two hours away). A rental car can be obtained to drive to Aesculapia.

COST:

 Aesculapia
Box 301
Wilderville, OR 97543

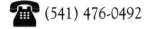 (541) 476-0492

ALCHEMICAL HYPNOTHERAPY INSTITUTE

"After the summer intensive, I continue to experience lots of transformation. I feel all kinds of release taking place...a healing, life changing experience."

—Alchemical Hypnotherapy participant

Alchemical hypnotherapy is "a therapeutic process designed to assist clients in working with their Inner Guides to change their lives." These Inner Guides live within the subconscious mind and can be accessed through the hypnotic state. They can show the direction to health, happiness, relationships, prosperity, and the fulfillment of individual spiritual purpose.

Its advocates consider it appropriate for such issues as addiction recovery (and compatible with twelve-step programs), survival of childhood abuse, co-dependency, physical illness (in conjunction with medical treatment), weight management, smoking cessation, stress management, decision making and success enhancement relating to career, and enhancing creativity.

The therapeutic process of alchemical hypnosis synthesizes techniques from Gestalt, Regression Therapy, Neuro-Linguistic Programming (NLP), psychosynthesis, and shamanism with the ancient science of alchemy as translated to the modern world by Dr. Carl Jung. It uses movement, psychodrama, hypnosis, emotional release, touch, breath, and sound to integrate the physical, emotional, mental, and spiritual areas of individual functioning. The process includes rescuing the inner child from the trauma, neglect, or pain of the past; contacting and working with the Inner Guides through trance and movement; contacting past-life memories within the collective unconscious to enhance creativity, resolve trauma, change karma, and alter contacts with significant others; and integrating subpersonalities (different voices within the self) to resolve conflicting desires and goals.

179

While the alchemical hypnotherapy process developed by David Quigley can be learned and practiced as a career, the Institute also provides personal growth training for those who want to experience the process for their own transformation rather than using it on a professional basis. This consists of one hundred hours (two weeks) of training. The Institute also provides weekend training courses and workshops on Healing the Inner Child, Wilderness Intensives (which combine outdoor activities such as hiking with the Alchemical process), and Personal Empowerment Seminars (in which the Inner Guides are brought into the body to transform posture, movement, voice, and being in the world).

Room and board varies according to location (generally resorts in California such as Malibu, Santa Ana, Sacramento, as well as other areas across the United States including Chicago, Salt Lake City, Atlanta, Portland, the Colorado Rockies, and Sedona, Arizona).

COST:

 Alchemical Hypnotherapy Institute
2310 Warwick Drive
Santa Rosa, CA 95405

 (707) 537-0495

BREAKTHROUGH

These five-day intensive co-dependency workshops are specifically designed for individuals impacted by family or relationship dysfunction in childhood or adult life. It's intended as an addition to long-term outpatient counseling although persons who are not currently seeing a therapist are welcome.

Breakthrough is considered appropriate for persons with any of the following characteristics:

• Repressed childhood memories

• Unreleased anger or grief

• Compulsive behavior (food, work, love)

• Involved in dysfunctional relationships

• Interested in personal growth

Experiential techniques, lecture, and play allow participants to address and release emotional pain of years of living in painful family systems. Some of the group therapy is conducted in same-sex groups so that sensitive issues can be comfortably discussed. Although the program is conducted in a structured group setting, there is some flexibility in the program guidelines which allow individual needs to be addressed. The atmosphere provides nurturing, safety, and an absence of shame.

All groups are conducted by master's level therapists who begin the process by conducting a personal intake interview over the phone. Participants must be over the age of seventeen, have six months abstinence and a solid recovery program if a recovering alcoholic or addict, be free of mood-altering chemicals such as tranquilizers and pain medication (antidepressants and lithium are reviewed individually in the screening process), and be physically and emotionally able to handle group therapy for at least six hours a day.

Each participant leaves with specific directions for follow-up care and a referral to a therapist (if one is needed). At the end of the workshop, old dysfunctional patterns have been broken and new possibilities are established.

The program begins on Sunday afternoon and ends Friday after lunch. Groups are held monthly for ten to twelve persons.

Participants stay at the Bon Secours Spiritual Center. Participants stay in private, basic rooms. A pool is available during the summer.

COST:

 Ann Smith Counseling and Training
4309 Linglestown Road, Suite 105-E
Harrisburg, PA 17112

 (717) 545-7252

www.annsmith.com/frmain.htm

THE CENTER FOR ATTITUDINAL HEALING

"It is time to heal the fear and negative thoughts, not just our bodies."

—Gerald Jampolsky, M.D.

"The workshop gave me the chance to work through some important issues in a self place. I now have a reference point of what peace really means."

—Center for Attitudinal Healing participant

Originally founded in 1975 as an alternative to traditional health care for children and adults faced with life-threatening illness, The Center for Attitudinal Healing has since expanded to provide support for other populations experiencing physical and emotional pain. This may include (but is not limited to):

- Persons with long-term illness

- The disabled

- Caregivers of persons with long-term illness or special needs

- Persons dealing with bereavement

- Anyone who is trying to cope with the challenges of everyday life

Attitudinal healing is "a process of letting go of painful, fearful attitudes." A conscious choice is made to favor peace over conflict and love over fear. The Center defines health as inner peace and healing as the process of letting go of fear. (The founder of attitudinal healing and the Center, Dr. Gerald Jampolsky, has written numerous books which explain the process in detail.) Although there is a spiritual element to attitudinal healing, it and the Center are nonsectarian.

Retreats are held periodically throughout the year at the Santa Sabina Retreat Center in San Rafael, California. Lasting two

183

and one-half days, they provide both experiential and didactic processes. Level I offers an introduction to attitudinal healing, empathetic listening (listening with the heart), and unconditional love and forgiveness. Level II provides a deeper exploration of attitudinal healing, including an investigation of life choices.

COST:

 The Center for Attitudinal Healing
33 Buchanon Drive
Sausalito, CA 94965

☎ (415) 331-6161

healingcenter.org

CHOICES COUNSELING CENTER
CO-DEPENDENCY ADULT CHILD PROGRAMS

"There have already been some positive changes in my life. It opened up a warm, spiritual part of me. Most of all, it taught me to be honest with myself."

—Choices Counseling Center participant

Preoccupation and extreme emotional, social, or physical dependence on another person or thing restricts personal freedom and choice. Persons who grew up with an alcoholic parent or who have lived with a substance abuser may find themselves in a codependent condition which causes difficulty relating to others, dealing with feelings (especially anger), and maintaining a sense of healthy self-esteem. Letting go of a traumatic past isn't easy, but it's possible to uncover feelings and resolve issues with the help of expert professionals.

Psychotherapy is available in every community on an outpatient basis. More intensive programs for persons new to the recovery process as well as those who are "stuck" over certain issues are available through the Choices Counseling Center in Florida. Participants may participate in a weekend program which runs from Friday night to Sunday afternoon or a five-day program beginning on Sunday night and ending Friday afternoon (or may combine the two for a week-long experience). Both programs focus on group process and provide many opportunities to identify and confront defenses.

Although long-standing problems can't magically be erased through programs like this, an investment of three to seven days can make a big difference in your ability to enjoy life and feel at peace with yourself. It can help you get more in touch with your spiritual side, gain increased self-awareness, and start making life-enhancing choices instead of being locked into unhealthy and rigid patterns. Improved relationships and a decrease in compulsive/addictive behaviors can also be benefits of participation.

185

A thirteen-page questionnaire must be completed when registering for the program. This provides insight as to participants' family history, current relationships, sexual behavior, health problems, religious and spiritual orientation, and alcohol or drug history. Programs can then be specifically tailored to meet the needs of each individual and the group.

Programs are held throughout the year. While most take place in a hotel in Orlando, a few are offered in other locations. Some programs are offered for couples or specifically for men. Meals are included.

COST:

Choices Counseling Center
P.O. Box 144
Winter Park, FL 32790

☎ (800) 741-3443 or (407) 628-3443

HEALING THE FATHER WOUND

"The retreat was what I needed to get on with my life. I made light years of progress in one weekend."
—Healing the Father Wound participant

Fathers are the means through which children learn about men. Beliefs about what men are or should be, how men should act, and how to act around them are formed by the father experience we had in our youth. Those lucky enough to have had a loving, nurturing dad had an optimal opportunity to develop positive feelings about masculinity. But many of us had fathers who were absent, distant, or abusive. The impact of this negative father experience can continue throughout adult life. Both males and females may have problems with self-esteem and with relationships because of the hurt inflicted by faulty fathering.

Three-night weekend retreats addressing this pain are offered throughout the year by leaders of the men's movement. Limited to groups of twelve participants to ensure open communication and sharing, these retreats are segregated by sex since men and women have different expectations and needs from their fathers. The weekend includes yoga, movement activities, breathwork, experiential exercises, and emotional release. Hidden memories and feelings are uncovered and released, allowing the healing process to begin. It runs from Thursday night through Sunday afternoon.

Participants stay at Harbin Hot Springs, a rustic resort three hours north of San Francisco.

COST:

The National Men's Resource Center
P.O. Box 800
San Anselmo, CA 94979

 (415) 457-3389

HEALING WITH LOVE: HOLOENERGETICS®

"This seminar opened up a place in my heart that I never felt before and helped me to understand myself and love myself and others more."

—*Holoenergetics participant*

As a physician and author of *Healing with Love*, Dr. Leonard Laskow found that the use of loving energy and expanded human consciousness can heal and transform oneself and others. He developed the process of Holoenergetic healing to recognize and release dysfunctional patterns that often stem from unconscious interpretations of our experiences and childhood perceptions. Research has shown these techniques to influence the body as well as the mind in profound ways (stabilizing cardiac activity and influencing the growth of tumor cells and bacteria).

An introductory weekend course as well as a more comprehensive four-day course are offered. Through lecture and demonstration, participants learn to recognize what they want to heal or change, resonate with it energetically to understand its source, release the energy of the illness at its source, and reform a positive energy pattern using energy, intention, imagery, insight, forgiveness, and love.

Techniques include guided meditation for self-healing and distant healing, breathwork, and cognitive awareness of activating the immune system. The techniques detect subtle energies with the hand and mind, and establish a Healing Presence in alignment with personal spiritual essence.

Seminars are offered mostly in the western United States (Washington, Colorado, California, and New Mexico). Accommodations and meals are arranged by the participant.

188

COST: 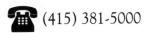 (tuition only)

 Healing with Love
20 Sunnyside Avenue, #334
Mill Valley, CA 94941

☎ (415) 381-5000

HOFFMAN QUADRINITY PROCESS

"The Hoffman Process was quite transformational for me. It made the world poetic again....After the process, I immediately rejuvenated my marriage and family relationships to their best levels ever, Then I made changes at work, creating a position with fewer hours and only my favorite kinds of work. I know of no other process that is so effective so quickly and so deeply."

—Quadrinity participant

Since it was created by Robert Hoffman in 1967, the quadrinity Process has enabled more than 30,000 people to make positive and lasting changes in their lives. Based on the principle that the negative, self-defeating patterns (thoughts, behaviors, and emotions) of adults has its roots in the experiences and conditioning of childhood, the Process seeks to resolve this original pain from childhood The goal is to realign and integrate the four divisions of being—the Quadrinity of intellect, emotions, body, and spirit.

Although conducted in a group setting, the Process is an individual, inner journey and healing. The intensive seven-day course includes such techniques as guided visualization, journaling, and cathartic work. A certified Hoffman Process teacher (with a seven-to-one student-teacher ratio) ensures that every student fully learns the techniques so they can be further developed and used after the week is over.

The Hoffman Quadrinity Process is held in scenic retreat centers around the United States and in twelve other locations (Argentina, Australia, Austria, Brazil, Canada, France, Germany, Hong Kong, Italy, Spain, Switzerland, and the United Kingdom).

Participants have found that the Process enhances their creativity, personal power, and energy. Once childhood pain, resentment, and anger are confronted, experienced, and

190

released, compassion and forgiveness develops, A spiritual awakening occurs as participants acquire the ability to connect with their inner perfect wisdom. The emotional freedom and self-knowledge that results can be used to make any aspect of life better, including career, relationships, and spirituality.

COST: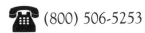

 Hoffman Institute
223 San Anselmo Ave., Unit 4
San Anselmo, CA 94960

☎ (800) 506-5253

www.quadrinity.com

THE INNER LIGHT 9-DAY INTENSIVE

"Three major shifts occurred for me: the fulfillment of my ultimate longing to know love, to finally 'belong,' and the loss of fear which has held me back all my life. I feel that I am just beginning to live. An ultimate, profound experience!"

—Inner Light participant

BodhiSoul Breathwork is a metaphysical process which uses natural breathing to release the negativity which has accumulated since before birth. The developer of the process and course feels that the gentle breathing exercises combined with other activities allows undesirable beliefs and behavior patterns to be uncovered, safely experienced, and integrated. Once this occurs, the transcendental nature and Inner Light of each participant's soul is released.

Letting go of excess emotional and psychological baggage (whether conscious or unconscious) enables true happiness to be experienced. Once freed of those thoughts and feelings which drain energy, participants can enjoy increased energy and a sense of personal empowerment to take charge of and enjoy their lives.

The nine-day intensive training course includes breathwork, writing an emotional autobiography, emotional clearing, group healing, and guided imagery.

When applying to take the course, each applicant must include completion/forgiveness letters to his or her mother and father, a written description of his or her ideal life, and a list of the five major fears and the five primary goals relating to taking the Intensive.

The course is held several times throughout the year at various sites throughout the United States. The recreational opportunities and prices vary according to the site where the Intensive is held (which can range from a yoga ashram in upper New York state to a state park in Colorado).

COST:

Inner Light Institute
P.O. Box 38280
Colorado Springs, CO 80937

INSIGHT AND OPENING RETREATS

These week-long intensives combine Holotropic Breathwork and Buddhist insight meditation. Much of the retreat is conducted in silence. Lectures and experiential activities use both Eastern and Western philosophy, psychology, and spirituality.

Holotropic Breathwork integrates observations and experiences from ancient spiritual practices and modern consciousness research. The sessions begin with theoretical preparation and technical instruction. Each participant is paired with a partner so that roles as the "breather" and "sitter" can be alternated. Through special breathing techniques, body work to facilitate energy release, diverse music sequences, and mandala drawing, emotional issues may surface. These can relate to birth and childhood or psychological death and rebirth. Because the experience can be so emotionally and physically demanding, it is not recommended for people with debilitating diseases, epilepsy, cardiovascular problems, or serious emotional problems.

Insight meditation (vipassana) begins by calming and concentrating the mind through a gentle breath meditation. This is followed by periods of sitting, walking, and eating meditation. As insight develops, the heart opens and love and compassion follow.

Through both disciplines, participants can heal their pain and open themselves up spiritually.

Retreats have taken place in Bennington, Vermont, and Yucca Valley, California. Accommodations are generally in dorm-type rooms at colleges and retreat centers. Vegetarian food is served.

COST:

 EastWest Retreats
11780 San Pablo Ave. 4-C #304
El Certito, CA 94530

 (510) 232-3098

JOHN BRADSHAW CENTER AT INGLESIDE HOSPITAL

John Bradshaw, a noted author, theologian, and educator, feels that many of us have lost our selves and consequently experience shameful feelings of being flawed, defective, empty, lonely, and hunted. This may be manifested as a loss of identity, intense neediness, substance abuse, eating disorders, trust disorders, "acting out" behaviors such as violence, abuse, or rebellion, "acting in" behaviors such as depression and physical problems, and intimacy dysfunctions (fear of abandonment/ engulfment).

The John Bradshaw Center at Ingleside Hospital sponsors seminars which foster awareness of the connections between current feelings and past unresolved issues that are bound by toxic shame. Individuals who come from dysfunctional families and who have been victims of incest or emotional, physical, or sexual abuse are assisted in identifying the origin of pain and in mastering the trauma.

The Center's five-day experiential workshops feature education on the shame-based syndromes, intensive group therapy focusing on shame reduction, skill-building exercises in setting boundaries, and development of new coping skills. These Original Pain Intensives are held Monday through Friday from 9:30 to 6:30.

After the Original Pain Intensive, participants may not have completely resolved all issues, but they're on their way to retrieving the authentic self. A sense of self-worth is reclaimed, along with the ability to live a happier life.

Lodging is not provided, but the Center can provide information on nearby hotel accommodations. Lunch and dinner is served daily at the Center.

Ingleside Hospital is located in Los Angeles. Participants can enjoy all that the city offers, in addition to the swimming pool and tennis courts located on the hospital grounds.

More information on John Bradshaw's philosophy and approach may be obtained by reading his books such as *Homecoming*, *Healing the Shame That Binds You*, *Creating Love*, and *Bradshaw on the Family*. Bradshaw also gives a number of two-day workshops throughout the year in other locations.

COST:

 John Bradshaw Center at Ingleside Hospital
7500 East Hellman Avenue
Rosemead, CA 91770

☎ (800) 845-4445 or (626) 288-1160

LIVING IN PROCESS

The Living in Process concept was originated by Ann Wilson Schaef (author of *Escape from Intimacy*, *Co-Dependence*, and *Native Wisdom for White Minds*, as well as other books). It focuses on confronting the addictive process, being present in the moment, and living in recovery. Addiction in this framework is not limited to substances but also includes addictive processes that are culturally supported, such as relationship, romance, sex addiction, work, and money issues.

Four- and five-day Living in Process Intensives are held throughout the United States. Taught by therapists and educators who have trained with Dr. Schaef, the program is educational and participatory in nature. It is not therapy, but instead offers a healing opportunity to experience the Living in Process System and community.

Along with the twelve-step model, the ideas and beliefs of Native Cultures are explored as a means of honoring life as part of all Creation. Participants work on personal and professional issues at their own pace. They work through past or present feelings that have been denied, suppressed, or distorted. Deeper processes are experienced as new levels of truth emerge. While working on personal recovery, participants support recovery in others in the group.

Accommodations vary depending on the location. Recent locations have included Seattle; Santa Fe; Philadelphia; Boulder City and Lake Tahoe in Nevada; Greenville, South Carolina; and Santa Barbara, California. Lodging is generally in cabins on parklands.

COST:

Waterdragon Enterprises
6231 Santa Maria Avenue
Las Vegas, NV 89108

 (702) 648-4383

MYSTIC PINES

"The further you reach, the higher you climb..."

—*Mystic Pines motto*

The motto of Mystic Pines indicates the focus on higher self-mastery and integration through healing experiences. Week-long workshops enable participants to learn or improve "tools" that can be used daily to become unstuck and move into wholeness. A comprehensive holistic system helps to discover, release, and heal energy blocks (physical, emotional, mental, or spiritual).

Some of the activities and tools are movement, massage, visualization, dreamwork, memory work, nature attunements and adventures, art, chanting and singing, psychic and spiritual reading, reflexology, acupressure, yoga, left-right brain integration exercises, chakra and auric cleansing, grounding, lifting, prayer, and spirit guidance.

Only six or less participants are scheduled for each workshop. Private, completely individualized retreats can be arranged.

Free time can be spent hiking, swimming, snorkeling, wind-surfing, fishing, and canoeing.

Mystic Pines is on a lake by the coast of Maine.

Participants stay in private rooms in cottages with kitchens. They prepare most meals on their own or dine out in nearby restaurants.

COST:

Mystic Pines
P.O. Box 19
East Orland, ME 04431

 (207) 469-7572

199

ONSITE

Onsite provides experiential therapy to address personal issues and enhance lives. It provides a dynamic personal and family systems approach to healing from pain.

Living Centered (seven and one-half days)

This program is designed for individuals whose lives have been disturbed by trauma, relationship problems, food, alcohol, drugs, gambling, divorce, co-dependency, abuse or losses. (Acute addiction is not treated.) Participants are taught the skills they need to change their behaviors through thirty hours of group therapy and an additional twenty-five hours of learning experiences. Family of origin issues are addressed. Repressed emotions are discharged through such activities as sculpture, group therapy, presentations, videos and psychodrama. Participants are assisted in seeing new choices for future actions. An individualized aftercare plan is developed so that the recovery process can continue once the participant gets home. Applicants must complete pre-program assessment forms prior to acceptance and enrollment.

Learning to Love Yourself (four and one-half days)

This workshop helps participants work through the trauma of being part of a distant or painful family system. Through experiential teaching, small-group work, self-worth exercises, and participation in a "family reconstruction psychodrama" (where one preselected participant does intensive work about his or her family origin, life traumas, neglect, current relationships, addictive and compulsive behaviors, and/or supportive systems), participants gain insight into the patterns that have shaped their lives. Some of these workshops allow children aged nine to eighteen to attend along with their parent(s).

Eating Disorder Program (six days)

Participants learn to address their relationship to food as it relates to family of origin issues, unresolved loss and shame, and the inability to identify feelings. Experiential techniques, psychodramatic tools, and journaling are used to experience feelings rather than medicating them.

Families (four and one-half days)

This intensive allows family members to confront the same truths and secrets caused by addiction, compulsions, and trauma. Participants learn to heal old hurt and resentments.

Onsite offers other programs besides those specifically for emotional healing. Most focus on personal empowerment or communication skills.

Grandparenting Course (three days)

Shows how to create connections with grandchildren.

Singles in Recovery (six days)

This program provides tools for building intimacy and understanding through social activities, small group therapy, same gender groups and experiential activities.

Couples Renewal Workshop (four and one-half days)

Couples learn how to better share feelings, communicate, negotiate, and experience intimacy.

Equine Interaction Therapy (six days)

In this program, small groups work with horses who are highly sensitive to people's emotions and, through their response to handling, can provide greater insight as to how participants relate to others as well as themselves.

Stress Management Program (seven days)

Consists of lectures, mindfulness meditation training and practice, yoga, group discussion, nutritional and physical fitness counseling, desert hikes, T'ai Chi, climbing walls and a challenge course.

Recreational activities include swimming and horseback riding.

Participants stay in a restored 1870s mansion or in luxury log cabins.

COST:

(depending on length and intensity)

Onsite
Cumberland Furnace, TN

email: intake@onsiteworkshops.com
www.onsiteworkshops.com

OPENING THE HEART WORKSHOPS

"Spring Hill saved my life. It's the equivalent of six months of therapy."

—Opening the Heart participant

These weekend inner journeys enable participants to "access their feelings, work through blocked emotions, build self-esteem, and live more authentically." Both Western psychological methods (gestalt, psychodrama, bioenergetics, music and art therapy) and Eastern traditions (such as meditation, witnessing, and inner work) are used. A variety of small group and individual exercises are incorporated into the workshops. Participants may choose not to participate in any activity they find threatening or uncomfortable.

The original Opening the Heart (OTH) for Individuals was initiated in 1976. Participants work towards accepting rather than burying their hurts. Specialized workshops include:

- **OTH for Couples**
  Communication and honesty is deepened as couples learn to express anger safely, move beyond blaming, and show love and appreciation freely.

- **OTH for Adult Children of Alcoholics**
  Designed for adult children of alcoholic, abusive, or dysfunctional homes, the workshop shows how to deal with issues such as an excessive need for control, low self-esteem, fear of abandonment, and difficulty with expressing feelings.

- **OTH for Men and Women Survivors**
  Adult survivors of sexual abuse are aided in their recovery by sharing stories, releasing feelings, and giving and receiving support.

- **OTH for Men**
  Male participants deal with their sadness, fear, and shame in a supportive environment. Special attention is given to healing painful father-son relationships.

- **OTH for Women**
  Myth, celebration, magic, dance, music, and visualization enable women to claim and celebrate their aliveness.

- **OTH for Gays, Lesbians, and Bisexuals**
  Individual sexual orientations are accepted and valued in a very supportive setting while issues such as rage and joy are expressed.

- **OTH for Therapists and Caregivers**
  Persons who give to others can receive something for themselves in these workshops which rejuvenate the spirit and recharge energy levels.

There are also weekend workshops for women survivors of sexual, physical, or domestic assault in adulthood; for musicians to increase their self-awareness; for healing the relationship with food (for undereaters or overeaters).

All the staff have had extensive training in Heart-Centered methods of counseling and healing. The staff of nearly one hundred includes psychologists, psychotherapists, social workers, substance abuse prevention counselors, psychiatric nurses, educators, musicians, and movement therapists. The staff reviews individual autobiographical material prior to the weekend to ensure that each participant's needs are best served.

At the end of the weekend, participants feel empowered to embrace the present and future instead of feeling ruled by the unresolved issues of the past. They feel that they have clarified their life direction and are capable of making significant changes in their lives.

Workshops are offered regularly throughout the spring, summer, and fall. They begin on Friday evenings and end early on Sunday evenings.

Spring Hill is close to the border of New Hampshire (in Ashby, Massachusetts) and is about a ninety-minute drive northwest of Boston. The country setting includes wooded trails and meadows.

Participants sleep in the conference barn on futon-style mats (with separate sleeping quarters for men and women). Tent sites for camping are also available. Vegetarian meals are served.

COST: (financial aid is available)

Spring Hill of Ashby
Spring Hill Road, P.O. Box 130
Ashby, MA 01431

OPTIONS UNLIMITED

Options Unlimited works with people traumatized by dysfunctional family systems caused or exacerbated by chemical dependency, catastrophic illness, mental illness, sexual, physical, emotional, spiritual abuse or neglect. They provide treatment to facilitate the recovery process of persons with codependency. By providing a safe place where participants can experience and express painful feelings, Options Unlimited enables healing.

An eleven-day program is offered. Up to seven participants live together closely, creating a new family setting where they can heal with the support of other people in similar circumstances. As participants get in touch with their inner child and re-experience a family situation, issues can arise and be resolved in new healthy ways.

The focus is on a twelve-step approach to recovery. Treatment modalities include humanistic, client-centered, gestalt, reality, and rational/emotive therapies. Psychodrama, guided imagery, and emotional discharge are some of the experiential therapeutic techniques offered.

In addition to the intense emotional work, participants play, exercise, and eat together. There's some opportunity for relaxation as well.

Potential participants are interviewed for a needs assessment. They must be free from mood- or mind-altering drugs and be involved with a therapist for aftercare.

Participants reside in a shared house. They cook some meals together and go out for others.

COST: 💲 (some insurance companies will reimburse on a full or partial basis)

Options Unlimited
1001 Capitol of Texas Highway
Building L, Suite 200
Austin, TX 78746

 (512) 447-7887

POCKET RANCH INSTITUTE

"It was really a special oasis of time and space in my life that genuinely changed the way I related to myself and to other people."

—Pocket Ranch participant

Pocket Ranch offers a unique therapeutic environment for adults who are seeking healing for psychological or spiritual crisis. By integrating a variety of approaches and addressing the interplay of mind, body, and spirit, the professional staff are able to develop highly individualized programs.

The STAR (Self-Analysis Toward Awareness Rebirth) program allows participants to discover and explore patterns and behaviors that were adopted in early childhood and conditioned by their family dynamics. Once aware of the roots of problems experienced in adult life, participants can work on releasing these obstacles to personal growth and happiness. One of the primary methods for taking participants into their past and uncovering the early decisions, negative experiences, and family messages which are still affecting their lives is a daily writing assignment. The methods for healing include guided imagery, individual and group processing sessions, breathwork, integrative bodywork, meditation, and art activities. Participants also re-experience their births as part of their program.

By the end of the program, participants are well on their way to healing deep wounds. They're better able to handle emotional crisis or distress in their lives and can live more fully and freely in the present.

The nearly one-on-one staff-participant ratio assures close personal attention. Staff is available to participants as they release chronically held emotional and physical pain.

The program, available about six times a year, is designed as a seventeen- or twenty-one-day intensive. Persons who do not have this time available to them or who don't need a structured environment and close supervision can design their own self-directed program for personal growth. Individual psychotherapy sessions, breathwork, bodywork, and sand-tray activities can be scheduled.

Participants stay in rustic cabins with private baths. All meals are provided.

The Ranch is located two hours north of San Francisco in northern California's wine country. Amenities include a pool, spa, sauna, and hiking trails.

COST:

 Star Foundation
P.O. Box 516
Geyersville, CA 95441

 (707) 857-3359

The Primal Institute

"I consider what I gained in therapy to be priceless. It is something I was searching my whole life for and yet it continually eluded me. I call it simply my self...Primal Therapy is the most wonderful thing in the world."

—Primal Institute participant

Dr. Arthur Janov, the founder of Primal Therapy and author of *The Primal Scream*, believes that optimal mental health can occur only when the buried hurts of childhood surface and are experienced by adults. According to Janov, many children feel unloved and learn to repress the pain that accompanies these feelings. The repressed feelings remain trapped inside and build up a constant tension throughout the body. In an attempt to alleviate the discomfort, adults may unconsciously try to fulfill the childhood needs that were never satisfied. But because they're not fully aware of exactly what these needs are, their efforts are not successful. Anxiety and depression may result.

Primal therapy enables participants to re-experience the repressed painful childhood events or experiences. Specially trained therapists assist in uncovering memories and with understanding and coping with the associated emotions. Both group and individual sessions are used.

Applicants fill out a questionnaire about physical and emotional symptoms as well as significant circumstances of their births and early childhoods. They are also required to write a two-page autobiography detailing why they want Primal Therapy. Those considered appropriate are interviewed prior to admission.

Due to the intense emotional nature of the therapy, the Institute's medical doctor provides a physical examination to ensure that there are no health concerns which would be adversely affected by the process. Participants must refrain from using coffee, cigarettes, alcohol, and all forms of drugs for forty-eight hours before the first session. To remove distractions and more quickly get in touch with their feelings, participants must spend anywhere from twenty-four to ninety-two hours alone in a hotel room before beginning the process.

After experiencing Primal Therapy, participants usually have less tension and psychosomatic symptoms. Work and personal relationships are improved. People feel more in control of their lives and can start to work on satisfying current needs rather than those in the distant past.

An eight day intensive is offered as well as a three-week session. Follow-up interviews and meetings are scheduled three months and a year after the intensive is completed.

Housing in Los Angeles is the responsibility of each participant.

COST:

(depending on length; medical insurance will often pay some of the cost for therapy)

  The Primal Institute
10379 Pico Boulevard
Los Angeles, CA 90064

☎ (800) 228-5777 or (310) 785-9456

www.primalinstitute.com

SAFE HARBOURS

Persons who were abused as children don't suddenly shed the psychological scars of this trauma once they reach adulthood. Survivors of physical, emotional, or sexual abuse experience pain from the past which can impact the ability to live life fully in the present.

A five-day intensive workshop offered by the California-based Safe Harbours counseling program allows participants to share experiences and explore new ways of coping. Structured group sessions focus on family dynamics, childhood experiences, old feelings and memories, and sexuality. The workshops are led by master's level nurse practitioners and licensed social workers. They're held several times throughout the year, mostly in northern California (but also in other locations such as Boston, North Carolina, and England). Some are for women only, whereas others accommodate both sexes.

By the conclusion of the five-day program, participants leave with improved self-esteem, confidence, and the ability to set goals for the future. Instead of remaining stuck in the past, they gain the knowledge and skills to move forward in their lives.

Participants stay in local hotels and take meals together.

COST: (some scholarships are available)

 Safe Harbours
2325 West Victory Blvd.
Burbank, CA 91506

☎ (818) 845-0729

Sober Vacations

"I consider this trip a milestone in my life. I met so many people who inspired me and who will serve as role models as I learn to live and grow in sobriety."

—*Sober Vacations participant*

Most people look forward to their vacations, but persons in recovery may be fearful about taking a vacation that changes their everyday habits and routines. The prospect of leaving behind the support system of a twelve-step program and being around vacationers who may be drinking heavily can be daunting.

But anyone in recovery can feel comfortable with a trip sponsored by Sober Vacations International. Begun by two brothers who are recovering alcoholics, this travel agency specializes in arranging sober vacations. Most of their vacations take place at Club Meds in the Caribbean, but they also sponsor cruises, tours of Europe, and rafting and ski trips.

In addition to the numerous recreational and sightseeing opportunities of each vacation, there are at least fifteen meetings each day, beginning with the 7 A.M. Attitude Adjustment meeting and ending with the midnight moonlight meeting. All are based on the twelve-step programs. The vacations are primarily intended for persons recovering from drug or alcohol addiction but can also be enjoyed by persons in Overeating Anonymous or adult children of parents with substance abuse problems.

Enjoying a vacation sober is something that many persons in recovery previously thought would be impossible, but Sober Vacation participants find great pleasure in experiencing the beauty and wonder of a week in paradise. The vacations can be emotional at times as issues surface, but the fellowship of people from all over the world provides warmth and love. Participants learn from and are inspired by their fellow recoverers.

The vacations give a spiritual lift and enable personal growth. When the vacation is over, participants have widened their network of friends and can return to their everyday lives feeling refreshed and energized as they continue with the work of their twelve-step program at home.

Rooms are double-occupancy, with Sober Vacations International matching roommates according to age and smoking preferences.

COST: (including airfare from and to Miami)

 Sober Vacations International
26560 Agoura Road, Suite 106
Calabasas, CA 91302

(800) 762-3738 or (818) 878-0008

www.sobervations.com

TEXAS MEN'S INSTITUTE

"Truly a lifetime experience that any American male should have. I'm only sorry I didn't know about it sooner. My life will never be the same."

—*Texas Men's Institute participant*

The Texas Men's Institute offers a variety of weekend programs to help men understand and accept their maleness. All the activities focus on healing the emotional problems common to all men and on enhancing the physical, intellectual, and spiritual well-being of men (and the women who relate to them).

They hold an annual Men's Gathering every spring which addresses the emotional, sexual, and spiritual wounds that men received from their parents. Participants acquire new perspectives on healing these wounds so that life can be lived more passionately and powerfully in the present.

The Texas Men's Institute also holds an annual Father's Day Gathering focusing on father/son relationships in the past and present. Men may attend alone or with a friend, son, or father. The workshop provides practical ways of improving current relationships with fathers and others as well as healing the painful memories of deceased dads.

There are a few retreats for both men and women. The Wildhearts gathering examines the similarities as well as the differences between the sexes. It addresses a variety of issues: sexuality, gender conditioning, money, freedom versus intimacy in a relationship, anger and violence, power and control, boredom, and lack of passion. They also offer canoe trips which combine outdoor adventures (canoeing, fishing, swimming, and hiking) with programming (discussions, exercises, singing, games) to improve relationship skills.

At the end of one of these weekends, participants have an enhanced awareness of and appreciation for what it means to be a man. Both men and women can feel better about themselves and their ability to relate to others of the same or opposite sex.

The spring and summer workshops are held at the Bosque Creek Ranch in central Texas or on the Brazos River in north-central Texas. Participants camp out with their own gear. Meals are provided.

COST:

 Texas Men's Institute
P.O. Box 311384
New Braunfels, TX 78131

VISION FOUNDATION

Ken Keyes, author of *The Power of Unconditional Love* and *Your Road Map to Lifelong Happiness*, provided workshops that brought healing in five days and those workshops continue under the guidance of Lee McFadden. The focus is on neuro-healing and areas of the unconscious mind that were damaged in childhood. Childhood strategies that developed as a result, but are harmful to adult life, are explored and healed. Reconciliation between the Inner Child and Inner Adult is fostered.

In a group setting, participants work on unloading a lifetime of suppressed fear, grief, anger, and rage. They learn to stop blaming themselves for childhood traumas and to feel safe in situations that previously caused discomfort.

After the five days, self-esteem is increased. A greater number of choices for the present and future seems possible. Life becomes more enjoyable.

The workshops are held at the Vision Foundation center in California.

Participants stay in local motels.

COST: (tuition only)

Vision Foundation
2995 Woodside Road
Suite 400
Woodside, CA 94062

 (800) 545-7810 or (650) 342-4733

stress.to//workship.html

WOMAN WITHIN®

"The experience changed my life...I came home as a whole person. I have never been a whole person in my life."

—*Woman Within participant*

Woman Within provides a number of healing and empowering experiences for women. The basic course is Woman Within Initiation. This three-day weekend intensive is appropriate for any woman who is ready to face the fears and wounds of the past so that the present can be reclaimed. It's geared for women who are struggling to achieve passion, balance, and wholeness in their personal and professional lives.

Participants enjoy a safe and supportive atmosphere for the removal of the masks and defenses they've been using. The initiation rites allow women to leave behind the ways of relating as a child and reclaim the wholeness of a woman. The need to be like a man is left behind and the values of the feminine are reclaimed. The angry, rebellious adolescent is left behind as the spiritual, wise woman within is reclaimed.

The intensive is not to be considered or pursued as therapy (although it can be a valuable adjunct). Activities include small and large group activities, guided meditations, physical movement, and individual processes.

Other weekend seminars include Women Healing Incest, Healing the Wounds of Shame, and Couples Weekends.

Programs are offered throughout the United States, Canada, and Europe. Accommodations are generally at retreat centers and are shared. Meals are served.

COST:

 Woman Within, Inc.—Mid-Atlantic
5 Steele Dr.
Cranbury, NJ 08512

 (609) 799-4031

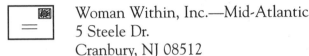 Woman Within, Inc.—Midwest
920 Indian Spring Dr.
Delafield, WI 53018

(414) 646-2717

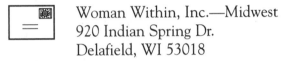 Woman Within, Inc.—Texas
P.O. 42339
Houston, TX 77242-2339

(713) 661-5943

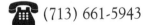 Woman Within, Inc.—Canada
1135 Fraser Ave.
Sarnia, Ontario N7S 4V2

(519) 542-1621

 Woman Within, Inc.—England
144 Humber Rd.
London England SE3 7LY

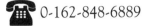 0-162-848-6889

BODY PROGRAMS

Life is less than wonderful when you're not feeling well. You can't reach your full intellectual, emotional, and spiritual potential if you're physically not up to the challenge. Getting the most out of life requires sufficient energy to cope with daily demands and to pursue those activities that give your life meaning.

The vacations in this section can restore your physical well-being. They don't necessarily claim to be able to cure severe illnesses, but they can show how to live more effectively with a chronic disease (such as arthritis, gastrointestinal problems, chronic fatigue syndrome, and diabetes) and reduce its limiting or uncomfortable effects. After participating in one of these programs, you will feel much more in control of your body. You'll know how to maximize your health so it's the best it possibly can be.

If you aren't ill but don't feel as well as you'd like, you'll find a number of health-promoting possibilities in this section. Once you experience improved health and energy by quitting smoking, beginning to exercise, losing weight, or changing your eating habits, it will be easier for you to accomplish what you want in the other areas of your life, such as career, hobbies, or relationships.

And even if you enjoy optimal health, you'll still want to explore this section. It is well worth your while to learn how to maintain this level of health. As we age, changes do occur and a more proactive approach is required to ensure that health remains good. By learning about the new theories and practices of nutrition, exercise, and medicine, you can prevent problems in the future.

The Comprehensive Programs section in the Holistic Vacations chapter also contains programs that promote health for the physical body as well as the mind and spirit.

BLACK HILLS HEALTH AND EDUCATION CENTER

"I found a whole new way of living. After twelve days, I have lost five pounds. I can climb a mountain and I have conquered the highest mountain of all—fear."

—Black Hills Health and Education participant

"Treat the body right and it will achieve wellness" is the philosophy behind the Black Hills Health and Education Center. Recognizing that it can be difficult for most of us to make basic changes in our lifestyle, Black Hills offers participants an escape from their normal environment and routines. Unlike traditional spas where participants are passively pampered, Black Hills actively involves participants in learning experiences.

Participants learn how to exercise appropriately through classes, aerobic equipment, and hiking on the many trails around the facility. They learn to manage stress and to deal with specific health problems such as hypertension or diabetes. Instead of confining nutrition education to a list of foods to eat and foods to avoid, Black Hills provides experiential learning in healthy cooking, shopping, and ordering in restaurants through field trips and classes.

Some traditional spa services are available, such as massage and whirlpools.

Medical history questionnaires are completed by each applicant and screened prior to entrance. The professional staff (physicians, nurses, nutritionists, therapists, and counselors) develops an individualized exercise and nutritional plan for each participant.

The program length is either twelve to twenty-five days.

221

As the name indicates, the Center is located in the Black Hills of South Dakota. Nearby attractions include caves, hot springs, parks, and monuments.

Participants stay in semiprivate rooms in the lodge or in their own motor homes.

COST: to
(depending on length)

 Black Hills Health and Education Center
Box 19
Hermosa, SD 57744

(800) 658-5433 or (605) 255-4101

CAMP/RESORT REDISCOVERY

Unlike other health-oriented camps or resorts, Camp/Resort Rediscovery caters to people forty and over. It allows participants to improve general health, fitness, and health knowledge. Held twice a year (January and June), the program is staffed by professionals and student interns from the University of Maryland's Health & Development program.

No one is coerced into participating in any activity, but the variety of recreational possibilities ensures that there is something for everyone: walking, jogging, hiking, square dancing, aerobic exercise, swimming, stretching, tennis, archery, volleyball, fishing, canoeing, horseback riding, ropes course, yoga, and riflery.

Each day includes at least an hour of health education. Topics include assessing basic physical fitness, osteoporosis, loneliness, dental care, nutrition, sexuality, stress management, coping with loss, and psycho-social aspects of aging.

Participants learn to take an active role in promoting their own health through physical activity and knowledge.

The week-long session is held at the Coolfont Resort and Spa in Berkeley Springs, West Virginia. Participants are housed in lodges or chalets with up to three other people. Breakfasts and dinners are included in the package.

COST:

Camp Rediscovery
2007 Pelden Road
Adelphi, MD 20783

 (301) 431-3733

223

CANYON RANCH

"...more than a retreat, more than a vacation. Canyon Ranch turned my life around!"

—*Canyon Ranch participant*

Canyon Ranch offers typical spa amenities and services such as a weight room, aerobics classes, tennis courts, saunas, massages, and mud treatments. But it goes far beyond the average spa by offering a two-page menu of services.

Its medical services include acupuncture, agility evaluation and training, bone density evaluation, Chinese herbal consultation, chiropractic services, Exceptional Sex workshop, Integrated Body Mechanics workshop, podiatry consultation, sleep apnea evaluation and intervention, and sports medicine injury evaluation.

The Behavioral Health services include biofeedback, Healing the Inner Child Consultation/Workshop, Hypnotherapy, Life Regressions, Sleep Disorders, Smoking Cessation, and Stress Management Consultation/Workshop.

Nutrition workshops include Foods That Fight Disease, Grab 'N Eat, Traveler's Guide to Eating and Exercise, and Winning Strategies for Eating Out.

Canyon Ranch offers a week-long Life Enhancement program in a small group format. It focuses on personalized concerns and issues, including smoking cessation, weight management, stress reduction, and heart disease risk reduction. Guidance is provided by physicians, psychologists, registered dietitians, movement therapists, exercise physiologists, and certified health educators.

Specialized week-long programs include:

- **Woman to Woman**
  This program for midlife women focuses on healthy living, maintaining balance, sexuality, and personal growth.

224

- **Spiritual Pathways**
  Classes in yoga, T'ai Chi (body movement to conserve and develop life energy), chi gong (use of breath to strengthen internal organs to calm the mind), meditation, breathing, spirituality, and inner life.

- **Elder Camp**
  Persons over sixty develop positive approaches towards aging, eating, and physical and emotional health.

- **Arthritis Week**
  Participants with arthritis learn how to prevent problems and maintain mobility.

Regardless of the specific program, Canyon Ranch is dedicated to ensuring that the awareness and vitality developed during the week continues once the participant gets home. As their brochure notes, Canyon Ranch is "where you experience the optimal — and learn how to make it practical. For life."

Participants stay in private rooms. Three meals are provided each day. Canyon Ranch is not a vegetarian spa, although it can accommodate vegetarians. It offers a varied menu, with choices that include lobster, lamb chops, cheesecake, and hot fudge sundaes! Canyon Ranch is located in the Arizona desert. This environment is very conducive to mountain biking and hiking (two of the most popular forms of exercise at the Ranch).

COST:

Canyon Ranch
8600 E. Rockcliff Road
Tucson, AZ 85715

 (800) 726-9900 or (520) 749-9000

www.canyonranch.com

COOPER WELLNESS PROGRAM

"I got far more from the week than I ever anticipated. In one month I have lost ten pounds, improved my cholesterol profile and am on a regular exercise program. I wish everyone could have the opportunity for this same pleasant, life-changing experience."

—Cooper Wellness Program participant

Enormous numbers of persons participate in some form of aerobic exercise, but not everyone is fortunate enough to learn the philosophy, physiology, and practice of aerobics from the foremost expert. Individuals who choose to spend a few days to two weeks at the Cooper Aerobics Center are given the rare opportunity to learn an exercise routine and lifestyle practices from the physician who literally wrote the book(s) on aerobics: Dr. Kenneth Cooper. His center provides the information and support to make those changes which result in optimal health.

Participants are screened for risk factors by a team of physicians, psychologists, exercise physiologists, and nutritionists. Everything from hearing to vision to body fat composition to pulmonary function is measured. Once this six-hour exam is completed, individual programs are developed.

Programs include workshops and lectures on behavior changes, antioxidants, mind/body partnership, aerobic walking, healthy dining, fats and cholesterol, relaxation, and resistance weight training.

Group and individual exercise sessions offer professional instruction in walking, jogging, treadmill, stationary bicycling, swimming, tennis, racquetball, toning/flexibility, yoga, and aquatics.

Meals low in sodium, calories, fat, and cholesterol are provided three times a day, along with cooking classes and trips to heart-healthy restaurants off-campus.

Follow-up after thirty days and "On Track" newsletters ensure that participants apply what they've learned once they're home.

Stays of one to two weeks are recommended for maximum permanent, life-enhancing changes. For participants with less time and money, four-day and daily rates are available.

Participants may stay at the Guest Lodge at the Cooper Aerobics Center (a colonial-style hotel located on the center's thirty acres) in single or double rooms, or may choose alternative lodging off-campus (for which special rate arrangements are available).

COST: to

(depending on length; meals included; lodging extra)

 The Cooper Aerobics Center
12230 Preston Road
Dallas, TX 75230-9967

(800) 444-5192 or (972) 386-4777

www.cooperinst.org

DUKE UNIVERSITY DIET AND FITNESS CENTER (DFC)

"What I learned applies not only to weight loss, but to life goals."

—*Duke University Diet and Fitness Center participant*

As the only university-based weight control and fitness program in the United States, DFC's staff is comprised of expert professionals in the fields of medicine, exercise physiology, nutrition, psychology, and massage therapy. The DFC program focuses on each of the four crucial components of weight loss: nutrition, fitness, behavior, and medical management.

Women generally lose ten to twenty pounds and men twenty to thirty during a four-week period. Best of all, 70 percent maintain the weight loss they achieved at the Center a year after completing the program.

A four-week program is recommended for first timers, but a two-week program is available for individuals with less available time.

The program begins with a full medical evaluation: complete history and physical; laboratory tests including cholesterol, triglycerides, and glucose levels; and a treadmill test to screen for heart disease and evaluate fitness. Physicians monitor progress throughout the program.

DFC takes an "anti-diet" approach, stressing healthy eating rather than a quick-fix diet. Meals are low in calories, fat, and sodium. Nutrition lectures, group workshops, cooking classes and demonstrations, and field trips to restaurants and grocery stores ensures that participants become nutrition experts.

A personalized fitness plan is developed. Goals include reducing body fat to a healthy level, increasing metabolism to lose weight, and toning the body. Fitness activities include walking,

228

no-impact aerobics, aqua jogging, step classes, swimming, weight training, and aerobic equipment such as rowing machines, treadmills, stair climbing machines, and stationary/recumbent bicycles. An exercise physiologists evaluates each participant's initial condition and adjusts the plan as needed throughout the program.

Since DFC believes that the mind is as important as the body when it comes to lifestyle change, clinical psychologists teach lifelong weight management techniques and strategies. Private consultation, classes, and group discussions help stress management, motivation, and self-esteem. Unhealthy habits such as emotional eating are unlearned.

Because the DFC program is not just about losing weight but is also about setting and reaching goals in all life areas, a personal development seminar is included. Investment in Excellence, a videotaped course used in major corporations and the U.S. Military, is facilitated by DFC staff members through discussion and workbook activities.

Duke University is located in Durham, North Carolina close to mountains and beaches. A variety of cultural and recreational activities are available.

Housing is not provided. Most participants stay in one-bedroom furnished apartments across from the Center.

COST: 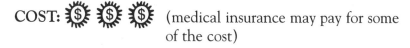 (medical insurance may pay for some of the cost)

 Duke University Medical Center
804 West Trinity Avenue
Durham, NC 27701

 (800) 362-8446 or (919) 684-6331

dmi-www.mc.duke.edu/dfc/home.html

GLOBAL FITNESS ADVENTURES

"Global Fitness was just a great experience for me. I have really become aware of so much in terms of health, nutrition, and my spiritual self. Your trip has changed my consciousness—I'm much more positive and in tune with my inner self. I'm feeling more healthier, happier, and empowered than I've ever been..."

—GFA *participant*

If you like the idea of a spa vacation but feel you might be bored staying in one spot for a week, you'll want to consider the traveling spa experience that Global Fitness Adventures offers. The small group sizes (eight to twelve participants) and intimate locations allow a highly personalized program that promotes both physical and mental health. While exploring ancient cultures and enjoying vigorous wilderness hiking, participants combine the adventure of travel with the healthy lifestyle of a stationary spa.

A typical day focuses on a hike of five to eighteen miles (depending on each person's fitness levels and desires). It includes yoga, deep breathing exercises, muscle-toning classes, and calorie-burning activities unique to the area (such as horseback riding, biking, fishing, whitewater rafting, snorkeling, scuba diving, and kayaking). Massages and Jacuzzis are available. Evening activities feature group discussions and motivational lectures.

Gourmet natural meals (mostly vegetarian) reflect the culture of the area. No sugar, caffeine, or alcohol is served. Participants stay in luxury hotels.

Recent adventures have includes Aspen, Colorado; Sedona, Arizona; Dominica, Caribbean; Bali, Indonesia; Kaui, Hawaii; Santa Barabara, California; and Lake Corno, Italy. Each locale has unique features and offerings.

With all these adventures, you can enjoy the discovery of new places while having ensured that you live and learn a healthy lifestyle that you can take back home with you.

COST:

 Global Fitness Adventures
P.O. Box 1390
Aspen, CO 81612

☎ (800) 488-TRIP

www.aspen.com/globalfitnessadventures

Hawaiian Wellness Holiday

"Now that I follow Dr. Deal's recommendations, my health is radically improved and I don't get sick anymore."
—*Hawaiian Wellness Holiday participant*

Hawaii has long been a favorite spot for sightseers who want to witness its magical beauty, but now it can also be a vacation destination which heals and revitalizes. Dr. Deal's Hawaiian Wellness Holiday provides participants with a personalized diet, weight loss, detoxification, rejuvenation, and exercise program.

Health lectures and nutritional counseling inspire participants to eat naturally, to find delicious but healthier substitutes for unhealthy foods, and to identify and correct the underlying metabolic causes of health and weight problems. As a psychologist and chiropractor, Dr. Grady Deal believes that traditional medical regimens are often unsuccessful in curing illness and promoting health. His focus is on the benefits of the natural therapies and alternative diagnostic methods used throughout the world by alternative physicians, nutritional chiropractors, and naturopaths. By determining and cleaning out the toxins throughout the system, including those arising from food allergies or metabolic disorders, symptoms can be minimized, weight stabilized, and diseases such as cancer, arthritis, and heart disease prevented.

The natural foods served are a combination of vegetarian, macrobiotic, raw foods, Fit for Life, juice fasting, and Dr. Deal's Delicious Detox Diet protocols. Fish and eggs are also available.

Exercise includes daily scenic hikes and walks, yoga, stretching, breathing classes, high/low impact aerobics, body sculpting, aquacize, computerized exercise equipment, and weight training.

Therapeutic treatment such as chiropractic adjustments, acupressure, reflexology, and massage are elements of the program as well.

Herbal laxatives and self-administered colonics are optional treatments to cleanse the body.

Participants stay at condominiums or resort hotels with private ocean or garden view rooms on the island of Kauai (known as the garden island of the South Pacific). The location lends itself to wonderful snorkeling and sightseeing opportunities.

COST:

 Hawaiian Wellness Holiday
P.O. Box 279
Koloa, Kauai, HI 96756

 (800) 338-6977 or (808) 332-9244

planet-hawaii.com/drdeal

233

THE HEARTLAND SPA

"An uplifting, self-revealing, motivating experience that I'd not exchange for any other. The Heartland has made a life-changing impact on me. I intend to take good care of myself from now on..."

—Heartland Spa participant

As a full service spa, Heartland provides services such as massage, sports and exercise activities, and education and practice in healthy eating. But Heartland is unique in several ways. In addition to standard aerobic classes, yoga, walking, and body building, Heartland offers classes in self-defense, martial arts (such as kung fu), boxercise (incorporating basic body moves with both aerobic and anaerobic exercises), ballet, country line dancing, body sculpting with inexpensive resistance equipment such as hydro-bands and surgical tubing, Capoeira (a Brazilian combination of dance, music, and martial arts), and mind-body exercise incorporating interpretive dance and psychological techniques for self-discovery, expression, and creativity.

Heartland is the first spa in the United States to offer a Challenge Course. This indoor and outdoor course of games and challenges is incorporated into the daily regimen. Participants walk tightropes, scale twelve-foot walls, leap from a trapeze thirty feet in the air, and swing across a body of water on a rope like Tarzan. Confidence is built as participants push through self-imposed limits that have held them back for years. They leave with an appreciation of the resources they have to achieve peak performance consistently in their daily lives.

A registered dietitian provides personal nutritional counseling based on the Inner Diet Assessment which identifies and develops strategies for overcoming the psychological barriers to successful weight management.

Heartland is not one of those spas in which participants wear fancy exercise and leisure clothes. The spa provides shorts, T-shirts, and sweatsuits for participants to wear all the time.

Participants may stay in private rooms or may be assigned a roommate. Meals are mostly vegetarian, with some fish served.

The spa is located eighty miles south of Chicago. The spa provides van service to and from downtown Chicago.

Two, five, and seven-day programs are available.

COST:

 The Heartland Spa
Kam Lake Estate, RR #1, Box 181
Gilma, IL 60938

☎ (800) 545-4853 or (312) 357-6465

www.heartlandspa.com

HILTON HEAD HEALTH INSTITUTE

Whereas some spas focus on changes which can be superficial and short-lived, the Hilton Head Health Institute uses comprehensive education and behavior modification to develop individualized programs which participants can follow throughout their lives. Their Health and Weight Control programs help participants to:

- Reach and maintain a healthy weight

- Control food cravings

- Improve physical fitness

- Reduce cholesterol

- Lower blood pressure

- Increase energy and reduce fatigue

- Quit smoking

- Manage stress

- Reduce disease risk

Programs last five, twelve, or twenty-six days. Regardless of length, each program begins with a health evaluation and medical screening of each participant. Males forty-five years or older, females fifty or older, smokers, diabetics, and individuals with known heart disease, high blood pressure (above 145/95), high cholesterol, or a family history of coronary heart disease prior to age fifty also undergo an exercise stress test on a treadmill (unless results of a stress test within the last six months can be provided). Once the Institute's physician completes the evaluation and screening, personalized nutritional and exercise programming begins.

Four to five low-calorie, nutritionally balanced meals and snacks are served each day. Meals are high in complex carbohydrates, moderate in protein, and low in fat, sugar, and sodium. Calorie amounts per day generally range between eight hundred and twelve hundred calories.

Walking is the primary recommended exercise, but participants also may attend supervised classes in low-impact aerobics, bench (step) aerobics, hand-weight training, aerobic walking, aqua exercises, calisthenics, and conditioning.

Many lectures, seminars, and workshops (as well as individual instruction) are provided. Topics include motivation, behavior modification, craving control, stress management, health promotion, weight control, and disease prevention.

Individual counseling addresses the unique stresses that each participant faces at home and at work so that habit changes learned at the Institute can be transferred to the real world.

Special programs include the Stop Smoking Program (using behavior modification techniques, individual/group support, and nicotine replacement therapy where appropriate) and the Psychotherapeutic Program (six one-hour group sessions discussing participants' resistance to losing weight and living a more healthy life and offering methods to overcome this resistance).

Participants typically lose between two to five pounds a week, as well as inches from the waist, abdomen, legs, and arms. Blood pressure and cholesterol are significantly reduced. Energy is increased and a positive mental outlook developed.

Thanks to the Institute's Lifetime Maintenance Plan, the majority of participants maintain their weight loss six to eighteen months after completing their program. The ongoing support includes lifetime access to the Institute's toll-free hotline for advice and consultation, preferential rates for return visits, regular personal correspondence from staff to monitor progress, a quarterly newsletter providing health information, audiocassettes and reference materials, and a list of graduates in the local area who can be contacted for peer support.

The Institute is located on a barrier sea island off the coast of

South Carolina. It is accessible by car or by plane (into Savannah, Georgia and then by limo, or directly into Hilton Head on smaller planes).

Participants stay in villas with golf course views. Villas are usually shared (although private ones are available for an extra fee); however, each participant has a private bathroom and bath. The villas are located within walking distance from the Institute.

As a world class resort, Hilton Head is renowned for its golf and tennis facilities. Participants can enjoy these activities during their free time, as well as racquetball, swimming, fishing, cultural activities, and sightseeing in Savannah (less than an hour's drive) or Charleston (two hours away).

The Institute's founder and Executive Director, Peter M. Miller (a clinical psychologist), has written nine books, including *The Hilton Head Metabolism Diet*, *The Hilton Head Executive Stamina Program*, and *The Hilton Head Over-35 Diet*. These books can provide further insight into the Institute's philosophy and approach.

COST:
(depending on length)

Hilton Head Health Institute
14 Valencia Road
P.O. Box 7138
Hilton Head, SC 29938-7138

 (800) 292-2440 or (803) 785-7292

HIPPOCRATES HEALTH INSTITUTE

"I am convinced that the Hippocrates program is the best way to regain and maintain health. I am back to work full-time and most of my illnesses have disappeared. The rest are under control. I feel like a human being again."

—*Hippocrates Health Institute participant*

For more than thirty years, the Hippocrates Health Institute has promoted super nutrition and revitalization techniques. One of the primary techniques they use is a carefully balanced diet of organically grown, enzyme-rich live foods. The diet does not include any meat, dairy products, or cooked foods. Fresh wheatgrass juice is taken daily to rid the body of waste matter and toxins.

The programming also includes health talks by resident and guest lecturers, cooking classes, exercise (swimming and water aerobics in the ozonated pool, walking, stretching, yoga, or T'ai Chi), massages, and counseling.

Some participants have experienced drops in their cholesterol levels of up to one hundred points during a three-week stay. Others have lost over twenty pounds. Hippocrates can provide many testimonials from former participants who enjoyed relief or cure from conditions as wide ranging as cancer, lower back problems, arthritis, obesity, colitis, bronchitis, chronic fatigue, candida, anemia, and allergies, but a serious illness is not a prerequisite for participation. Individuals who just want to maintain or improve their current good health are also welcome.

Most participants stay for the three-week Health Encounter program, but shorter or longer stays can be arranged. Participants stay in dormitories, semiprivate, or private rooms.

The Institute is located in West Palm Beach, Florida (twenty minutes from the Palm Beach International Airport) on a twenty-acre subtropical, wooded estate. The tranquil setting (complete with one hundred-year old palm and banyan trees, a lotus pond, and peacocks roaming the grounds), aids the rejuvenation process. The attractions of Disney World, Universal Studios, and Seaworld are two hours north by car. A renowned theater and a museum are nearby, as is shopping on Worth Avenue in Palm Beach.

Among the many benefits promised by the Health Encounter system are alertness, a clear complexion, emotional stability, improved relationships, healthy blood cholesterol and triglyceride levels, and reversal of degenerative diseases. Other benefits include improved digestion, a more limber, painless back, muscular flexibility and strength, oxygenation of cells, release of tension, and increased energy.

COST:  to

(depending on length and accommodations)

 Hippocrates Health Institute
1443 Palmdale Court
West Palm Beach, FL 33411

 (561) 471-8876

www.hippocratesinst.com

New Age Health Spa

Like most spas, New Age has indoor and outdoor pools, steam and sauna rooms, weight and exercise rooms, and tennis courts. What sets New Age apart from the average spa is its offerings like Zen meditation, T'ai Chi, hypnotherapy, astrological charting, and Tarot card reading. There are also opportunities to learn winter activities such as cross-country skiing and snowshoeing.

The most unique feature of New Age is its Alpine Tower. This free-standing, fifty-foot high climbing structure with rope ladders, swinging logs, and a seesaw provides many climbing challenges. There are at least nineteen different ways to climb it and many different goals to be achieved. When participants work together on it, the experience provides growth in teamwork, mutual respect, trust, and communication. Done as a solo experience, individuals learn how to face challenges, overcome inhibitions, take risks, focus, and build self-esteem.

Walking is the most emphasized physical activity . Participants walk between three to six miles every morning before breakfast. Full day guided hikes are available a few times each week.

Meals are mostly vegetarian, with some fish and poultry. Entrees are available in three sizes: large (six hundred calories), medium (four hundred calories), and small (two hundred calories). Juice fasting is available as well.

Located in the Catskill Mountains, the spa is approximately a two and one-half hour drive from New York City. There is also a direct mini-van service from Manhattan.

Rooms are private, but New Age will arrange for a roommate if requested to take advantage of the double-occupancy rates.

There is no set length of stay, other than a minimum stay of two nights.

COST:

 New Age Health Spa
Route 55
Neversink, NY 12765

☎ (800) 682-4348 or (914) 985-7600

www.newagehealthspa.com

NEW LIFE HEALTH CENTER

"Through the treatments and lectures, diet, teas, meditation, and support, I was given a new lease on life. It's six years later and I am happier than I've ever been."

—*New Life Health Center participant*

Eastern and Western medicine is combined at the New Life Health Center to promote health and happiness. While much of the emphasis is on the body, the mind and spirit are not neglected. Individualized programs are developed so that participants can learn to heal themselves.

The Center has successfully treated accident injuries, asthma, back disorders, cancer, candida, chronic pain, colitis, chronic fatigue syndrome, depression, diabetes, eating disorders, gastro-intestinal disorders, hypertension, immune deficiencies, nicotine/drug/alcohol addiction, PMS, sexual problems, sports injuries, weight problems, and work injuries. Testimonials are available from a large number of participants and physicians.

Healing techniques include:

- **Acupressure**
  Manipulation on specific points and areas of the body corrects posture imbalance and stimulate circulation of energy and blood.

- **Acupuncture**
  Painless acupuncture is used to relieve energy imbalances and to strengthen the immune system.

- **Herbal teas**
  Healing herbs are selected and prepared for specific conditions. The teas balance, strengthen, and rejuvenate the body.

243

- **Cupping**
  Glass cups placed on the skin to create a vacuum are used to draw toxins from the skin, blood, muscles, and connective tissue. The process releases muscular and nervous tension while stimulating energy flow.

- **Moxa heat treatment**
  Burning the herb mugwort strengthens the immune system and improves blood circulation.

- **Mahayana yoga**
  This dynamic exercise includes static postures, work with partners, breathing, acupressure massage, and meditation techniques. It develops physical flexibility and strength, mental concentration, and emotional stability.

- **Corrective exercises and meditation**
  Relaxation techniques, deep abdominal breathing, meditation, prayer, and exercises create a balanced posture to allow optimal flow of internal healing energy.

- **Fasting**
  Supervised fasting eliminates toxins.

- **Natural diets**
  Participants prepare, eat, and attend lectures on balanced natural meals.

Program length is either one or three weeks.

Healing begins with a private consultation from the Center's founder, Bo-In Lee (an acupuncturist and yoga/martial arts/meditation teacher). Mr. Lee determines the root causes of each participant's illness or lack of health and develops a comprehensive program. The Center also has a staff medical doctor who can provide Western diagnosis through blood tests, X-rays, CAT scans, and so on.

Participants stay in double-occupancy or single rooms.

The Center is located in the Boston area.

COST: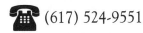

 New Life Health Center
12 Harris Avenue
Jamaica Plain, MA 02130

☎ (617) 524-9551

www.anewlife.com

OPENING YOUR HEART

Over the past two decades, Dr. Dean Ornish has demonstrated that individuals with blocked coronary arteries don't have to undergo surgery to restore blood flow to the heart. Lifestyle changes can prevent, reduce, or even reverse severe heart disease.

The Preventive Medicine Research Institute offers one-week retreats throughout the year to teach Dr. Ornish's approach. The retreats are designed for both people with heart disease and those without heart disease (but who have risk factors such as a family tendency or who just want to ensure that they remain healthy).

Participants learn stress management, moderate exercise techniques, and smoking cessation. They are instructed in adhering to a very low-fat diet (10 percent—with no meat, chicken, fish, or nuts). Dr. Ornish lectures at each retreat and has support staff of physicians, nurses, nutrition specialists, exercise physiologists, and counselors.

Accommodations are at the Claremont Resort and Spa in Oakland, California. Participants stay in private rooms and are served three low-fat meals a day. Amenities include tennis, golf, hiking, swimming, and water volleyball, as well as spa services such as massage.

After the retreat, most participants report having more energy, enhanced awareness, a reduction in the frequency and severity of cardiac symptoms, and an improved sense of well-being.

COST: 🌼 🌼 🌼 (limited scholarships are available)

 Preventive Medicine Research Institute
900 Bridgeway
Suite One
Sausalito, CA 94965

 (800) 775-7674

PACIFIC OASIS FOR PERFECT HEALTH

Ayurveda is a four thousand-year-old system of treatments from India that include meditation, exercise, yoga, massage, diet, herbs, and daily/seasonal routine. Panchakarma is a specialized Ayurvedic therapy designed to remove stress, fatigue, and impurities while restoring physiological balance. According to Ayurvedic beliefs, everyone should receive at least one week of Panchakarma each year to alleviate the imbalances that may especially occur with seasonal changes.

Pacific Oasis for Perfect Health offers three-, five-, and seven-day Panchakarma programs. They include such treatments as:

- **Abhyanga** (energizing herbalized oil massage)

- **Shirodhara** (relaxing oil steam on forehead)

- **Swedana** (herbal steam bath used for deep relaxation and for moving toxins from the tissues to the colon)

- **Bastis** (gentle medicated enemas for eliminating impurities)

- **Aromatherapy** (aromatic oils to create balance and harmony)

- **Gandharva veda** (invigorating music that re-establishes harmony with nature's cycles)

Optional treatments that are not included in the treatment package but which may be purchased separately are eye treatments, herbal steam inhalation, herbalized nasal drops, herbal paste massage, and a dry massage with silk gloves.

A consultation with a medical doctor trained in Ayurveda is required prior to beginning the program. After accounting for the mind/body type, the season, and any present imbalances, the physician designs a unique program to meet individual needs. Pacific Oasis can arrange for a consultation with doctors in its area or the participant can seek out a local physician. Ten days prior to beginning Panchakarma, participants adhere to a

247

home program. This involves a simplified diet, daily routine, and the internal use of small amounts of oil to oleate the digestive tract.

Pacific Oasis is not a residential clinic. However, they can send a list of the many bed and breakfasts, motels, and hotels in central Vancouver.

COST:

 Pacific Oasis for Perfect Health
#7-6137 Tisdall Street
Vancouver, British Columbia, Canada
V5Z 3M9

 (604) 266-1162

Pritikin Longevity Centers

"Getting slim with the Pritikin Approach gives you important benefits in improved health. While you begin to look better on the outside you'll be doing yourself a world of good on the inside."

—Nathan Pritikin, founder

After being diagnosed with coronary insufficiency and a high cholesterol level in 1958, Nathan Pritikin ignored conventional medical treatment advising medications, inactivity, and a daily diet that included steak and eggs. Instead, he started a vigorous exercise program and reduced fat in his diet. Within a short time, he cleared up the cholesterol/fatty deposits in his coronary arteries and enjoyed twenty-seven more years of good health. In 1976, he established the first Pritikin Longevity Center to teach his nutrition and exercise methods to others.

The Centers are not spas or diet programs. The main focus is on education for nutrition, stress management, and exercise. A thirteen-day program is available for persons without any health problems who want to learn Pritikin living. It's also open to persons with mild hypertension, weight problems, or diabetes controlled by oral medication. The twenty-six-day program is open to everyone, including those with serious weight problems, advanced heart disease, or insulin-requiring diabetes.

The program has a strong medical component. Pritikin physicians consult with participants' personal physicians prior to the start of the program. They conduct a complete history and physical exam oriented to risk factor analysis. This includes blood chemistry tests and a treadmill tolerance test. From these methods, a personalized exercise prescription is developed. The tests are administered at the end of the program as a comparison.

249

Pritikin physicians monitor progress throughout the program. They often take participants off some of their medications and are available twenty-four hours a day.

The exercise program consists of daily exercise classes of warm-up activities and thirty minutes on the treadmill. Walks along the beach and swims in the ocean or pool are also encouraged.

Participants eat six times a day. Daytime snacks and meals are served buffet-style. Dinner is sit-down, with table service. The Pritikin Eating Plan is mostly vegetarian, with poultry or fish served twice a week. Carbohydrates form the bulk of the diet, with fat less than 10 percent and protein less than 15 percent. Salt, sugar, fat, or cholesterol is not added to the food. Cooking and nutrition classes are an integral part of the program.

Topics in the daily classes include understanding heart disease, preventing cancer, and developing a plan of action for going home. Group and individual counseling also focuses on stress management and smoking cessation.

Follow-up after graduation from the program includes a monthly newsletter, a toll-free hotline for assistance with following the Pritikin lifestyle, and a local alumni network that can provide support.

Dramatic results are achieved, particularly after the twenty-six-day program. An average of thirteenpounds are lost. Over 50percent of diabetics leave without further need for insulin. More than 83percent of hypertensive individuals who entered the program on medication lowered their blood pressures and left drug free. All participants are reported to leave with a renewed sense of energy and vitality.

Participants stay in private rooms at the Centers' hotels.

Both Centers are oceanside in Miami Beach, Florida, and Santa Monica, California. Tennis and golf are nearby.

COST:

 Pritikin Longevity Centers
1910 Ocean Front Walk
Santa Monica, CA 90405

 (800) 421-9911 or (310) 450-5433

 Pritikin Longevity Centers
5875 Collins Avenue
Miami Beach, FL 33140

 (800) 327-4914 or (305) 866-2237

www.pritikin.com

RANCHO LA PUERTA

Rancho La Puerta offers a very well-rounded fitness program, addressing aerobic conditioning, strength training, stretching, coordination, and relaxation. More than sixty exercise classes are offered each day, assuring that each participant can find some means of exercise that appeals to them. Miles of hiking trails also encourage walking. Tennis, volleyball, and basketball courts are available, as well as a putting green. Spa services include massage and herbal wraps.

Unique offerings of Rancho La Puerta are special weeklong classes. These have included:

- **Aikido**
  Participants deepen their sense of selves, improve their state of attention, and "transform the capacity to become a black belt in daily life."

- **Pilates**
  This discipline addressed the entire neuromuscular system, increasing balance and joint mobility while relieving back pain and neck tension. The Pilates methods can enhance strength, stamina, and focus for the participants, just as they do for professional athletes and dancers.

- **Waterworks**
  Participants learn state-of-the-art aquatic exercise, including water circuit training, waterwalking, underwater toning for thighs and tummies, aquatherapy, water volleyball, and swimming.

To ensure a distraction-free environment, television, telephones, and newspapers are not allowed.

The Ranch is located on the California-Mexico border (about one and one-half hours from San Diego). Complimentary transportation to and from the San Diego airport is provided.

Participants stay in one-bedroom villas. Meals are largely vegetarian, with fish served a couple of times a week.

COST:

 Rancho La Puerta
P.O. Box 463057
Escondido, CA 92046

☎ (800) 443-7565 or (619) 744-4222

www.rancholapuerta.com

St. Helena Health Center

"The McDougall Program and St. Helena Health Center make an unbeatable team. Together, they have made it possible for me to change my diet and lifestyle and to get well and stay well."

—*St. Helena/McDougall participant*

As a fully accredited acute-care hospital and health center, St. Helena is renowned for specialized live-in health programs. The focus is on wellness rather than illness and self-responsibility. The approach is on treating the whole person because the body's health affects physical, emotional, social, and spiritual well-being.

In conjunction with physician and author John McDougall, St. Helena offers a twelve-day program aimed at making the lifestyle changes necessary to live a longer, healthier life. The program is appropriate for those with a weight problem, high cholesterol, heart disease, high blood pressure, adult onset diabetes, rheumatoid arthritis, multiple sclerosis, and intestinal disorders. Individualized goals may include controlling weight; managing stress; reducing risk of serious health problems; increasing endurance for exercise or work; decreasing dependence on medications; and improving cholesterol, blood sugar, and triglyceride levels.

The McDougall Program utilizes a low-fat vegetarian diet that is high in fiber and complex carbohydrates, has zero cholesterol, and is low in sugar and salt. Three meals are served daily. Classes show how to plan, shop for, and prepare healthy foods at home and follow this approach when dining at restaurants.

Physical conditioning is another component of the program. Exercise physiologists develop an exercise routine for each participant. A pool, gym, and walking paths are available.

Group discussions, individual counseling, biofeedback techniques, and group relaxation exercises teach participants how to reduce the negative effects of stress.

Graduates of the program have access to the McDougall team of professionals via the toll-free phone line for questions and advice. They also receive ongoing support through a newsletter and by attending retreats throughout the year.

St. Helena also has a seven-day Nicotine Addiction program. The curriculum offers lectures, walks, group discussions, gym sessions, stress management groups, and water exercise classes. Participants learn strategies for behavioral control and gain a better understanding of addiction so they can remain nicotine-free.

Other programs include Pulmonary Rehabilitation (ten days), Cardiac Rehabilitation (ten days), and Pain Rehabilitation (twenty-six days). Individualized alcohol and chemical recovery programs are available.

The Center is located seventy miles north of San Francisco in the Napa Valley. Shuttle service is available to and from area airports.

Participants are accommodated in semiprivate (or private) hotel-style accommodations. Recreational amenities include pool, whirlpool, sauna, therapeutic massages, gym, and scenic walking paths.

COST: 💲💲 (Nicotine Addiction program)

💲💲💲 (McDougall program)

   St. Helena Health Center
Deer Park, CA 94576

 (800) 358-9195 or (707) 963-6200

www.drmcdougall.com/sthelena.html

255

STOP SMOKING RECOVERY PROGRAMS

"It wasn't near as hard as I thought it would be. I should have done this years ago!"

—*Stop Smoking participant*

If you're like many smokers, you've thought about or tried stopping but haven't been able to put your good intentions into actual practice. Advertised as a revolutionary program for the person who has "tried everything" to stop smoking, this intensive and comprehensive program treats the nicotine habit as a drug addiction. It offers a long-term program of recovery designed to prevent relapse. The course content includes nutrition, exercise, the twelve steps, dealing with feelings, developing supports, dealing with compulsions, proper withdrawal, and after-care planning. Led by a former staff member of the Palm Beach Institute who developed a comprehensive inpatient treatment program for nicotine addiction, participants leave the program with the motivation and skills to quit smoking permanently.

Instead of returning from your Florida "vacation" with a souvenir like a doll made from sea shells, you'll be bringing back something much more important: a healthier you. For less than the cost of a pack of cigarettes per day for a year, you'll gain the resolve and the knowledge to be a nonsmoker for the rest of your life. By kicking the habit, you'll save money, add years to your life, and generally feel better all around.

The program is held monthly, beginning on a Wednesday in the late afternoon and ending early on the following Sunday. Participants stay in semiprivate rooms at a resort hotel in

West Palm Beach, Florida. Only six clients are admitted per program.

COST:

 Stop Smoking Recovery Programs
P.O. Box 16656
West Palm Beach, FL 33416

 (800) 547-7867 or (561) 585-8901

THE TEMPLE BEAUTIFUL

In ancient Egypt, the Temple Beautiful provided a place for purifying and healing the body so that a state of higher awareness could be achieved. Edgar Cayce (a famous psychic who advocated holistic living and alternative medicine remedies) wrote in depth about the healing phenomenon of the original Temple Beautiful. He believed that individual consciousness could be awakened when the atoms, cells, organs, and systems of the entire human body were influenced by the Divine. A.R.E. (Association for Research and Enlightenment) Medical Clinic combines conventional medicine with the alternative medicine practices of Cayce and others so that each participant can have a life-changing experience.

A.R.E.s medical staff screens each applicant prior to admission (based on written information supplied by the applicant as well as medical records forwarded by the personal physician) and evaluates the medical status upon entrance into the program as well as at the end of the program. Laboratory tests are performed to assess various physiological factors. While A.R.E. physicians are not a substitute for participant's personal physicians, they do provide counseling as to the lab tests, diagnosis, nutritional program, and overall physical condition.

In addition to the physical benefits, Temple Beautiful participants leave with a heightened consciousness and deeper spiritual insights. Participants attend lectures on meditation, prayer, movement, dance, practical home remedies, biofeedback, nutrition, dream symbology, and creative living. There is an exercise period each day. Biofeedback, therapeutic full-body massages, hydrotherapy, reflexology, acupressure, colon therapy, osteopathic manipulation, and energy medicine therapies (such as the electromagnetic balancing machine for pain and stress relief) are also used. Guided imagery, music, art, journal keeping, and group work complete the program.

The basic diet at A.R.E. is consistent with the Cayce readings: low in fat, low in animals with an inappropriate acid-alkaline balance, focus on vegetables and fruits, and elimination of processed and fried foods.

Because treatment is so highly individualized based on each participant's unique health needs, the program is limited to fifteen or less participants. Each leaves with a personalized program to follow at home.

The program is offered monthly. The original is eleven days, but a shorter version is available for seven days.

Participants live on the A.R.E. campus in Phoenix in semiprivate housing at the lodge.

COST: 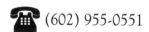 (some of the services and tests are reimbursable through insurance that covers out-patient office care and diagnostic testing)

 A.R.E. Medical Clinic
4018 North Street
Phoenix, AZ 85018

☎ (602) 955-0551

VEGA STUDY CENTER

The macrobiotic dietary approach emphasizes the importance of natural foods to physical and emotional health. Macrobiotic diets are based on whole, unrefined grains and fresh vegetables. The diet is low-fat, low-protein, high-complex-carbohydrate, and high-fiber. Food preparation is considered to be just as important as the selection of appropriate foods. Certain emotional or physical conditions or climates and seasons demand specific approaches, such as adjusting the salt or water used in cooking or steaming, boiling, and baking. A dynamic approach is needed to individualize the diet to each person's needs (which are never static, but typically change from day to day).

As a nonprofit, world-renowned macrobiotic study center, Vega offers one- to four-week courses in macrobiotic learning and living. Macrobiotic Lifestyle Essentials is the basic two-week course for persons new to macrobiotics or long-time practitioners seeking renewal and updated information. The program includes a complete macrobiotic cooking course, advice on adjusting macrobiotics for personal needs, and techniques for stress management and emotional stability. Other courses include one-week sessions on Healing From Head to Toe (macrobiotic home remedies), Cooking for One! (macrobiotic cooking and eating for busy single persons, including techniques for when traveling away from home), and Women's Week of Spirituality (drumming sessions, guided imagery, images and myths, in conjunction with macrobiotics).

There are specialized three- and four-week courses for persons who want to develop professional expertise as cooks or teachers. Weekend getaways are available for individuals to gain some exposure to the macrobiotic lifestyle. Two-week Cancer and Healing programs are available for persons recovering from cancer.

Leisure activities include using the center's saunas and salt baths, local sightseeing, student-planned social activities, visits to San Francisco, or attending cultural events in Chico (a nearby university town).

Vega is located in the northern California countryside, one and one-half hours north of Sacramento. Taxi service is available from the airport.

Participants usually share a room with one to three other persons. Most have a half-bath; tubs and showers are located nearby each room. Private rooms or stays at nearby motels can be arranged. Locally grown organic grains and produce are served, along with Vega's own home-made miso, soy sauce, umeboshi plums, pickles, and stone-ground naturally-leavened bread.

Programs are held throughout the year.

Vega can also provide information about the annual George Ohsawa Macrobiotic Foundation Summer Camp. Held in the Tahoe National Forest, the camp incorporates lectures and workshops on macrobiotics and healing with recreational activities such as campfires, swimming, hiking, and so on.

COST:

 Vega Study Center
1511 Robinson Street
Oroville, CA 95965

 (530) 533-7702

www.vega.macrobiotic.net

WE CARE HEALTH CENTER

"I feel better than I have in years. I have more energy and have lost ten pounds. I'm ready to live again!"
—*We Care Health Center participant*

There is no shortage of spas and health retreats designed to improve the participants' physical and mental well-being. But the We Care is unique in its design for rejuvenation of the entire body from the cellular level on out. While most health programs address diet as the major cause of health problems, We Care focuses on total health of the colon. Believing that "life and death begins in the colon," the We Care staff have developed a program to remove the toxins which accumulate in our bodies from preservatives, additives, artificial colorings, and chemicals that are in our food, water, and air we breathe.

According to We Care, the symptoms of an unhealthy colon include gas, headaches, irritability, chronic fatigue, dulled senses and perceptions, and cold hands and feet. Untreated colon problems such as constipation, colitis, and diverticulosis increase the risk of colon cancer. But once the toxins are removed, energy levels improve and a sense of well-being is maintained.

The detoxification is accomplished through fasting with an all-natural liquid diet, lymphatic massage, colonics, reflexology, herbal glow, salt glow, and skin brushing. Other activities include nutritional classes so participants can develop healthy eating patterns, exercise (including biking, swimming, walking, and yoga), and stress release groups where members learn to trust, give, and receive as a means of achieving emotional well-being. Other available treatments include scalp treatments, acupressure, massages, facials, iridology, and aromatherapy.

To prepare for the revitalization program, participants should eat only fruit, raw and steamed vegetables, juices, and herb teas for four days prior to coming.

Although trained colonic therapists administer the treatments, there are no medical doctors on the premises. Participants' health must be stable enough to not require monitoring by a physician and to tolerate the treatments.

Testimonial letters from participants enthusiastically document substantial weight loss, changed eating habits, increased energy, enhanced appearance, stronger immune systems, and optimized emotional health.

Participants stay in private accommodations. Packages are available for three, six, or eight days.

The center is located ten minutes from the Palm Springs airport in the California desert. Only ten participants can be accommodated at a time.

COST:

 We Care Health Center
18000 Long Canyon Road
Desert Hot Springs, CA 92241

 (800) 888-2523

www.wwb.com/company/c008252.html

WEIMAR INSTITUTE

"At Weimar I discovered the answer to my body's needs! It has made a tremendous impact on my lifestyle. I came home not with just a head full of 'I shoulds,' but with a heart full of motivation."

—Weimar Institute participant

Weimar's NEWSTART® (Nutrition, Exercise, Water, Sunlight, Temperance, Air, Rest, and Trust in Divine Power) program offers eighteen days of health improvement designed to last a lifetime. Although the primary goal is to heal the physical body, it incorporates spirituality into the approach. Although run by Christian health professionals, persons of any or no religious affiliation can feel comfortable with the program.

It is primarily geared towards persons with significant health problems such as hypertension, angina, obesity, arthritis, high cholesterol, diabetes, allergies, and conditions related to stress and aging. The Institute reports great success in treating these health concerns, such as 50 percent of all hypertensives stopping medication and returning to normal blood pressure, persons with pain from arthritis, diabetic neuropathy, and angina experiencing dramatic relief, and persons whose cholesterol levels dropped 40 percent.

NEWSTART® physicians begin the program by evaluating each participant's condition through a comprehensive history and physical exam, treadmill exercise test, and blood chemistry panel. They formulate an exercise prescription from this information and evaluate progress during the program. A treadmill test and blood chemistry panel at the completion of the program serves as a comparison.

Three vegan (no animal products, including dairy) meals are served daily. Water is the beverage of choice; caffeine, sodas, and alcohol are not allowed.

Walking is the major form of exercise. Group calisthenics are encouraged. There is some exercise equipment, but the Institute encourages a simple, low-tech approach.

Participants attend cooking classes, receive counseling, and enjoy therapeutic massage and hydrotherapy treatments.

The Institute also offers a two-day diabetic reversal seminar that shows how to counteract the effects of adult-onset diabetes. The seminar includes lectures on scientific knowledge, exercise, a whole-plant food diet, and lifestyle choices that can reduce the need for insulin or oral agents.

Accommodations are in private or shared rooms in a lodge.

Weimar is located in the foothills of the Sierra Mountains about an hour away from Sacramento. Group activities, shopping trips, and weekend outings are provided.

COST: 💲 (diabetes seminar) to 💲 💲 💲
(some of the cost may be covered by insurance and may be tax-deductible)

Weimar Institute
P.O. Box 486
Weimar, CA 95736

 (800) 525-9192 or (916) 637-4111

www.weimarinstitut.net

WILDWOOD LIFESTYLE CENTER AND HOSPITAL

"Wildwood literally saved my life! I experienced not only great physical improvement but inner peace and spiritual rewards."
—*Wildwood participant*

Hospitals are not typically considered a vacation destination. But in the case of Wildwood, it just may be the healthiest thing you've ever done for yourself! Wildwood, in addition to being a fully licensed hospital for acute care, runs a lifestyle center which offers seven-, fourteen-, and twenty-two-day programs to improve health problems such as overweight, smoking/emphysema, heart disease, high blood pressure, arthritis, connective tissue disease, stress, diabetes, depression, hypoglycemia, and allergies.

The Wildwood physician evaluates participants' medical history as soon as they arrive. The physical exam includes a blood chemistry profile, EKG-exercise stress test, lung function, chest x-ray, and a comprehensive computerized life inventory/fitness evaluation. Based on this information, a personalized conditioning program is developed. Personal counseling and periodic consultations with the physician ensure that each individual program stays on course. Nutrition lectures, cooking classes, and a natural food diet help participants develop a healthy eating style which can last a lifetime. Exercise options include warm-up activities and guided hikes on trails. Health lectures are also a part of each day. The center has a Christian focus (although persons of any religion or faith system are welcome) and sees prayer as part of a healthy lifestyle.

After a twenty-four-day program, participants experience a significant reduction in blood pressure, lowered resting pulse, lowered cholesterol and triglyceride levels, weight loss of twelve to thirty-five pounds, a cessation of unhealthy habits such as smoking or excessive caffeine or sugar consumption, and enhanced emotional and spiritual well-being. With shorter stays, results may be less extensive but still significant.

The stop-smoking program is especially noteworthy. It's a medically supervised seven-day live-in program. The focus is on making the decisions necessary to live life free of tobacco products. Participants totally abstain from cigarettes. Withdrawal symptoms are controlled by a nonstimulating diet, exercise, rest, and exercising willpower while relying on Divine help. New habits are formed by avoiding activities that trigger smoking desires and developing alternative coping resources.

Located in the north Georgia mountains ten miles southwest of Chattanooga, Tennessee, on five hundred acres with dogwood and wild azalea tress along the trails, the center provides its own shuttle service from the Chattanooga airport or bus terminal.

Guests stay in private rooms, each with a garden patio.

COST: 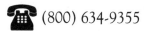 (depending on length)

 Wildwood Lifestyle Center
Wildwood, GA 30757

☎ (800) 634-9355

www.tagnet.org/wildwood

SELF-IMPROVEMENT VACATIONS

*I*t can rightfully be said that every vacation in this book leads to self-improvement. Whether you acquire skills in poetry writing or lose a few pounds, you're improving yourself in some way. You're effecting change in your life and growing as a human being.

But the vacations in this chapter have a primary focus on self-improvement in a general sense. It's not so much that they teach a specific skill such as a foreign language or yoga. Instead, they develop self-knowledge and self-confidence with the ultimate goal of relating more effectively to yourself as well as to others. Your life can be changed through the increased understanding and appreciation of yourself that you'll gain by a weekend or week at one of these programs. When you believe in yourself, you can successfully tackle new challenges and deal with other people.

The first section, Personal Empowerment Programs, contains vacations that empower individuals with the skills and attitudes needed to reach their unique personal potential. Techniques can be as varied as firewalking, role playing, lectures, and art therapy, but the goals are similar: to improve self-awareness, self-confidence, creativity, and independence.

The second section, Relationships Enhancement Programs, provides information about personal development vacations with a focus on improving communication and intimacy skills with spouses/partners, relatives, friends, co-workers, and supervisors.

PERSONAL EMPOWERMENT PROGRAMS

No one can give you personal strength and power. Nothing can make you believe in yourself if you're resistant to doing so. Personal empowerment ultimately comes from yourself. Only you can change your consciousness, attitudes, and emotions to create the conditions where you feel good about yourself and life.

But many of us don't know where to begin. We may know that we want to make some changes in our lives. We may desperately want to be happy with ourselves and become the individuals we long to be, but the people and routines of our everyday lives can make this quest difficult.

If you've been feeling for some time that you want to develop the skills and attitudes to reach your unique potential but felt that you didn't have the time or knowledge to do this in a meaningful way, consider the following vacations. The programs in this section don't magically raise your self-esteem, heighten your consciousness, enhance your creativity, or develop a direction for the rest of your life. It will require work on your part both during and after the vacation. But if you're committed and open to change, each program can provide the tools, techniques, and experiences that you need. You'll discover and enjoy the best possible you. What better souvenir could there be from a vacation?

ANTELOPE RETREAT AND EDUCATION CENTER

"…this has been the most self searching week of my life. I realize that I have to slow down my life and be more aware of my surroundings wherever I am….a really remarkable experience with lasting lessons."

—Antelope participant

Unstructured retreats are offered year-round at this small center. During the summer, there are special programs which focus on Native American teachings and vision quests. Each program allows participants to expand awareness of themselves and the natural world while finding the source of vision and guidance which exists within them. The quests, modeled after those practiced by indigenous cultures for thousands of years, involve going into the wilderness to connect, heal, and discover creativity, personal power, and spirit.

The Center offers one-day quests for individuals who aren't sure that they're ready for a longer experience. Most participants do a three-day quest with two days of preparatory work and one day of integration after the experience. Fasting is part of the quest.

There are special women's quests which include group time, solo time, sweat lodges, and a two-day vision quest. The Sacred Hoop week includes Dakota teachings as another way of understanding personal life journeys. The Survival and Nature Awareness week teaches basic survival skills (shelter, water, fire, and food) while exploring alternative paths to spirituality.

Participants stay in shared accommodations in a ranch house or in small yurts. Family style meals are served to participants when not fasting.

The Center is located in the foothills of the Rockies, just north of Colorado. Van service is available from the airport in Hayden, Colorado.

Recreational activities include swimming, hiking, and cross-country skiing.

COST:

 Antelope Retreat and Education Center
P.O. Box 156
Savery, WY 82332

 (307) 383-2625

www.anteloperetreat.org

AVATAR

"Don't let what you're being get in the way of what you might become."

—Harry Palmer, creator of Avatar course

"For me, Avatar has been an opening, a tremendous boost of energy, a clean start to my life, and the most important 'process' I have ever done."

—Avatar participant

More than one thousand Avatar masters (trained and licensed teachers who deliver the Avatar course) in thirty-two countries offer a one-week course focusing on managing and changing beliefs. The Avatar philosophy is based on the importance of beliefs and their ability to create or attract the situations and events which individuals experience as their lives. By changing the consciousness of being, participants learn to live life deliberately, creatively, and playfully.

Instead of lessons which are purely intellectual and word-based, Avatar provides experiential lessons as well as self-paced readings which enable participants to examine and manage their beliefs. They learn to "discreate" (cause to vanish or self-destruct) their limiting beliefs while creating the reality they prefer. Unlike other self-help systems, there are no specific beliefs taught (other than the assertion that belief precedes experience). Each participant discovers those beliefs which are right for him or her.

The three sections of the course are:

I. Creativism
Exercises allow participants to explore the beliefs with which they've designed their lives, determining which are limiting or self-sabotaging and which are life-expanding.

II. The Exercises

Participants learn to perceive reality without judgment, separation, or distortion. By connecting their current functioning with the future they wish to create, a sense of harmony with the universe is achieved.

III. The Rundowns

Any beliefs which participants choose not to retain are discreated. Through the use of expanded consciousness techniques, rundowns allow changes in body sensations, interpersonal conflicts, dependencies, compulsions, and negative emotions such as blame and self-pity.

Avatar classes are usually held at sites with scenic vistas and amenities such as hot tubs, hiking trails, and so on. A few seminars are held in large cities, but most are conducted at beach or mountain sites. Locations have included Santa Fe, New Mexico, Malibu, California, Boulder, Colorado, the Hawaiian Islands, and the Caribbean (such as the coast of Belize). Some courses are given once a month, while others are run seven days a week year-round and can be started on any day.

Persons who aren't sure if they want to commit the time and money for the full course may begin with a free one-day seminar on Creativism. Sufficient information is provided for determining whether the full course would be beneficial.

Upon completion of the course, participants have the power to create the professional and personal lives they want. Limitations, doubts, and excess baggage are forever shed. Goals are more easily set and reached. The moment-to-moment flow of life can be more fully appreciated.

COST: 💲 💲 (tuition only; living costs vary according to accommodations and location)

(312) 432-4300 Nationwide Headquarters

800 numbers of the more popular locations include:

 (800) 334-0048 New England

 (800) 565-2055 Upstate New York

 (800) 682-2534 Boulder, Colorado

 (800) 299-5509 Northern California

 (800) 334-0048 Caribbean

BOULDER OUTDOOR SURVIVAL SCHOOL

"It was one of the hardest things I've ever done in my life, and I know I reached my lowest low. But I also reached my highest high and am glad I pushed myself to do it! You've restored my spirit."

—Boulder Outdoor Survival School participant

Boulder Outdoor Survival School (BOSS) is dedicated to "the instruction and preservation of primitive survival arts and to the development of people through experiences within the natural world and its cultural traditions." It is not a boot-camp military survival program or a desert meditation school or a Native American revival group. Instead, its field courses are designed for those who want to test themselves physically, mentally, and emotionally by a new way of engaging with life in the wilderness. Participants increase their self-awareness and self-confidence, their interpersonal skills as part of the group experience, their appreciation and understanding of the environment, and their spiritual awareness and connection with the sacred forces of the natural world.

Unlike other wilderness experience companies, BOSS participants are taught how to live in a natural environment through knowledge and technique, not technology. Instead of using synthetically-insulated sleeping bags and storm-proof tents, participants use a wool blanket. Rather than carrying seventy pounds of gadgets and supplies on their back, participants carry only the blanket, an Army poncho, knife, and a change of clothes. Instead of eating chemically processed trail foods, participants try hunting and gathering skills as well as provided grains, rices, potatoes, vegetable proteins, and nuts.

The standard course is twenty-seven days. It begins with twenty-four hours of orientation followed by three days of intense hiking. During this phase, the only food and water is what the participants find for themselves. This simulates a survival situation where the desert is experienced on its own terms. The second phase is a group expedition where the basic skills for wilderness travel are taught: shelter construction, navigation, orienteering, fires, water, edible plants, trapping, cordage, and trail safety. It consists of two weeks of hiking, personal instruction, and traveling in small hunter-gatherer bands. Two meals a day are provided during this phase. After a brief independent hike, participants are ready for the Solo/Quest. For three to five days, each is on his or her own to enjoy the opportunity for self-discovery, independence, and solitude (with food available/optional). Following activities consist of student expeditions where small groups navigate at their own pace.

There are abbreviated courses of seven or fourteen days that provide the same experiences in a shorter time frame (such as a two-day Solo/Quest). Some of the seven-day courses are reserved exclusively for women so they can participate without the dynamic of coed instruction.

All courses are held during the summer in the desert of Boulder, Utah (in the south-central part of the state).

The average weight loss is ten to fifteen pounds during a twenty-seven-day program, so participants must be in good physical shape and check with their doctors before attending a course. Prescription medications and the use of other drugs are forbidden since the combination of heat, thirst, strenuous activity, and drugs does not make for a healthy mix (although some necessary drugs may be approved). Final acceptance is contingent upon passing a fitness test immediately prior to starting the course.

COST: (seven to fourteen days)

 (twenty-seven days)

 September 15 to April 30:
Boulder Outdoor Survival School
P.O. Box 1590
Boulder, CO 84716

(800) 335-7404 or (303) 444-9779

 May 1 to September 14
Boulder Outdoor Survival School
P.O. Box 1345
Boulder, UT 84716

(800) 335-7404 or (801) 335-7404

CAMP WINNARAINBOW

"It's never too late to have a happy childhood at the Camp Winnarainbow. This will be just like kids camp, only you can make love and don't have to brush your teeth."

—*Wavy Gravy, Camp Director*

Since 1986, Camp Winnarainbow has specialized in teaching children and adults performing and circus arts. Most of its summer program is for children, but one week in June is reserved for adults-only. Its director is Wavy Gravy (a prominent counter-culture hero during the fifties and sixties).

Campers from all walks of life and all levels of experience (including complete beginners) learn tricks of the trade from seasoned circus professionals. Skills taught are clowning, magic, storytelling, acrobatics, juggling, stilt-walking, mask-making, trapeze, and improvisation. Participants range in age from eighteen to seventy-five.

Participants can learn skills which can be used to entertain children and others as a part-time business or as a volunteer, but there are other benefits from the week. The whimsical camp unleashes creativity, uncovers a talent in every participant, reduces depression, and alleviates shyness and fear. It's a very empowering experience.

The week culminates in a cabaret on Saturday night. Participants show off their skills in a mini-amphitheater in front of an audience.

Free time activities include swimming in a lake, careening down a 350-foot waterslide, and listening to rock music.

There is also a spiritual element to the camp, especially on the last day which is dedicated to environmental concerns and a conscious awakening. A "Ceremony of All-Species Day" is performed. Each camper dons a mask or costume he or she creates

279

and which represents a species of animal. A speech from the perspective of that species is made to the rest of the campers.

The camp is both drug and alcohol free.

It's located five miles north of Laytonville in Mendocino County, California on the Black Oak Ranch's scenic five hundred wooded acres.

Participants live in communal teepees or private tents. Sleeping mats are provided, as are three gourmet meals. Vegetarian alternatives are always available.

COST:

 Camp Winnarainbow
1301 Henry Street
Berkeley, CA 94709

www.well.com/user/arainbow/

DANCE OF THE DEER

"Shamanism involves healing and empowerment through personal transformation and direct experience as well as the healing of our families, communities, and environment. By following the shaman's path, we can truly learn to inhabit the earth and our being with gentleness and respect."

—*Brant Secunda, director of Dance of the Deer Foundation*

Dance of the Deer Foundation sponsors seminars, pilgrimages, and study groups throughout the United States and Mexico (as well as Europe and other locations throughout the world). All experiences focus on exploring and keeping shamanic traditions alive. Especially as practiced by the Huilchol Indians of Mexico, shamanism is an ancient healing tradition as well as a way of life. Participants experience Huichol ceremonies (drumming, song, and dance, including the sacred Dance of the Deer), vision quests, shamanic health and healing, dream studies to guide and empower their lives, and pilgrimages to places of power in nature.

By the end of the experience, participants have learned to walk the shamanic path, discovering the sacredness of their lives and their responsibilities as human beings on the earth. They return to their lives with knowledge and skills that can help them establish more balanced and healthful lives.

Typical pilgrimages and retreats are to the Catskill Mountains of New York (three days), Mount Shasta in California (five days), Alaska (ten days), Puerto Vallarta, Mexico (ten days), Tuscany, Italy (fourteen days), and the German Alps (five days). They're held throughout the year. Depending on the time of the year and place, there are special ceremonies to honor the mountains, ocean, and summer solstice.

Participants camp out or stay in cabins.

COST:

 Dance of the Deer Foundation
Center for Shamanic Studies
P.O. Box 699
Soquel, CA 95073

☎ (408) 475-9560

www.shamanism.com

DOLPHIN CAMP

"The dolphins teach in a loving, gentle and playful way; and are the most powerfully enlightening, empowering, liberating, and enjoyable lessons I've learned to date. I will treasure forever what I refer to as 'my dance with the dolphins.'"

—*Dolphin Camp participant*

Many people consider dolphins to be magical creatures with an intricate language and social structure. Swimming with dolphins can be an exhilarating experience. Dolphins respond to each person individually, communicating in unique ways. The dolphins help participants learn to trust, tap into intuitive potential, enrich sensory awareness, and play with a childlike sense of joy.

Six- and seven-day Dolphin Camp programs provide participants with daily opportunities to swim and interact with wild dolphins in the ocean and semi-captive swim situations. The program also provides classes, experiential exercises, and discussions which explore what was learned about or from the dolphins and how to transfer it back to the everyday world. Content includes communication skills, sensory awareness flotation, brain dominance evaluation, whole brain synchronization, group dynamics and leadership, stress release, and healing energies.

The training expands self-concept, clarifies life vision, and supports the healing process. Dolphin Camp participants have eliminated depression, enhanced creativity, and enjoyed improved health.

Dolphin Camps are held a few times a year, usually in the Florida Keys and occasionally in Mexico's Yucatan Peninsula. Participants stay in double-occupancy rooms at resort hotels. Pool, spa, tennis, and hot tubs are available. Three meals a day are provided.

COST:

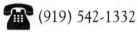 DeLano Training Systems
1654 Hamlet Chapel Road
Pittsboro, NC 27312

☎ (919) 542-1332

DOW CREATIVITY FELLOWSHIPS

"As we look to the future...more individuals are going to demand personal creative outlets. It becomes our responsibility to make available to every individual the opportunities for constructive growth."
—*Alden B. Dow, architect and inspiration for the Dow Creativity fellowships*

Lots of us have creative ideas and projects we wish we could develop further, but the distractions of our lives don't allow us to pursue these projects. Imagine getting away from it all for a couple of months to devote yourself to a creative endeavor.

That's exactly what could happen if you were chosen for a Dow creativity fellowship. For eight weeks during the summer, you could escape from your normal routine and environment. You'd live on the campus of Northwood University (about 125 miles north of Detroit). The fellowship would provide for travel expenses to and from Midland, room, board, and a small stipend for materials.

Applicants must submit a description of the project, the specific accomplishable goals for the residency, a list of needed facilities and equipment, a resume, and three references. Applications are welcomed from all disciplines and areas of interest including the arts, sciences, and humanities. Former projects included a creative writing program for prisoners, technological improvements in filmmaking, and a math curriculum emphasizing creative problem solving. Other projects have focused on music, architecture, business, textiles, choreography, and theology. While there are no requirements related to age or academic experience, fellows must have the maturity and motivation to work independently. The major factor for selection is the inherent quality and uniqueness of the project idea. An average of four fellowships are awarded each year.

Your completed project might bring you fame and fortune. It might enhance your career or start you off on a rewarding avocation. And while you might never again have the luxury of an all-expenses paid sabbatical, once your creative juices have flowed for eight weeks you'll try harder to find some time and space in your life for future dreams.

Upon completion of the program, fellows make oral presentations of their projects to the Creativity Center board members and Northwood University staff. At the fellows' requests, notice of accomplishments will be directed to the appropriate media. Projects remain the property of the applicant.

Fellows live in a large furnished apartment on their own. The apartment is equipped with a kitchen, but weekday lunches are provided at the Creativity Center on the campus. There are facilities for indoor and outdoor recreation and the visual and performing arts.

 Northwood University
Alden B. Dow Creativity Center
3225 Cook Road
Midland, MI 48640

 (517) 837-4478

www.morthwood.edu/abd/index/html

ENNEAGRAM PERSONALITY TYPE TRAINING

"The training for me was a cross between summer camp and a spiritual retreat, fun yet somehow sacred."
—*Enneagram Personality Type participant*

The Enneagram is a geometric depiction of the nine personality types of human nature: The Reformer, The Helper, The Motivator, The Individualist, The Thinker, The Loyalist, The Enthusiast, The Leader, The Peacemaker. Proponents believe it to be more comprehensive and profound than other modern personality typologies such as Myers-Briggs or the DSM-III(R). The Enneagram personality theory encompasses both psychological and spiritual elements. Each personality type shows the full range of human potential (from dysfunctional, neurotic conditions to optimal states of psychological health, expanded consciousness, and transcendence beyond the self). The focus is on a pathway for personal growth unique to each type.

Enneagram Personality Types, Inc., offers five-day training programs which emphasize the inner workings of the personality types. Each type's early developmental roles, core dynamics, psychic structures, paths of integration and disintegration, stress and security points, and internal symmetries are analyzed. Nine hours of classes are given each day. In addition to lectures and readings, there is ample time for group discussion and sharing.

Graduates of the course develop insight into the underlying motivations of all the types, as well as an understanding of how they relate to one another. Many of the graduates teach the Enneagram in their own workshops and/or use it in conjunction with other areas of their professional expertise (such as teaching, counseling, medicine, business management). But the workshops are as valuable personally as they are professionally. The information enables personal growth and transformation by showing participants how to become fully integrated and balanced and how to best relate to the important people in their lives.

287

Training programs are held throughout the year at conference centers in Bangor, Pennsylvania (seventy-five miles west of New York City in the Poconos), and Menlo Park, California (on the San Francisco Peninsula in an urban area). Participants are accommodated in double-occupancy rooms and are served three meals daily.

COST:

 Enneagram Personality Types, Inc.
222 Riverside Drive, Suite 10
New York, NY 10025

☎ (212) 932-3306

EUPSYCHIA INSTITUTE

"People need to be gently brought to the awareness that thought is creative and that we are indeed responsible for our choices and our ways of viewing our reality....It is empowering to know that if you are helping to create your problems, you can also create the solutions."

—*Jacquelyn Small, founder, Eupsychia Institute*

The concept "Eupsychia" was coined by Abraham Maslow (one of the founders of transpersonal psychology and the originator of self-actualization theory). It means "good psyche" or well-being in Greek. Dr. Maslow expanded the meaning to encompass the idea of a community of persons who explore and follow their spiritual values and who work towards an optimal future for all of us. Jacquelyn Small, as a social worker/therapist, founded Eupsychia Institute to perpetuate Maslow's dream.

The Institute offers a variety of extended personal, interpersonal, and transpersonal wellness retreats and programs. All programs attempt to birth a new consciousness and healing force which enables self-empowerment and fulfillment of each participant's life purpose.

"Healing Into Wholeness" is a fourteen-day retreat which combines aspects of mainstream mental health and addictions treatment with the spiritual psychologies. It's intended for persons who are experiencing spiritual hunger, critical life transitions, blocked creativity, grief/loss, patterns of addiction, repressed trauma, illness, depression, burnout, and relationship and gender concerns. To access the unconscious mind and release hard-to-reach patterns holding dysfunctional and outworn habits in place, a variety of psychospiritual therapies are used. These include integrative breathwork, psychodrama, shadow work, the enactment of myth/symbol/story, expressive artwork, movement and play, sacred ceremony, mask-making, guided imagery, and journal work. Daily yoga classes, body-work, exercise, meditation, silent time, nature outings, nutritional counseling, and twelve step meetings promote wellness within the body as well as the spirit.

"Psyche's Treasure House: Exploring Myth, Symbol, and Story as Our Link to Immortality" is a six-day intensive. It focuses on the myths and tales of our ancient ancestors as a means for understanding our own mythic stories and realities. Through such methods as integrative breathwork, guided imagery, T'ai Chi, large and small group process, dialogue, mandala artwork, and sacred music, participants learn psychospiritual approaches to heal the self as well as to help others.

"Psycho-Spiritual Integration: A Psychology of Being for the Closing of an Age" is a six-day retreat blending psychological health with spiritual essence. Participants learn to let go of the past and let a higher Self guide from within. Topics covered include Activating the Inner Healer, The Purpose of the Open Heart, Creating Sacred Space, and The Powers of Invocation, Inspiration, and Intention. As with all of Eupsychia's offerings, it is highly experiential (with large and small groupwork, integrative breathwork, guided imagery, sacred artwork, ritual, chanting, and storytelling.)

Eupsychia also offers weekend conferences with nationally known experts in the psychological and spiritual fields. Participants learn how to develop their sensory awareness, to imagine a personal and societal renewal of depth and substance, and to recognize the soul's sacred purpose.

Retreats, intensives, and conferences are held throughout the United States in hotels and retreat centers. Locations have included San Diego, Orlando, Minneapolis, Salt Lake City, and Dahlonega, Georgia. Participants are accommodated in double-occupancy rooms and served vegetarian meals.

COST: 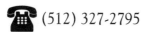 (weekend conferences and six-day retreats)

(fourteen-day retreats)

 Eupsychia Institute
P.O. Box 3090
Austin, TX 78764

(512) 327-2795

www.jacqunelynsmall.com

FEMININE VOICE OF LEADERSHIP

"[The program] helped awaken me in so many ways."
—Feminine Voice of Leadership participant

This five-day wilderness program is "a personal journey through the uncharted wilderness of the self for women who are searching for a deeper, richer connection to their own power, strength, and leadership style." Designed for women who are not comfortable with traditional masculine leadership styles, it incorporates backpacking and camping with growth exercises and discussions.

Participants develop intuition, explore language and communication for women leaders, evaluate personal and group risks, honor diversity, and experience feminine ways of being in the world.

The course is conducted in Alaska's Chugach Mountains. Participants share in all the daily tasks and chores of wilderness living.

COST:

Alaska Women of the Wilderness
Box 773556
Eagle River, AK 99577

☎ (907) 688-2226

GATEWAYS TO CREATIVITY

"A remarkable experience. I explored hidden realms of my creative self that had been waiting to unfold. Gateways offers camaraderie and support as you begin the process of transformation. An opportunity to do self-work, the work you have not had the time for. An opportunity to nurture the soul."

—*Gateways to Creativity participant*

While there are other week-long programs that provide creative experiences, few are conducted by professional art therapists. The leaders of this program (offered for one week in July each year) have graduate training and expertise in art expression, creative behavior, and Gestalt and family therapies.

Creativity is used as a catalyst for personal transformation. Participants work with clay, paint, cloth, paper, and masks in a safe, structured, and supportive environment. No previous art education or talent is necessary. A telephone interview is required of all applicants.

Many of the participants are social service or health professionals or artists, musicians, dancers, writers, or actors who would like to apply the insight and techniques that they gain to their work. But anyone who is interested in enhancing their creativity and ability to express themselves could benefit.

The experience increases self-esteem and confidence, clarifies personal and professional life choices and goals, and opens the door to playfulness.

Participants are housed in dorm accommodations at a private school in Massachusetts (two hours west of Boston and three hours north of New York City). Three meals are served each day, with vegetarian options available.

COST:

 The New England Art Therapy Institute
216 Silver Lane
Sunderland, MA 01375

☎ (413) 665-4880

javanet.com/~cccneati

HAWK, I'M YOUR SISTER

"I came to Montana feeling like an orphan. I came off the river feeling renewed and nurtured by the water and the landscape, by the solitude and companionship, and especially by the example and knowing of so many women. I cannot recall ever being so validated in my woman-ness. I felt the void inside me filling up."

—*Hawk, I'm Your Sister participant*

A variety of women's wilderness canoe trips are offered by the Hawk, I'm Your Sister organization. In a safe, supportive, non-competitive environment, women of all ages and degrees of outdoors experience learn to feel comfortable in forests, canyons, deserts, rivers, lakes, and seas. Participants acquire skills in canoeing and camping while sharing chores of food preparation and clean-up, filtering water, and digging latrines.

All of the nine-day trips involve strenuous physical effort. Participants rise at dawn and are on the river for five to eight hours a day. Hardships are not deliberately built into the trips, but varying wind, weather, and water level conditions can present unexpected challenges. All participants are urged to improve their physical condition prior to the trip and must fill out a simple medical information form certifying that their general health is good.

In addition to physical strength, participants also discover and increase inner strength as they learn to be self-reliant, enjoy the simplicity of outdoor life, and reach goals they've set for themselves.

By escaping from the overcivilized and secular world, participants can confront some of the self-demeaning negative patterns that have become a part of their everyday lives. They can reconnect with their spiritual sides and discover more natural ways of living and being. The knowledge, insights, and confidence gained from the trips can be used in the civilized world once the trip is over.

295

Special trips include writing retreats which deepen the creative vision, leadership training for young women, and couples workshops (with couples defined simply as pairs of people without concern for gender or sexual intimacy). All include camping and canoeing.

Nine-day possibilities include the Missouri River in Montana, Heron Lake in New Mexico, the Green River in Utah, the Sea of Cortez in Baja California, Mexico, and the lower canyons of the Rio Grande in Texas. There is even a three-week trip open to women and men in Siberia and other Russian locations.

Trips are scheduled throughout the year.

All major equipment is provided (such as canoes, paddles, life jackets, and cooking and eating utensils). A sleeping bag and personal gear are the responsibility of the participant. Meals are nutritious and generous, with fresh vegetables and fruits, whole grains, chicken, and fish rather than the dried food typical of camping trips. Vegetarian meals and other dietary restrictions can be accommodated when noted in advance. Transportation is provided from the closest airport to the departure point, but travel costs and arrangements to this pick-up point are the responsibility of the individual.

COST: 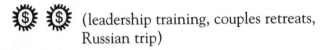 (most trips and writing retreats)

(leadership training, couples retreats, Russian trip)

 Hawk, I'm Your Sister
P.O. Box 9109
Santa Fe, NM 87504-9109

 (505) 690-4490

THE INSTITUTE FOR TRANSFORMING LEADERSHIP

Every summer the center for Psychology and Social Change (affiliated with the Department of Psychiatry at Harvard Medical School) holds an intensive residential retreat. The summer program enables participants to learn and practice an extraordinary level of leadership. Believing that leadership is defined and driven not so much by plans and proposals as by our actions and interactions with those around us, the Institute combines self-exploration exercises with presentations of leading-edge theory.

During the Institute's six days, participants are exposed to new paradigms of knowledge. Included are:
Ecopsychology—Focusing on and encouraging mutually beneficial relationships within and among humans and the earth.
Gaia Theory—Proposing that humans are one of many interdependent parts with other species and the biosphere.
Transpersonal Psychology—Combining modern Western psychology with traditional wisdom traditions of the world.

But the Institute goes far beyond mere intellectual understanding. Direct experiential learning methods bring the theory to life. These include meditation, holotropic breathwork, facilitated group discussion, guided awareness walks, and solo time in nature.

Each participant leaves with increased awareness of the deep interconnections between each other and the universe. Along with a heightened sense of self, the expanded world view allows new possibilities and resources to emerge for leadership and social change.

To sustain the development which occurs during the Institute, participants may join an Internet discussion group and use a summer program private web page.

Anyone who is looking to become a leader or improve their leadership efforts in any context could benefit from this mind/body/spirit program. The new ways of engaging with the self, others, and the natural world can be transforming for all personal and professional relationships and activities.

Participants stay in shared accommodations at the Merriam Hill Center in Greenville, New Hampshire. Transportation between Boston and New Hampshire is provided.

Partial scholarships are available. To qualify, participants must submit a brief essay describing the context of their work/project and how attendance at the summer program would affect their leadership efforts.

COST: (nonprofit organizations and self-employed individuals) to 💲 💲

Institute for Transforming Leadership
Summer Program
Center for Psychology and Social Change
P.O. Box 398080
Cambridge, MA 02139

 (617) 497-1553

www.cpschange.org

THE INTUITION CRUISE

"The best sustained week of my adult life. An experience that is not only worth doing again, but one that the spirit dare not go without. An Intuition Cruise provides both the physical and the spiritual awareness of the Beyond-That-Is-Without and the Beyond-That-Is-Within."

—*The Intuition Cruise participant*

Cruising can be a very relaxing mode of vacation travel, but it tends to be a little mindless. However, there is a cruise which goes far beyond the typical cruise experience in providing opportunities to acquire new skills and knowledge. The Intuition Cruise specifically focuses on the unlimited aspects of consciousness and the mind.

Whether the cruise participant has been exploring the field of intuition for years or is just beginning to develop an interest in the field, The Intuition Cruise can challenge and expand his or her intellectual and spiritual being. Half the experience is just being at sea (noted by famous psychic Edgar Cayce to enhance human intuitive abilities); the other half is being in the company of other seekers and experts in intuition and transformation. Although there's time for rest and recreation, there's also a full program of scheduled and unscheduled discussions, presentations, experiential workshops, mind-body exercises, metal bending parties, shared consciousness experiments, and free trials of mind expansion/intuition technologies. Internationally-known authors, intuition trainers, intuitive counselors, parapsychologists, psychic researchers, and representatives from transformational organizations provide formal and informal learning experiences. Topics include:

- **Intuitive training**
- **Parapsychology**
- **Mind-body health**

- Mind expansion
- Personal growth
- Spirituality
- Conscious living
- Business
- Investing
- Sports
- Hypnotherapy
- Dreams
- Psychic ability/ESP

Two- to three-week cruises are scheduled during the year. In the past, they've been on the Dolphin Cruise Line's ship. Destinations have been the Western Caribbean (Playa del Carmen/Cozumel, Montego Bay, Grand Caymen) and the Eastern Caribbean (Nassau, San Juan, St. John, and St. Thomas).

Participants choose either single- or double-occupancy cabins. Meals are served more than six times a day.

COST:

   (depending on accommodations; airfare extra)

 The Inner Voyage
765 Greenwich Street, Suite #4
New York, NY 10014

☎ (212) 989-1615

LEADERSHIP TRAINING PROGRAM

"I learned to let go of my need to have answers, to live and love the questions. It deepened my roots and strengthened my wings for being at home in the mystery of a man's heart..."
—Leadership Training Program

The Men's Council Project Leadership Training Program connects men with the wisdom of the natural world and their own indigenous intelligence. Although designed for men interested in the leadership of men's groups, community service organizations, therapists, counselors, teachers, doctors, and others who work with boys and men, it is also appropriate for men seeking a growth experience.

During a week-long wilderness encampment, men learn powerful tools for personal and community development. Activities include building sacred containers, calling for the blessings of ancestors, guiding personal and group ritual process, fasting and solo time, sweat ceremony, storytelling, drumming, moving to inner and outer rhythms, exploring the male lineage, and developing mentoring skills.

At the end of the week, participants have connected to the deep masculine and feminine, identified and owned their shadow sides, and developed unique leadership talents.

The program is held in July in Saphire Canyon (a private wilderness area near Estes Park, Colorado).

COST: (on a sliding scale, with some work/study scholarships available)

Men's Council Project
P.O. Box 17341
Boulder, CO 80301

 (303) 499-9926

LifeLaunch

"This experience provided me with new tools for renewing myself and making my life work again. I'd recommend it to anyone who wants to live his or her own life, and not somebody else's."

—LifeLaunch participant

LifeLaunch is designed to help adults in their middle years develop personal and professional plans to get the most out of their lives. While many of the participants are seeking assistance with the challenges of career changes, the seminars are also designed to help individuals plan for retirement or to aid couples who want to renew their relationship. Individuals who don't need or want to make major changes but still would like to discover and tap into hidden interests, talents, and dreams could also benefit from the course.

The seminar is taught by Frederic Hudson, author of *The Adult Years—Mastering the Art of Self-Renewal*. Dr. Hudson's mission is to help adults "learn new ways to renew their lives, manage necessary transitions, and find new tools and models for the critical leadership challenge ahead in the creative chaos of the twenty-first century—beginning with day by day living."

Through discussion, exercises, and coaching, participants increase their confidence, trust, and commitment to the future. They leave energized and determined to create success at home and at work.

The four-day seminar is available every other month. It's held from Thursday afternoon through Sunday noon.
The seminar is held at an ocean-front hotel in Santa Barbara, California. Participants stay in single- or double-occupancy rooms. Meals are not included.

COST:

 The Hudson Institute of Santa Barbara
3463 State Street, Suite 520
Santa Barbara, CA 93105

 (800) 582-4401 or (805) 682-3883

www.hudsoninstitute.com

MERRITT CENTER

The Merritt Center provides holistic experiences that renew and empower. A number of weekend retreats and workshops are offered throughout the year for men and women of all ages. There are also a number of week-long retreat programs for persons at least fifty-five years of age.

General offerings during the past years have included:

- **Me and My Shadow**
  Participants learn from their shadow side as they move through the fears of yesterday, today, and tomorrow.

- **Couples: Growing Together**
  Couples learn how they can grow together and enjoy unconditional love, support, and adventure together.

- **Magic of Menopause**
  The myths of menopause are explored, along with the magic that can be found during this special time of life.

- **Women's Journey**
  Women find their inner woman of wisdom and playful child as they become empowered and discover their centers.

- **Empowerment Weekend**
  Participants are guided through the "what ifs," the limiting beliefs and power systems, and emotional clearing so they can apply the Empowerment Model in their day-to-day life. A special empowerment weekend is available for those who wish to change their self-image and redesign the image of their bodies.

The workshops for seniors have included:

- **The Adult Journey**
  Participants explore their location in the cycle of life and what to do to complete their personal missions.

- **Laughter and Play**
  The physical and mental benefits of laughter are emphasized, along with experiential play activities.

- **Communication: It Isn't Just Talk**
  Participants learn how to communicate effectively through listening actively and expressing naturally.

Participants stay in double-occupancy guest rooms in the lodge. Meals are provided (but no red meat is served).

Leisure activities and amenities include massage, bodywork, hot tubbing, T'ai Chi, yoga, hiking, and a flotation tank for relaxation.

The Center is located ninety miles north of Phoenix.

COST:

  Merritt Center
P.O. Box 2087
Payson, AZ 85547

☎ (800) 414-9880 or (520) 474-4268

www.merritt-az-retreat.com

MONROE INSTITUTE

"The Gateway experience is something that should not be missed by anyone seeking knowledge and higher truths."
—*Monroe Institute participant*

As a nonprofit research educational and research organization, the Monroe Institute is devoted to the premise that forced consciousness contains all solutions to the questions of human existence. Its founder, Robert Monroe, developed and patented technology that uses audio signals to help people reach altered states of consciousness which are not ordinarily available to the human mind.

Participants use stereo headphones with a different frequency for each ear. The brain responds by "hearing" a third frequency (the difference between the two incoming frequencies). Both hemispheres are brought into unison (hemispheric synchronization, or Hemi-Sync) amplifies brain responsiveness and maximizes available brain power. These Hemi-Sync programs can expand consciousness, achieve deep meditative states, eliminate tension, maximize fluency of mental processing, improve concentration, control insomnia, improve self-esteem, combat depression, control pain, and strengthen the immune system.

The Institute's standard program is the Gateway Voyage. This six-day intensive program focuses on expanded consciousness. Progressive, guided Hemi-Sync tapes (about six a day) are the main program, along with group discussions and informal lectures. Out-of-body experiences are not guaranteed, although they often occur.

Participants spend much of their time in Controlled Holistic Environmental Chambers (CHEC). Just large enough for a single mattress, the units provide isolation from external light and extraneous sound. From a central control room, an audio network feeds sound patterns and special exercises to each unit

306

under the direction of a team of trainers. Participants hear the sounds through headphones during the day and speakers at night. They can control the lighting in the unit for both color and intensity. When each exercise is completed, participants record their thoughts and feelings about the experience on an audiotape.

Some time is spent away from the CHEC to eat, exercise, attend group debriefing sessions and lectures, receive individual counseling, hike or swim.

While every individual's experience can be different, most experience increased awareness and personal empowerment. There is the universal conclusion that each of us is more than our physical body and that we can perceive that which is greater than and goes beyond the physical world. Each participant can ask the questions and find some answers that are personally meaningful and transformative.

The Institute is located in the Blue Ridge Mountains of Virginia.

Before being accepted into the program, applicants must complete a form describing their physical health, mental health history, phobias, previous mind training activities, drug use, and goals for the experience. Once accepted, participants are sent some tapes to prepare for the program.

COST:

 Monroe Institute
Route 1, Box 175
Faber, VA 22938

 (804) 361-1252

www.monroeinstitute.org

NATIONAL OUTDOOR LEADERSHIP SCHOOL

"I've realized that I can live simply and that the basic essentials of life are all I need."

—*National Outdoor Leadership School participant*

National Outdoor Leadership School (NOLS) makes very clear in its brochure that it is not an adventure travel school, nor is it a wilderness therapy/survival school. Its instructors are not guides, counselors, or therapists. They don't cook, set up tents, or carry gear for participants. Instead, they teach how to do it so participants can learn and apply new skills on their own. Personal growth and increased self-knowledge often result from the experience.

NOLS's classroom is the wilderness and its courses are extended expeditions, ten days to three months long. Groups of eight to seventeen students travel with two to four instructors. Participants sleep outdoors, prepare their own meals, and take care of themselves under challenging conditions, The activity can be strenuous (carrying a backpack that weighs fifty-five to eighty-five pounds at altitudes up to twenty thousand feet) and the weather can be extreme.

Courses include thirty days backpacking through Wyoming's Wind River Range, twenty-one days horsepacking through the Rocky Mountains in Wyoming, twenty-one days rock climbing in Wyoming, thirty-five days snow and ice climbing in the Himalayas of India, twenty-two days sailing in twenty-two-foot longboats in Mexico, and thirty-five days kayaking in Alaska rivers.

The average participant in many of the courses is nineteen years old. For persons twenty-five and older who prefer to be with their peers and may not have time for a longer course, there are courses with a minimum age requirement of twenty-five (where the average age is thirty-six). These courses are generally fourteen days and are similar to the others: sea kayaking in Mexico or Alaska, backpacking in Wyoming, and cross country skiing on the Teton Range in Wyoming. There are even courses exclusively for those fifty and older.

Participants must be in good physical condition (used to at least thirty minutes of aerobic activity three to five times a week) and must complete an application detailing their reasons for applying.

COST:

(depending on length & location; some scholarships available)

National Outdoor Leadership School
288 Main Street
Lander, WY 82520

☎ (307) 332-6973

www.nols.edu

NEURO-LINGUISTIC PROGRAMMING (NLP)

Neuro-Linguistics is an applied scientific approach to changing behavior and attaining goals. The mind's natural language and imagery is used to repattern thoughts and feelings. Negative emotions and dysfunctional habits are cast aside in favor of more successful ways of viewing and dealing with the world. Unlike other models of human behavior which focus on the "why" you do what you do, NLP focuses on the "how."

The enhanced understanding of the dynamic relationship between mind (neuro) and language (linguistic) and its impact on body and behavior (programming) can be used to facilitate communication and change in such human endeavors as management, sales, parenting, education, health, counseling, and creativity.

Topics addressed include verbal and nonverbal rapport with others, effective and active listening, "as if" frames which actively engage the imagination in making actions more productive and give increased command over feelings, accessing and anchoring states of excellence and inner resources, reframing limitations into opportunities, and replacing or modifying unproductive behaviors.

Skills can be applied on a professional basis by counselors, salespersons, consultants, trainers, and anyone else who needs to gain rapport with people and communicate more effectively in the course of conducting business. Job seekers and job changers will also find them helpful. Outside of the business realm, the skills promote personal growth and build loving relationships.

Proponents strongly believe that NLP brings success and balance to lives and careers. Lasting, self-directed changes in motivation and relationships are made possible through optimal thought patterns acquired through the training.

There are a number of programs offering training in NLP. Each offers a unique approach and setting while teaching the philosophy and practice of this psychology of inter- and intra-personal intelligence and communication.

Advanced Learning Systems

A twenty-one-day certification course is offered several times throughout the year through Advanced Learning Systems.

The course is held at a resort hotel on the Kona Coast, Big Island, Hawaii. To enable participants to enjoy the beach in the morning hours, the training is held from noon until eight p.m. each day.

COST:

 (800) 700-4657

NEW YORK TRAINING INSTITUTE

"...the knowledge...requires me to stretch to new areas of personal growth and change — which is not always easy yet compels me forward."

—New York Training Institute participant

In addition to the twenty-four-day certification program held over nine weekends from October through May, New York Training Institute (NYTI) offers a variety of two-day weekend courses throughout the year. While none of them teach all the basic concepts and patterns of NLP as does the certification training, they all incorporate NLP philosophy and techniques. Examples include:

- **NLP & Fitness**
  Techniques to enhance and maintain a healthy relationship to food and exercise.

- **Mindmapping**
  A whole-brain process to organize thoughts and ideas in minutes rather than hours.

- **NLP & Healing Chronic Illness**
  Designed for persons with conditions such as heart problems, diabetes, cancer, and immune deficiency disorders.

- **Divorce Without War**
  Tools for psychological/financial/social/family preparation, legal meditation, and redesigning life after divorce.

- **The Evolved Self**
  A process for accessing innate wisdom, natural genius, and creativity.

As the first NLP center in the country, NYTI only offers training and does not provide lodging. Accommodations in New York City are the responsibility of each participant.

COST: (weekends)

 (certification program)

 NYTI/NLP
145 Avenue of the Americas, 5th Floor
New York, NY 10013

☎ (212) 647-1660

www.nlpcenter.com

NLP Comprehensive

"The NLP Practitioner training has given me an increased sense of self and I have learned to love and accept myself at a higher level."

—NLP Comprehensive participant

The practitioner certification training offered by NLP Comprehensive is twenty-four-day (summer residential) or twenty-seven-day (fall-winter weekend format).

Training is available in Colorado, Illinois, Ohio, and California.

NLP Comprehensive also offers an annual international conference, usually held in Denver. The four days are filled with a variety of half-day workshops and full-day institutes on personal evolution, business, health, sports, therapy, finances, education, and general NLP. Examples of past offerings include:

- **Playing the Game of Money Successfully**
  Options, strategies, and resources are developed to create a desirable relationship with money.

- **Living the Dream with Resilience Power**
  Participants learn to navigate the ups-and-downs of everyday life so that they never stop living their dreams.

- **Love, Grace, & Gratitude**
  Participants learn authentic thanksgiving for life so that they move from fear and isolation to love and a celebration of ultimate belonging.

Hotel accommodations and meals are not included in the price for the weekends, but are part of the package for the longer programs.

COST: 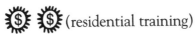 (weekend tuition)

(residential training)

 NLP Comprehensive
5695 Yukon Street
Arvada, CO 80002

 (800) 233-1657 or (303) 940-8888

www.nlpcomprehensive.com

NLP UNIVERSITY

Dynamic Learning Center offers a number of programs each summer. Many of the programs are geared for persons already certified in NLP who are looking for advanced courses, but there are two courses for persons who are new to NLP. The Basic NLP Skills Core Course covers the essential "building blocks of NLP." This twelve-day course is for those participants who wish to use NLP only for personal applications. The NLP Practitioner Certification Path is a twenty-seven-day program which qualifies individuals to practice NLP on a professional basis. This course is a combination of the Basic Skills Core Course and a specialized track in either Health and Well-Being or Business and Organizations. The health option covers the use of basic NLP skills and tools in promoting mental and physical well-being. The business and organizations option covers the basic skills for attaining the inner maps and skills of effective leadership.

NLP University is held on the University of California campus at Santa Cruz, seventy-five miles from San Francisco. A shuttle is available from the airport. The campus offers such recreational amenities as a swimming pool, tennis courts, track, and weight room.

Participants stay in large student apartments in private bedrooms. The residential package includes three meals each day in the campus dining hall.

COST: 💲 💲 (Basic Skills Core Course) to

💲 💲 💲 (Practitioner Certification Path)

   Dynamic Learning Center/NLP University
Box 1112
Ben Lomond, CA 95005

 (408) 336-3457

www.nlpn.com

NEW WARRIOR TRAINING ADVENTURE

"New Warrior Training is an authentic initiation into the cauldron of mature masculinity. This was the most powerful training I've ever done, and the changes it started in me have been both deep and positive."

—New Warrior Training Adventure participant

The Mankind Project, as a national not-for-profit corporation, runs weekend adventures for men who seek to "reclaim the sacred masculine for our time through initiation, training, and action in the world." Physically and emotionally challenging activities on group and individual levels focus on developing a mature and healthy male self. Participants are initiated into manhood and encouraged to engage in authentic self-examination.

Unlike men who have yielded to social pressures to repress the warrior parts of themselves and instead substitute a distorted shadow, New Warriors have confronted this destructive shadow. They have reclaimed the focused, aggressive energy that empowers the inner masculine self. This enables passionate and compassionate living.

The (mostly volunteer) staff serve as guides and mentors, but participants choose their own level of commitment during the process. While adventures are highly individualized, most participants discover both the treasures and obstacles buried within themselves. They confront their dependence on women and their mistrust of other men.

Participants must be in reasonably good physical condition and be willing to examine deep fears and wounds from the past.

Several days after the training, a graduation ceremony is held to welcome participants back into the larger community. A small voluntary team called an Integration Group is available to help integrate the training into daily living.

Weekend training adventures (running Friday through Saturday) are held at sites all over the country. Recent locations have included Denver, Houston, Chicago, Indianapolis, Philadelphia, Santa Fe, New York City, Memphis, San Diego, Louisville, Detroit, Tucson, and Washington, D.C.

Accommodations vary according to the location.

COST:

 The Mankind Project
P.O. Box 230
Malone, NY 12953-0230

 (800) 870-4611

www.mkp.org

NINE GATES TRAINING

"Nine Gates and Gay Luce have profoundly changed my life. Access to my inner self has increased my self-esteem and self-worth. I can now live at a depth which is nourishing and be true to myself."
—*Nine Gates participant*

Dr. Gay Luce, a noted author, teacher, and facilitator of healing and transformation, founded Nine Gates as a means of empowering individuals with the wisdom and practices of ancient spiritual systems. Participants pass through nine "gates" to become unobstructed and enjoy more personal power throughout their lives. Ritual, movement, energy work, emotional mastery, theater, music, and art are utilized throughout this experiential training.

Participants feel that the training adds a new and important spiritual dimension to their lives. Being in greater touch with personal feelings and energies enriches intimacy with the self and with others.

Gate 1 helps participants release limiting and nonfunctional behavior patterns by confronting survival issues and discriminate real from imaginary danger. Celtic traditions are emphasized, along with breathing, movement, diet, and exercise training.

Gate 2 involves bonding, healing, and sexual vitality. Taoist and Hindu tantric traditions are used as a resource for creativity and transformation.

Gate 3 focuses on purifying the emotions and strengthening the will. Native American traditions and ceremonies enable participants to experience their sacred nature and personal power, as well as to discover the hidden beliefs which dominate and limit.

Gate 4 heals the heart through unconditional love. The Sufi tradition lets participants make the leap of consciousness into loving without expecting something in return.

Gate 5 awakens joy and celebration in the contexts of Christian gnosticism, Hindu devotion, and Jewish, Islamic, and other traditions.

Gate 6 emphasizes communication. Taoist traditions are used to help participants experience speaking and listening as forms of meditation. Exercises to awaken throat energies are also utilized.

Gate 7 uses Polynesian Kahuna traditions to explore intuition and soul consciousness. Participants begin to understand the relationships between our thoughts and imaginings, and experience the ability to construct or alter their lives according to their goals and desires.

Gate 8 focuses on cosmic knowledge, death, and rebirth practices derived from Tibetan Buddhist, Egyptian, and other traditions enable participants to develop the skills of consciousness needed during final moments (their own or someone else in transit). When death is no longer feared, the remainder of life can be lived more skillfully.

Gate 9, through the use of Tibetan Buddhist practices, focuses on transcendence. This is the most spiritual and complete of all the gates, allowing participants to find their essence and realize a sense of fellowship with all life.

The training is usually held in California on a private ranch in Sonoma or a desert retreat in Joshua Tree.

It's usually held at least twice a year. Part I (involving Gates 1 to 4) is held in the spring; Part II (Gates 5 to 9) is held in the fall. Each part is nine days.

COST: (entire program)

 Nine Gates, Inc.
220 Redwood Highway, Suite 61
Mill Valley, CA 94941

(800) 995-4459 or (415) 927-1677

www.ninegates.com

OPTION INSTITUTE AND FELLOWSHIP

"I found a new way of viewing life, one that enables me happiness....I am forever changed and forever grateful."
— *Option Institute and Fellowship participant*

Year-round programs for individuals, couples, families, and groups who wish to improve the quality of their lives are offered by the Option Institute and Fellowship. The focus is on choosing to be happy by changing thoughts and visions of the world to something positive. Living in the present is seen as preferable to regretting the past or worrying about the future.

Programs range in length from three days to eight weeks. They include:

- **The Happiness Option (weekends)**
  Designed for first-time visitors to the Option Institute, this program shows how to create and sustain feelings of optimism, peace of mind, clarity, and personal power and joy. Participants learn how to stop the self-defeating habit of judging themselves while recognizing and changing the hidden beliefs which prevented them in the past from feeling comfortable and in control of their own lives.

- **Loving You/Loving Me (weekends)**
  This program for couples (spouses, lovers, and significant others) maximizes the power and potential of loving intimate relationships. Participants learn to develop an accepting attitude, a sense of personal authenticity, listening skills, conflict resolution, and techniques for enhanced physical and emotional intimacy.

- **Inward Bound (five days)**
  The Activa Meditation process uses internal, meditative processes as well as physically active and interactive experiences to allow participants to develop the ability to instantly cultivate and maintain a sense of peace and focus throughout everyday activities.

319

- **Empowering Yourself: Going For (And Getting) What You Want (five days)**

  Experiential sessions allow participants to design a clear vision of what they really want in relationships, career, money, health, and personal happiness. The program then teaches how to design useful perspectives to help achieve these desires.

- **Living the Dream (either four or eight weeks)**

  The Living the Dream program goes beyond being a mere course or seminar. It's actually a living laboratory where every aspect of the experience is integrated into the learning experience. Participants learn to recreate themselves in whatever ways they choose. Areas of focus include personal growth, love relationships, sexuality, health, personal authenticity, money, work, parenting, giving and receiving, and death and dying. The loving and supportive atmosphere encourages risk-taking, celebrates individuality, and challenges each participant to live their visions. This intense experience is appropriate for those at a turning point in their lives (career change, divorce, death of a spouse, graduation from college, midlife transition, or retirement) or who work in a helping profession and want to gain a new perspective on their work by applying a loving and accepting attitude towards themselves and their clients, as well as anyone who wants to be more effective and happier in any area of life.

There are also individualized programs for families of special needs children, teaching parents (as well as support people and assisting professionals) in using a loving and accepting approach to working with children with a vast range of difficulties and dysfunctions.

The Institute is located in the Berkshire mountains of Massachusetts (three hours driving time from New York City and Boston airports). There are local bus and limousine connections from these airports. The eighty-five-acre property includes ponds, meadows, and forests with streams and waterfalls. Recreational activities include swimming in the

Institute's pond, canoeing, river tubing, hiking on the Appalachian trail, cross-country and downhill skiing, plays and concerts, and exploring nearby New England villages.

Participants generally are housed in double-occupancy rooms in guest houses. There a few private rooms with private baths. Three vegetarian meals are served daily.

Programs are held throughout the year.

The founder of the Institute, Barry Neil Kaufman (in conjunction with his wife, Samahria Lyte Kaufman) has written a number of books which can provide further insight about the Institute's philosophy and approach. These include *Happiness Is a Choice, To Love Is to Be Happy With,* and *Son-Rise.*

COST:  (three to five days)

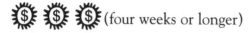(four weeks or longer)

(three-month volunteer experiences where participants serve full-time in the kitchen, office, housekeeping, and building and maintenance departments are available)

 Option Institute and Fellowship
2080 South Undermountain Road
Sheffield, MA 01257

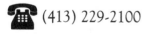 (413) 229-2100

www.option.org

OUTDOOR LEADERSHIP TRAINING SEMINARS

Since 1973, this organization has been offering programs which emphasize personal growth, leadership training, and ecological consciousness through such activities as whitewater rafting, rock climbing, mountaineering, backcountry skiing, and general wilderness travel. A variety of educational, psychological, and philosophical strategies are used to expand each participant's physical, emotional, and spiritual capacity. American Indian ritual, Taoist philosophy, meditation, relaxation techniques, and problem-solving practice all add to the transformational potential of the outdoor experience.

While the organization's primary focus is the training and preparation of wilderness guides and leaders through five-week to five-month courses, they have also developed a special series of workshops entitled Breaking Through Adventures. These workshops are designed for personal rather than professional growth. They use the spirit of the wilderness as the guide to celebrating our interdependence with one another and the earth. The goal is to establish a meaningful community while exposing and changing self-limiting beliefs and behaviors. Examples of these courses include:

- Two-day Centered Rock Climbing workshop which uses a unique internal approach of centering exercises, relaxation, and self-awareness to counter fear and develop balance and trust on carefully graduated climbs in Colorado.

- One-week Canyon Quests in Utah which include backpacking and hiking, wilderness navigation, singing and drumming, meditation, T'ai Chi, and a short solo.

- Six-day Breaking Through in Colorado featuring camping, climbing, hiking, whitewater rafting, centering, and wellness training, Native American ritual and ceremony.

- Seven-day Mountain Quests in Colorado with two days of training, preparation, and ritual at a wilderness basecamp, three days and nights solo in the wilderness on the buddy system, one and one-half days celebration and reconnection with the group including music, art, song, movement, and storytelling to share visions.

All the wilderness experiences allow participants to discover their deepest connections with themselves, nature, and other men/women. The personal growth attained by these experiences can be applied to everyday circumstances in the "real world." Participants have learned to make decisions and take action under stress, cope with the unexpected, draw upon untapped reserves, and enjoy a sense of wholeness.

Most of the programs are for men and women, but a few are for men or women only.

No previous outdoors experience is necessary. Climbs and challenges can be moderated for older individuals or persons with disabilities.

COST:

 Outdoor Leadership Training Seminars
P.O. Box 20281
Denver, CO 80220

☎ (800) 331-7238 or (303) 333-7831

www.olts-bt.com

OUTWARD BOUND

"I was at a point where I needed to make some decisions about how I would spend the rest of my life. Outward Bound helped me to do this. I discovered more parts of myself than I ever knew were there. The experience affected me profoundly."
—*Outward Bound participant*

Outward Bound courses range from alpine mountaineering in Colorado's Rocky Mountains to dog sledding in Maine to sea kayaking through the Everglades of Florida. But regardless of the specific activity or location, they all share a common element: combining physical challenges with inward journeys involving the heart, mind, and body. Using wilderness environments as its classroom, Outward Bound enables participants to regain connection with the environment while gaining self-confidence, assertiveness, and independence.

In small group settings of eight to twelve students, Outward Bound instructors teach technical skills and safety procedures relating to such activities as whitewater rafting, sailing, sea kayaking, alpine mountaineering, rock climbing, canoeing, bicycling, desert/mountain backpacking, canyon exploration, dog sledding, skiing, and winter camping. The group tests these new skills in problem-solving exercises on extended expeditions. Every course also features a "solo" experience away from teammates for a day or two to develop self-reliance and spend some time in reflection. When the activity is completed, the group discusses the relevance of what was learned so they can transfer the learning into daily life at home and work.

The noncompetitive atmosphere enables participants to develop a sense of self, both as an individual and member of a team. In addition to the physical skills, personal skills in leadership, problem-solving, decision-making, and communication are developed.

No prior outdoors or athletic expertise is required. The thorough instruction ensures that even total novices can participate in the program of their choice. Participants do need to be in reasonably good physical condition (as certified by a physical examination within the last year) and be open to trying new experiences.

Special Outward Bound courses include those for adults only (over twenty-one or over fifty), men only, women only, couples, parents and children, managers/executives, teenagers (fourteen to sixteen), youth-at-risk who have motivational and behavioral difficulties, educators, health professionals, and special mental/physical health needs such as Vietnam veterans, adult children of alcoholics, persons recovering from eating disorders, and survivors of cancer.

Participants sleep in sleeping bags or tents under the stars, carry their own packs, and cook their own meals.

Courses range from five to eighty-three days and are held all over the United States and the world.

Academic credits can be awarded for most courses.

COST: 💲 to 💲 💲

(participants are liable for the transportation costs of getting to the pick-up point—usually an airport or hotel convenient to the beginning of the wilderness experience. Scholarships, low-interest loans, and zero-interest deferred payment plans are available)

Outward Bound
384 Field Point Road
Greenwich, CT 06830

 (800) 243-8520 or (914) 424-4000

www.outwardbound.org

PATHWAYS

Pathways is the perfect program for anyone who has ever wanted an African bush experience that goes beyond a photo or traditional safari. Far more than a recreational "time-out" holiday in the bush, it provides a retreat where participants discover a sense of wholeness. Dysfunctional patterns of thinking and behaving are changed as individuals expand their awareness of themselves and the environment.

Although the experience is facilitated by a mental health professional, it is not a medical or clinical treatment program. The experience focuses on the natural environment where participants can observe and learn from animals.

As a holistic program, it offers individually designed activities for the mind, body, and spirit. These include bush trail hiking, yoga, relaxation exercises, Reiki healing, meditation, visualization exercises, dream analysis, group dynamics, insight facilitation, and individual counseling.

The program is appropriate for individuals who have some issues relating to stress, trauma, loss, difficult relationships, or co-dependencey, as well as those who want to enhance their self-awareness or spirituality. It can also be customized for business and corporate groups who want to reduce their stress levels and improve communication.

Participants can book the experience for several days or a longer period as desired.

Individuals learn to relax some of their need and mechanisms for control. They rediscover and celebrate the mysteries of life. This leads to new priorities and healthier relationships with the self, others, and the environment.

The experience takes place on private game reserves in the North or East Transvaal areas of South Africa. Safety is ensured through the supervision of a professional game ranger. Participants arrange for their transportation to and from Johannesburg.

Accommodations can range from primitive/economy to fairly luxurious, depending on individual preferences and finances.

COST:

(depending on length and accommodations)

   Sharon Rosen
008 Prestwick
Illovo, 2196
Johannesburg, South Africa

082 852 4523

www.tecnet.co.za/pathways

PERSON CENTERED EXPRESSIVE ARTS THERAPY

"The Creative Connection is the enhancing interplay among movement, art, writing, and sound...which stimulates self-exploration. As our feelings are tapped (in creative expression) they become a resource for further self-understanding and creativity."

—Natalie Rogers, Founder of Person Centered Expressive Arts Therapy

Traditional psychotherapy takes a very verbal approach to examining and dealing with emotions. Expressive arts therapy offers an alternative to talking about feelings. Expressive arts such as movement, art, music, writing, sound, and improvisation allow creative energy to be tapped and healing to occur.

Person Centered Expressive Arts Therapy (PCETI) combines the humanistic psychology of Carl Rogers with the creative process. PCETI retreat programs enable participants to express their innate creativity through experiential arts sessions in a safe, supportive environment. Group members are encouraged and empowered to delve into their emotions rather than concentrating on the aesthetics or craftsmanship of the art they're involved in. The goal is expression, release, and insight rather than a product which is professionally rendered or artistically pleasing.

Both the six-day Door to Creativity Program and the more advanced nine-day Nurturing the Creative Self program enable participants to connect with their nonverbal means of expression in a community which accepts, understands, and validates all individuals. Group members enjoy the freedom to be, to create, and to communicate. No artistic ability or training is needed; PCETI believes that all people have the ability to be creative.

By delving into emotions through the expressive arts, participants achieve new levels of self-awareness, understanding, and insight. As each person's inner essence is uncovered, a sense of wholeness and healing develops. Creative blocks are broken through and enhanced communication and connection with other people is made possible.

The methods learned in the program can be applied in settings as far reaching as health care, education, and business. The training benefits participants professionally (especially those who can use it in a helping capacity in their jobs) as well as personally. Academic credit is available.

Programs are held in the spring, summer, and fall at three locations: Northern California, the Catskill Mountains of New York, and the Midlands of England. Participants stay in double-occupancy lodging at retreat centers and are served three meals a day.

COST: to   (depending on length)

Person Centered Expressive Therapy Institute
P.O. Box 6518
Santa Rosa, CA 95406

PHOENICIA PATHWORK CENTER

"Thoughts and opinions create feelings, and both of them together create attitudes, behaviors, and emanations which, in turn, create life circumstances. These sequences must be connected with, understood, and fully recognized. This is an essential aspect of the Pathwork."

—The Guide, The Pathwork

From 1957 to 1979, Eva Pierrakos channeled teachings by a spirit entity of enormous wisdom known as the Guide. Topics focused on self-responsibility, self-knowledge, and self-acceptance. Ms. Pierrakos recorded these channelings and organized them into a series of 258 lectures known as The Pathwork. Those who study and experience the lectures are empowered to follow a spiritual path of self-purification and transformation.

Whereas most channeled material focuses on the essential goodness of human beings, the Pathwork recognizes the "dark side" of human nature. Rather than fear and avoid this negativity, the dark side should be investigated, understood, accepted, and, ultimately, transformed. Misconceptions about the nature of reality are dissolved while the unconscious is made conscious.

The Phoenicia Pathwork Center is the spiritual home of the Pathwork. It offers weekend and week-long workshops which include a history of the Pathwork, a Core Energetics class (to release muscular tension and thereby release a harmonious flow of life energy), a process group (to share, reveal, and release blocked emotions and find and change misconceptions into true concepts), and prayer and meditation.

Persons who have experienced the Pathwork find it highly transformative. A fuller life results from the increased consciousness and self-acceptance. Obstacles such as restlessness, boredom, fear, doubt, and addiction to thinking can be dealt with more readily by applying the teachings to everyday life.

Week-long intensives can be individualized to enable participants to meet and connect with their innermost knowing.
Individual spiritual retreats can also be arranged for participants who wish to develop a uniquely personalized experience
with a minimum of structure.

The Center is located on three hundred acres of a high mountain valley at the edge of the Catskill Wilderness Area. Miles
of hiking trails are available. Other amenities include a swimming pool, tennis courts, a barn for social events and dance,
and an organic garden. The center can be reached by car or bus
in about three hours from New York City.

COST:  (weekend)

 (weeklong)

 Phoenicia Pathwork Center
P.O. Box 66
Phoenicia, NY 12464

 (914) 688-2211

www1.mhr.net/~wmoeller/welcome.htm

331

QuantumQuests International

"It was a wonderful, exciting, and positive experience. Issues I've wrestled with for years came to light. The ability to eliminate repeating patterns that have created negativity and keep me stuck are now on their way to elimination. I feel light and more free and joyful, and better equipped to make the positive difference I know I'm here to do."

—QuantumQuests participant

QuantumQuests International specializes in audiotapes with guided meditations, subliminal messages, and audible affirmations. Its founder, Jonathan Parker, also offers two- to nine-day workshops which enable participants to look within the depths of their own minds and souls. Blocks acquired through past patterning and circumstances are cleared so that personal power can be restored.

Discussions, group interactions, Mind-Heart-Spirit meditations, visualizations, psychic expansion, and expert instruction reveal and activate universal forces to remold lives in a positive direction. Topics of The Call to Power and Pathways to Mastership workshops include astral projection and mind projection to other realities and dimensions; attracting your soulmate and twin flame; awakening and enhancing creativity; physical and emotional healing; turning stress into energy, vitality, and achievement; living in a state of eternal love; and discovering your life's purpose and destiny.

The higher levels of consciousness achieved at the workshops enable participants to continue a loving and joyful state of being during each moment. This personal transformation leads to enhanced personal achievement in the areas of work, leisure, finances, and relationships. Each individual becomes the master of his or her own destiny and feels empowered to cope with daily challenges with strength, judgment, and balance.

Workshops are held throughout the country (mostly in the Midwest and West Coast) during the year. Participants stay in hotels.

COST: (tuition only; lodging and meals vary according to location)

 QuantumQuests International
P.O. Box 7000
Ventura, CA 93006-7000

☎ (800) 772-0090 or (805) 650-1294

www.quantumquests.com

SACRED PASSAGE

"In almost every case, people come out with a sense of profound and deep relaxation, a tremendous release of tension and stress. A deep insight will often develop and many folks will come out with a powerful sense of their true dharma, or true path, finding a completely new way of living that is exactly true for them."

—*John Milton, founder, Sacred Passage*

"...one of the most powerful experiences of my life. Through your Sacred Passages, you provided the environment, program and personal energy which facilitated a quantum leap in: (a) my healing process, and (b) synthesis and sharp focus about my life purpose and work."

—*Sacred Passage participant*

Sacred Passage is a guided eleven-day wilderness solo experience designed to expand self-knowledge and a feeling of connection with the natural world. Like the Native American vision quest, it enables the integration of inner and outer nature.

Before the solo time, participants work with guides on two days of meditation and awareness training. From the base camp site, individuals then embark on a seven-day solo experience. Each individual's experience is highly variable and unique as there are no structured activities. The focus is on being present in the moment through the senses. Participants typically experience a release of negative emotions (such as fear, anger, sadness, and alienation) during the first few hours or days and then become more aware and open to the emotions, thoughts, and feelings that develop spontaneously through the freedom from environmental and interpersonal demands.

To ensure safety, there are daily checks (without actual contact) by a guide or companion passenger as well as a whistle to call for help from another person about one-quarter to one-half mile away. Participants are furnished with a simple shelter and food.

The locations include the Sangre de Cristo Mountains of Southern California; Baja California in Mexico; Chiricahua Mountains in Arizona; Lost Hollow (a valley of the Shenandoah Mountains in West Virginia); Maui, Hawaii; San Juan Mountains in Colorado; and the Himalayas in Nepal and Tibet. The Himalayan trips are extended in length to twenty-two days.

Participants are said to enjoy renewed creativity, vitality, relaxation, and inner clarity and peace as a result of their experience. Many develop new directions in both their professional and personal worlds.

COST: (U.S. and Mexico trips)

 (Himalayan trips)

 Sacred Passage
P.O. Box CZ
Bisbee, AZ 86503

☎ (520) 432-7353

www.sacredway.com

SHADOW WORK SEMINARS

"Through the creative theatre of Shadow Work I've discovered long lost energies, desires, and strengths. I'm renewed by this work."

—Shadow Work participant

First used by Carl Jung to describe the repressed or denied part of the self, the "shadow" can be positive or negative. The concern is that the true self is in shadow and needs to be brought into the light for full expression. Instead of editing or censoring these hidden parts, they need to be worked with in a way that frees up personal energy.

Examples of shadows being manifested in negative ways include involuntary repetition of behavior patterns (such as not being able to control eating, drinking, or smoking, or jumping from one self-defeating relationship to another) and reacting irrationally to certain traits on other people (which in actuality are denied traits that reflect one's own shadows).

Shadow Work weekend seminars begin with the facilitator asking, "What would you like to have happen?" Participants explain in their own words what is desired. Typical goals are to understand specific behaviors, to break through old patterns of behavior, to work with feelings like fear, grief, or anger, and to get help or assistance in unfolding more of the self.

Role plays and other tools are used to help reconstruct each participant's issue so the shadow can be identified and viewed objectively. Facilitators suggest new perspectives and facilitate powerful techniques for reintegrating the energy of the shadow.

The work is done in a group setting that provides a strong sense of safety and trust. Since it can feel uncomfortable and even risky to expose shadows that were previously hidden, individuals proceed at their own comfort level without any pressure to go beyond what feels right.

Other weekend seminars include the Power of Paradox, which explores the paradoxical territory between deep growth and intense fun in working with shadows, and En-Compass, which translates the principles of Shadow Work for use in business and organizational settings.

Seminars are held a number of times throughout the year. Recent locations have included Texas, Wisconsin, Colorado, Oregon, Indiana, and Washington, D.C. Costs and facilities are variable depending on the locale and whether held in a hotel or retreat center.

COST:

Shadow Work Seminars
13076 Buckhorn Rd.
Loveland, CO 80538

 (970) 203-0400

www.shadowwork.com

Sundoor Foundation for Transpersonal Education

> "I found the core of who I am, my joy in being alive, and a sense of connection to all that is. To anyone considering the course, I will say, 'Take it!' You will find what you are looking for and more: you will find how to live your passion."
>
> —*Sundoor participant*

Walking on fire has a long history that crosses through many divergent cultures and religions. Vikings, Buddhists, Christians, Cherokee, and Apache Indians have all used the experience as a means of spiritual awakening. Over one-half million Americans have experienced a firewalk. Major corporations such as Digital Equipment, Metropolitan Life Insurance, and Colombo Yogurt have offered firewalking seminars to their employees.

Sundoor offers weekend seminars and eight-day trainings which incorporate firewalking (with certified instructors) with other activities to improve health, mental attitude, and relationships. Exercises and learning experiences include conscious breathing and board/brick/steel bending (with bare hands).

The state of mind created by these activities alters physiology and behavior and enables people to walk over glowing coals with total immunity (although there are very infrequent instances of burned feet). These same states also enable peak performance and full potential to be realized at work, in relationships, and throughout all other areas of life. The old blocks which previously interfered with success no longer seem problematic once participants become more self-confident and realize their own personal power.

Seminars and intensives are held throughout the year in San Francisco, other California locations, and all over the United States. Participants stay in hotels.

338

COST: (weekends, tuition only)

 (week-long seminar, all-inclusive)

Sundoor
P.O. Box 669
Twain Harte, CA 95383

(800) 755-1701 or (209) 928-1700

www.sundoor.com

UNIVERSAL EXPERIENCE

> "There was so much I learned about myself that I never realized affected my way of living. I took with me from The Universal Experience a new life, a conscious life with open eyes. I feel more alive and joyous than ever."
>
> —*Universal Experience participant*

Several of the programs in this book recreate the birth experience to enable participants to heal the wounds that occurred during this first transformational experience. But the Universal Experience is the only program that addresses the opposite end of the life journey: death.

This three-day workshop enables participants to have an encounter with their own deaths. Discussions and activities develop an appreciation of the mysteries of death. The core of the experience is letting go as a way of releasing fear and expanding freedom. Old fears, hurts, and struggles are abandoned as the here-and-now is focused upon. The meaning of close relationships and the connection to everything in life is explored.

Far from being depressing, the Universal Experience provides an uplifting reconciliation of life's ultimate challenge. Obviously it transforms each participant's personal relationship with death. But the greatest benefit is the effect it has on living...in the present, without fear.

Most of the workshops are offered in the countryside of Europe (England, Switzerland, and Germany).

Participants stay in dorms and eat vegetarian meals.

COST:

The Art of Being, Europe
Waldhaus Zentrum
CH-3432 Lutzelfluh, Switzerland

 (34) 61 07 05

www.theartofbeing.com

VALLEY OF THE SUN

"I can absolutely prove that everyone has memories of past lives locked away in their subconscious mind, and I contend that those lives are influencing today. In addition, the important people in this life have been with you before....Once you know the cause of your problem, wisdom can erase the karma."

—*Dick Sutphen, workshop facilitator*

In just two days, participants explore their past lives and connect the past to present influences. They come away with a better understanding of their needs, preferences, fears, dislikes, relationships (love and friendships), success blocks, sexual orientation, and so on. By understanding the past, the present and future can be improved.

The weekend includes some lectures, but focuses on subjective participation. Experiences include a Spirit-Guide/Angel contact session, altered-state sessions through meditation and hypnosis, and "automatic writing" sessions. All psychic techniques are designed to release the past.

Seminars are held from 10 A.M. to 5 P.M. on Saturday and Sunday. They're held in locations throughout the country, such as San Diego, Seattle, Chicago, Fort Lauderdale, and Philadelphia.

Accommodations at hotels must be arranged by participants.

COST: (tuition only)

 Valley of the Sun
P.O. Box 683
Ashland, OR 97520

☎ (800) 225-4717 or (541) 488-7880

341

RELATIONSHIP ENHANCEMENT PROGRAMS

None of us function in isolation. We live in a world filled with other people. We interact with numerous persons at work, at home, and in the community. We need to be able to develop and maintain satisfying relationships with these important people to be happy with ourselves and our lives.

Any personal growth and change must start from within. Others can't be expected or depended upon to do it for us. And it's futile to try to change anyone else. But attempts at self-improvement should include some work towards improving relationships. Learning to communicate better, develop intimacy, and resolve conflict will expand your personal power and happiness.

A week or weekend at any of the following programs can change the way you relate to other people. You can mend troubled relationships and make good ones even better. Whether it's with your partner, child, parent, or co-workers, you'll find that enhancing your relationship(s) adds pleasure and comfort to your life.

ART OF CONSCIOUS LOVING SEMINARS

"After twelve years of marriage, my wife and I discovered this seminar that has radically renewed our relationship. I can recommend this seminar to any couple who is serious about having a fun-loving, growing relationship."

—*Art of Conscious Loving participant*

The Indian practice of Tantra focuses on the spiritual aspects of sexuality and intimate relationships. Charles and Caroline Muir, leading experts on tantra yoga, offer tantra seminars which adapt the theories and techniques of this ancient art to contemporary Western form.

Techniques include sexual healing, breath control, transformative touch, varied positions, energy exchange meditations, and advanced lovemaking procedures. No explicit sexual activity or nudity takes place in class. Optional homeplay is assigned.

Most participants come as couples, but individuals are welcome, too.

Week-long seminars have traditionally been held in Hawaii (with some weekend seminars in Boulder, Colorado; San Diego, and Los Angeles), but week-long seminars are also available in Mexico. The Maui seminar takes place in a resort hotel on the island of Maui, with a spectacular vista that offers beaches, hillsides, jungle swimming holes, tropical flowers, and incredible sunsets. The Mexican seminars are held at the Rio Caliente healing spa in the village of La Primavera (a one-hour taxi ride from the Guadalajara Airport). This location offers natural hot mineral baths in the Rio Caliente River, spa services (massage, facials and manicures, and a steam room), hiking, and horseback riding.

By the conclusion of the week, participants have owned, befriended, and reveled in their sexual being. The newly discovered sexual energy increases general vitality, creativity, and

343

consciousness while healing and renewing relationships. While none of us are born skilled at sexual loving and relationships, this important skill can be quickly mastered with the right tools (and maintained through daily homework focusing on a ten-minute connection).

Participants stay in rooms with private baths and are served three vegetarian meals a day.

COST:

 Hawaiian Goddess Source School of Tantra Yoga
P.O. Box 69
Paia Maui, HI 96779

 (808) 572-8364

www.tantra.com/source/index.html

BODY, HEART AND SOUL

"My entire being feels! Every part of me is alive! I feel as if a dam has burst open....I will treasure this week always."
—*Body, Heart and Soul participant*

To be fully human and experience all aspects of existence, individuals need to embrace their sensual and sexual nature without guilt or shame. Body, Heart & Soul assists participants in reclaiming the often underdeveloped ability for true intimacy. Through weeklong workshops, men and women (attending as individuals or as couples) learn to enhance the quality of their love-making, deepen their communication with an intimate partner, and discover sexual energy as a path of spiritual awakening.

All the Body, Heart and Soul workshops include Tantric practices, movement and creative art, a variety of meditation practices, dreamwork, hypnosis, bodywork/breathing/energy processes, and opportunities for communication (verbally, bodily, and through all the senses).

There are four separate but interrelated weeklong workshops offered during the year. Everyone is required to take Part I first, while Parts II, III, and IV can be taken in any order after the first part.

Part I, The Healing Initiation, provides healing experiences for the sensual, sexual, and emotional wounds that most people carry. Participants learn how to dissolve the fears, guilt, shame, and restrictive beliefs that impede their natural capacity for experiencing pleasure. They also learn to honor both their personal boundaries and their desire for intimacy. A special ceremony provides a sacred initiation and celebration of manhood and womanhood.

Part II, Ecstasy and the Transforming Power of Sexual Energy, shows how to remain connected with one's personal sexual energy through all its changing rhythms. Participants learn to free themselves of all expectations and the perceived need to

345

perform. The release of ecstatic and orgasmic potential enables sexual intimacy as well as creativity and delight in everyday life.

Part III, Loving and Relating, explores intimacy with another human being. Participants learn to move through old barriers that have prevented or sabotaged love relationships. They discover how to become more truthful, playful, and passionate rather than remaining fearful and isolated.

Part IV, The Union of Sex, Love and Consciousness, guides participants in realizing their sexual energy and lovemaking as a path of spiritual awakening. As they learn to go beyond their personal plane of existence, they weave together sexual energy, heart, and consciousness through ancient and contemporary sacred rituals.

There are also Intimacy and Love weekend workshops for individuals and couples that introduce Body, Heart and Soul while providing a complete experience in itself. Participants are guided gently into experiences of touching and being touched physically, emotionally, and spiritually. They go deep into themselves at times and at other times become more open to others. By the end of the weekend, sexual fears and repression are lessened. Joyful acceptance of the self as a loving, sensual, and spiritual being is achieved.

Programs are held at a retreat center in a lush natural setting on the island of Maui. Meals are vegetarian, with occasional fish. Accommodation is in shared rooms (or private rooms at an additional charge).

COST:

 Transformational Adventures
P.O. Box 38
Paia, HI 96779

 (808) 572-2234

www.maui.net/~niyaso

CENTER FOR EXCEPTIONAL LIVING

"I really feel much freer, as if a heaviness in my heart has been lifted and now I have a chance to use all this energy in a positive way."

—Center for Exceptional Living participant

Judith Wright, a psychotherapist, sponsors weekend retreats at her Center for Exceptional Living. Most of the retreats provide opportunities for participants to connect deeply with the people who are important in their lives.

A favorite retreat is Joy and Intimacy. The goal is to bridge the gap most couples experience between their life ideals and their daily realities so that joy and intimacy can surface in the relationship. Each couple examines their past and current partnership, develops a new appreciation for intimacy and teamwork, and formulates a "play/action" plan to enhance the relationship.

The Mothers and Daughters Retreat enables participants to relate to each other as adult-to-adult women rather than parent-to-child. By learning what works in the relationship and what does not, both mothers and daughters can clear old patterns and develop new, healthier ways of relating.

There are also programs on Living a Conscious Life. These programs deal with "soft addictions" or habits which help us avoid feelings such as upset, pain, anxiety, fear, anger, or joy. These soft addictions include too much television watching, social drinking, compulsive shopping, compulsive masturbating, nail biting, chocolate stuffing, binging, and gossiping. Participants learn how to free themselves from these bad habits and addictions while moving toward a life of consciousness, grace, aliveness, and connection to spirit.

Retreats incorporate discussion and experiential exercises.

347

Participants stay in shared accommodations at the Center's residence in southern Wisconsin. Less than two hours from Chicago and forty-five minutes from Milwaukee, the Center provides opportunities for hiking and hot tubbing. All meals are served.

COST:

The Center for Exceptional Living
445 East Ohio Street, Suite 260
Chicago, IL 60611

 (312) 664-2700

GLOBAL RELATIONSHIP CENTER

"The course helped me discover and overcome patterns of past relationships that were preventing me from moving forward with a new, healthy relationship."

—*Global Relationship Center participant*

As adults, we've spent many, many years constructing and concealing barriers that prevent successful relationships and happy lives. But a weekend course can change a lifetime of these problem thoughts and behaviors.

"Understanding Yourself and Others" is a thirty-five-hour workshop that provides highly individualized education (not therapy) to participants who want to enhance their relationships. Based on the psychological theory of Alfred Adler, the course focuses on life decisions that were made as children but which may not work well in adult lives. The "protective walls" built of the things which caused shame, fear, hurt, or anger at some point in our lives are overcome to permit love for the self and others.

To assure individualized attention, each workshop is limited to twenty-four participants. Two certified instructors and assistants facilitate discussion, introspection, and roleplaying in an atmosphere of unconditional acceptance.

"Understanding Successful Attitudes" is a course which teaches how to turn personal and professional relationships into teams. The focus is on discovering one's own intentions and learning to read other people's intentions. Participants learn how to relinquish the need for control. They learn to be flexible in being the leader or follower, as dictated by each individual situation.

All the courses address intimacy as something which is desirable in all relationships — with the self, family, friends, romantic partners, co-workers, and supervisors. These enhanced relationships can then lead to increased self-esteem, success, and happiness.

Workshops are held in approximately fifty centers around the United States, as well as overseas.

Most of the sites are urban and don't have housing, but the Center will assist with arranging for nearby accommodations.

COST:

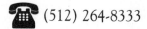 Global Relationship Center
25555 Pedernales Point Drive
Spicewood, TX 78669

(512) 264-8333

GRANDTRAVEL

Grandparents and grandchildren have historically enjoyed a special relationship. Freed from parent-child dynamics, both generations benefit from time spent together. Unfortunately, modern life often prevents grandparents and grandchildren from really getting to know each other. Busy schedules, geographic distance, and divorce may limit interaction to an occasional phone call or letter.

Vacation time is an excellent opportunity for grandparents and grandchildren to connect with each other. Traveling together enables the older and younger generations to share experiences which are both educational and entertaining. But intergenerational travel is not without its pitfalls. Grandparents may find it difficult to keep up with energetic youngsters. Grandchildren who don't know their grandparents very well and may not feel comfortable with older people may be apprehensive about traveling with a grandparent. Trips that don't take the needs of both generations into account can be a disaster.

That's where GRANDTRAVEL comes in. As a vacation program specifically designed for intergenerational travel, it provides unique features not available on other domestic or international tours. In addition to an experienced tour guide, escorts are available to supervise the children and provide learning and recreational activities. Itineraries (ranging from a week in Washington, D.C., or Manhattan to two weeks in New England, Hawaii, Kenya, or Italy) focus on activities which are shared by both generations, but also include separate activities for each peer group so grandchildren can spend some time away from their grandparents and vice-versa. Pre-departure counseling is available to help grandparents and grandchildren understand each other's needs before they travel together.

If you're a grandparent (or aunt, uncle, or friend) who would like to travel with a child (seven to seventeen years old), you'll want to consider GRANDTRAVEL. At the end of the trip, you

351

and your grandchild will have memories which will last a life-time. You'll have developed a greater knowledge and appreciation of each other which may not have occurred if you hadn't shared this special time together.

COST:

 GRANDTRAVEL
The Ticket Counter
6900 Wisconsin Avenue, Suite 706
Chevy Chase, MD 20815

☎ (800) 247-7651 or (301) 986-0790

www.grandtrvl.com

LOVE, INTIMACY, AND SEXUALITY WORKSHOPS

"The workshop is a simple and affordable program which quickly surfaces blocks that keep people from totally participating in life. I moved from being sad and 'victimy' to feeling, giving, and enthusiastic."

—*Love, Intimacy, and Sexuality Workshop participant*

Most of us want to love and be loved, but our fears, judgments, and disempowering beliefs and behaviors can keep us separate from others. Barriers to love and intimacy need to be broken down for life and relationships to be fully satisfying.

Weekend workshops by professional therapists, counselors, educators, and sexologists can show how to create intimate, nurturing, and enriching relationships. In a safe and supportive environment, participants learn to:

- Examine and discard limiting notions about sex, love, and intimacy

- Improve communication skills

- Increase self-knowledge, acceptance, and appreciation

- Heal wounds from abusive relationships

- Set personal boundaries

- Regain a sense of childlike innocence and ability to engage in joyful play

- Be nurtured and loved unconditionally

Participants of any age, experience, relationship status, or sexual orientation are welcome.

Most of the workshops are held throughout the year at the rustic, clothing-optional Harbin Hot Springs three hours north of San Francisco. Some are held in Michigan, New England, Australia, and Japan.

The sleeping accommodations are sleeping bags on the deck under the stars. Meals are served (with a vegetarian option).

COST:

 Human Awareness Institute
2814 San Carlos Ave.
San Carlos, CA 94070-1760

☎ (800) 800-4117 or (650) 571-5524

www.hai.org

LOVING RELATIONSHIPS TRAINING

"The LRT was the most supportive, loving growth experience I have undergone. It assisted me in taking the next significant step in my life. I endorse it unequivocally."

—Loving Relationships Training participant

Almost twenty years ago, Sondra Ray designed a training experience to enable individuals and couples to gain greater clarity, joy, freedom, love, and success in all relationships. These weekend training seminars, known as Loving Relationships Training (LRT), have become the longest running relationship seminar in the world and are still going strong!

Many people instantly think of intimate and romantic relationships when they learn about the seminars. In actuality, LRT stresses the relationship with the self. LRT leaders believe that better relationships with others (mate, family, friends, coworkers) and other things (body, money, career, spirituality, the universe) are not possible until each individual takes charge of the most primary relationship: the one with himself or herself.

All persons can benefit from this training, regardless of whether they are looking for a new relationship, leaving one, struggling in one, recovering from one, or enjoying one. Participants learn to shed old patterns of behavior by identifying and releasing unresolved past experiences. By opening the mind to new possibilities, the heart to more love, and the body to more energy, all relationships can be healed and more fulfilling.

Weekend training sessions are generally held Thursday and Friday nights and all day on Saturday and Sunday. There are many experiential activities (including a group rebirth), meditations, and discussions.

Both individuals and couples are welcome.

Seminars are held at hotels all over the country and throughout the world.

COST:

 Loving Relationships Training
P.O. Box 1465
Washington, CT 06793

☎ (800) 468-5578

NATIONAL MARRIAGE ENCOUNTER

"The Encounter left us with a beautiful feeling. We became reacquainted with each other and learned how to communicate with one another again."

—National Marriage Encounter participant

Marriage Encounter leaders believe that the future transformation of the world begins at the heart of the family: the couple. Over the course of a weekend (beginning Friday evening and ending Sunday afternoon), spouses examine all facets of their life together. The focus is on reflection and communication about strengths and weaknesses as individuals and as a couple, attitudes towards each other and the family, hurts, desires, ambitions, disappointments, joys, and frustrations.

A team of couples who receive special training after personally experiencing and benefitting from Marriage Encounter, lead the process. They share experiences or examples from their own lives and then propose questions for participants to think about and issues to resolve. All work is done in privacy as individuals and as a couple. Persons who do not want to discuss their private marital issues with strangers are relieved to find that the only group interaction is at mealtime.

Although founded by a Catholic priest and deeply rooted in the Christian faith, National Marriage Encounter is ecumenical or interfaith. It's equally effective for Catholics, Protestants, Jews, Muslims, and even atheists (although persons of unbelief or beliefs contrary to the Christian and Jewish faiths are warned that they will hear people share about the God in their lives, usually expressed in Judeo-Christian terms). Couples of all faith commitments are welcome to strengthen the meaning of their marriage in their own religious frame of faith.

The Encounter is also open to couples of any age or length of marriage. Couples married over fifty years find the weekend as helpful as newlyweds do.

357

It's valuable for all marriages, from good ones (to strengthen them even more) to weak ones (which need improvement) to those in transition (to clarify issues and establish the desired direction).

Diverse sites where Marriage Encounters have been held include retreat centers, churches, private homes, schools, campgrounds, and hotels. They're held throughout the country in numerous locations.

Marriage Encounter proponents believe that, because love is limitless, any marriage can be more. If couples are willing to invest in their marriages just as they spend time and money in home maintenance or for career advancement, they can enjoy a marriage which provides more satisfaction, growth, and security than any other endeavor.

Information on local Encounters or anywhere in the country can be obtained by writing to the national office.

COST: (no couple is ever refused the opportunity to participate because of lack of funds)

National Marriage Encounter
4704 Jamerson Place
Orlando, FL 32807

 (800) 828-3351

marriages.org

SHARED HEART TRAINING

"This training brought us more deeply into our hearts and feelings than any other workshop we've ever done. We came to a new level of intimacy that has been a turning point in our relationship."

—*Shared Heart participants*

Joyce and Barry Vissell, a nurse and physician, formed the Shared Heart Foundation to teach about personal growth, relationships, parenting, and healing. They've also written books such as *The Shared Heart*, *Risk to Be Healed*, and *Light in the Mirror*.

A number of three- to ten-day workshops are offered. The majority are weekend courses geared for couples. These programs focus on healing and growing as a committed couple. Participants learn how to remove the blocks keeping them from fully expressing their love. With the assistance of other couples who provide nurturing support, they reach a new level of joy, strength, and purpose in their relationship.

In addition to the couples programs, there are retreats for mothers ("to recharge, inspire, and bring quality mothering back to the family") and Living Your Purpose trainings (to help participants discover their unique gifts and become open to their destinies).

Most of the programs are held at the Vissell's Home-Center in the Santa Cruz mountains by the central California coast. Participants either camp out in their own tents or their camping vehicles or live in local lodging. Three vegetarian meals are served each day. Some programs are offered throughout California and the United States where private rooms in lodges are available.

359

COST:

The Shared Heart Foundation
P.O. Box 2140
Aptos, CA 95001

 (800) 766-0629 or (408) 684-2299

www2.cruzio.com/~sharedhf/

*N*ot all vacations take place on a beach or sightseeing bus. Some of the most life-transforming vacations occur in a classroom. Any of the programs contained in this chapter can enable you to learn a new skill or to improve beginning or dormant abilities. Acquisition or refinement of a skill could change your life in a number of ways. Anytime you learn something or develop your abilities (regardless of the specific area), you enhance your confidence and self-esteem. By learning and refining skills such as painting, drawing, pottery making, photography, writing, acting, cooking, or speaking a foreign language, you can then make the most of your leisure time by doing something more satisfying and productive than watching television. Some of these skills could even be parlayed into a part-time business such as making and selling handmade crafts or writing novels. The ability to speak a foreign language could boost your career in a present or future job. It's possible that some skills could develop into a major career change such as becoming a chef or opening up a restaurant or catering business.

Even if you're resistant to the idea of being cooped up in a classroom during your vacation, you should still look through this chapter. Some of the learning vacations do not take place in a traditional school setting. You'll find a program that teaches you safer driving techniques on a professional race track, a home building course where you work on an actual home, and a backpacking course through the mountains. The skills you learn and the experiences you have will stay with you throughout your life.

AMERICAN ACADEMY OF DRAMATIC ARTS

As the oldest school of professional actor training in the English-speaking world, the American Academy of Dramatic Arts offers a six-week summer program. While some participants have had professional experience, others are beginners who have always wanted to act. Educators and persons who do a lot of public speaking or make sales presentations might find that the training improves their style and gives them an edge in their nonacting professional life.

The core curriculum consists of:

- **Acting**
  Participants learn relaxation, concentration, involvement, and sense memory through exercises, improvisations, and scene study.

- **Voice and Speech**
  The course starts with the basic principles of voice production, placement, and control, and then emphasizes articulation, intonation, stress, and phrasing.

- **Vocal Production**
  Vocal problems are identified and correction is begun through collective and individual work on scales and songs.

- **Movement**
  The focus is on the development of imagination, coordination, and awareness of the body as an instrument of the actor.

Electives include fencing, mime, makeup, and musical theater.

Applicants must audition by delivering from memory two monologues (one comedy, one drama) of two minutes each. A regional audition can be arranged for applicants unable to travel to New York or California for the audition.

Participants can select either the New York location (in midtown Manhattan) or Pasadena (twenty minutes from Los Angeles and Hollywood).

The Academy will supply participants with information about living accommodations in the area.

COST:

 American Academy of Dramatic Arts
120 Madison Avenue
New York, NY 10016

 (212) 686-9244

 American Academy of Dramatic Arts
2550 Paloma Street
Pasadena, CA 91107

 (626) 798-0777

www.aada.org

APPALACHIAN MOUNTAIN CLUB

Outdoor activity can be a little intimidating to the beginner. If you would like to learn to canoe, kayak, raft, hike, backpack, climb rocks, horseback ride, ride a mountain bike, or explore a cave, but didn't know how to get started, consider a two- or three-day workshop at one of the Appalachian Mountain Club (AMC) sites. Offerings include:

- **Bicycle Weekend: Tuning Up, Maintaining, Repairing, and Riding**
- **Finding Your Way: Map, Compass, and Orienteering**
- **Introduction to Backpacking and Overnight Camping**
- **Hiking and Moving with Ease**
- **Introduction to River Canoeing**

There are several AMC sites in the Northeast, including New Hampshire's White Mountains, Maine's Acadia Park, the Berkshires in Massachusetts, and the Catskills in New York.

Participants stay in lodges with private, semiprivate, and dormitory accommodations. Meals are served family-style.

COST:

 Appalachian Mountain Club
P.O. Box 298
Gorham, NH 03581

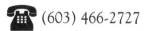 (603) 466-2727

www.volunteers.com/mtnclub.html

ARROWMONT SCHOOL OF ARTS AND CRAFTS

The visual arts are alive and well at Arrowmont. Clay, fiber-fabric, metals, enameling, drawing, painting, photography, marbling, stone carving, woodturning, and coopering are all taught at the internationally known visual arts complex. The week-long classes address both technical skills and the creative process.

Most courses are for all levels and can benefit beginning through advanced students. There is a minimum age of eighteen.

Two semester undergraduate or graduate credits are available through the University of Tennessee, Knoxville, for each week of study at Arrowmont.

The school's proximity to the Great Smoky Mountains National Park in Eastern Tennessee (three miles from the entrance) enables students to enjoy outdoor recreational activities as a diversion to their studies.

Students may live on campus in single, double, triple, or dormitory rooms with private or adjoining baths. The cafeteria provides three meals a day.

COST:

Arrowmont School of Arts and Crafts
P.O. Box 567
556 Parkway
Gatlinburg, TN 37738

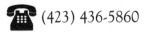 (423) 436-5860

AUGUSTA HERITAGE CENTER

Traditional music, dance, crafts, and folklore become a magical part of present-day lives with a weeklong class at the Augusta Heritage Center. The variety of creative activities, offered on all levels, ensures something of interest for almost everyone. At the end of the week session, participants have gained sufficient skills to continue the activity as a fulfilling hobby and ensure that these folk traditions never die out.

Dance classes include clogging, Cajun dance, Irish dance, swing dance, and dance calling.

Craft courses include basketry, white oak rib basketry, broommaking, bookbinding, paper marbling, calligraphy and Celtic lettering, Celtic stonecarving, wood relief and chip carving, banjo construction, fiddle and bow repair, mountain dulcimer construction, blacksmithing, fretted instrument repair, reedmaking and pipe repair, pottery, stained glass, traditional papercutting, African applique masks, quiltmaking, log house construction, stonemasonry, treenware (wooden spoon and bowl carving), traditional weaving, and rag rug weaving.

Folklore classes include herb gardening, herb foraging, Appalachian literature, Cajun cooking, Irish folklore, Gaelic language and song, and storytelling/African-American storytelling.

Music classes include autoharp, banjo, group playing (on autoharp, dulcimer, banjo, fiddle, or guitar), bluegrass, blues, improvisation, Cajun music, harmonica, fiddle, flat-pick guitar, hammered dulcimer, swing music, Irish music, tinwhistle, and a special vocal week incorporating everything from "Singing for the Confidence Impaired" to songwriting to vocal technique.

Evenings are always lively, with mini-classes, slide shows, discussions, student showcases, jam sessions, song swaps, craft showcases, and open craft and music studios.

Undergraduate credit is available.

Davis & Elkins College, the home of the Augusta Heritage Center, allows participants to use all campus recreation facilities (including tennis courts, indoor swimming pool, fitness trail, and Nautilus Center. Located in a small West Virginia town about a four-hour drive from Pittsburgh and Washington, D.C., the countryside offers a variety of outdoor activities: whitewater rafting, canoeing, caving, rock climbing, and backpacking.

Participants who wish to carpool may receive a listing of others who would like to drive together. The nearest major airport is Pittsburgh, although there are limited flights in and out of the Elkins airport. It's also possible to fly into Clarksburg, West Virginia, and take a cab or carpool into Elkins (about one and one-half hours by car).

Participants may stay in the campus residence halls with semiprivate rooms and common bathrooms. Three meals a day (including meatless entrees and a salad bar at all meals) are available in the cafeteria. There are also motels, bed and breakfast inns, and campgrounds within a few miles of the campus.

COST:

 Augusta Heritage Center
Davis & Elkins College
100 Sycamore Street
Elkins, WV 26241

 (304) 637-1209

www.augustaheritage.com

BENNINGTON SUMMER WRITING WORKSHOPS

During July of every year the campus of Bennington College in the Green Mountains of southwestern Vermont provides writers with the time and space to begin or finish their work while escaping from the demands of their everyday lives. It also offers constructive counsel and support through six hours of seminars per week, plus tutorial meetings with faculty and evening readings by visiting and resident writers. Faculty and fellow students read works in progress and completed works, offering suggestions for writing and rewriting. Prominent editors, publishers, and authors discuss publication and distribution of literature.

Participants may enroll in either two-week or four-week sessions, and elect to focus on poetry, fiction, or nonfiction. To keep class size small, enrollment is limited. Applicants must submit a brief writing sample (up to twenty-five pages of prose or twelve pages of poetry).

Undergraduate or graduate college credits are available.

Recreational activities on campus include tennis, soccer, and basketball. Restaurants, country stores, and a spring-fed lake are within walking distance. Theater, dance, and music performances and historic homes for touring are within a fifty-mile radius.

Participants live in comfortable single rooms in college houses and take meals at The Commons.

COST:  (two weeks)

(four weeks)

 Bennington Summer Writing Workshops
Bennington College
Bennington, VT 05201

 (802) 442-5401, ext. 160

369

CERAN-LINGUA INTERNATIONAL

The countrysides of Belgium and France are perfect places to learn French. At either CERAN center, participants are totally immersed in the language. French is the only language spoken from 8:30 in the morning until 10:30 at night. In addition to small classes of one to four students and language laboratories, meal times and evening activities (such as parties, films, musical performances, and lectures) offer a further opportunity for practice. In one week's time, students are exposed to sixty-sixhours of French.

Facilities for tennis, swimming, and golf are available, as is sightseeing, but the major focus is on the acquisition of language skills. Instruction can be geared for beginners with no knowledge of the language or for intermediate speakers. Prospective students with some knowledge of the language are required to provide a sample of their writing in French. To help the staff provide personalized instruction, all students must define their professional or personal reasons for taking the course.

Other languages taught at the centers include English, Dutch, German, Spanish, and Japanese.

The minimum stay is one week. CERAN recommends at least two weeks for gaining real proficiency in the language. Classes are held throughout the year.

Students stay in rooms or apartments on the campus. Single and double rooms are available; some have private baths. All meals are provided.

COST:

 Chateau CERAN
Avenue du Chateau, 16
B-4900 SPA NIVEZE-SPA
BELGIUM

+ 32 87 77 41 64

 CERAN Langues Provence
Monastere Saint-Pancrace
F-30130 PONT-SAINT-ESPRIT
FRANCE

 + 33 66 90 33 66

www.ceran.com

CORNELL'S ADULT UNIVERSITY

Cornell's Adult University makes it possible to attend an Ivy League school without worrying about SAT scores, grades, or four years of tuition. You can get a taste of its academic offerings in a relaxed atmosphere.

Week-long classes are held on the Cornell campus throughout the summer. Examples of recent offerings include:

- **Personality and Behavior**
  The focus is on nature versus nurture as a determinant of personality and group behavior. Personality tests, the relationship between intelligence and personality, ethnic-group, and male-female differences are also discussed.

- **Now You're Talking: A Public Speaking Workshop**
  Group activities, individual presentations, and private tutoring assist participants in developing effective public speaking skills.

- **Field Ornithology**
  Daily field trips give participants a chance to see some of the more than 120 bird species of the Finger Lakes region.

- **The Internet Workshop: For Users and Browsers**
  Hands-on experience using the Internet is the focus. Participants learn about information retrieval, the economics and laws of universal networking, Internet publishing, and getting connected to the Internet at home or work.

- **Wines and Cuisines: The Road to Perfect Combinations**
  Participants learn the art of blending food and drink through classroom study and field trips to restaurants that serve a variety of Asian and European cuisines.

- **A Long Look at the Short Story: A Fiction-Writing Workshop**
  The course enhances the ability to write descriptive passages, dialogue, characters, and plot.

There are also study tours throughout the year. These are usually two weeks long and can range from "The Natural History and Ecology of New Zealand" to "A London Theatre Study Tour."

Participants stay in campus residence halls in private rooms with baths and air-conditioning. Meals are served in the campus cafeteria.

Study tour participants stay in hotels while traveling.

Participants have full access to Cornell's and Ithaca's cultural and natural resources: concerts, plays, lectures, films, museums, libraries, shops, galleries, bookstores, coffee houses, restaurants, golf, tennis, swimming, sailing, hiking, parks, gorges, waterfalls, lakes, trails, and gardens.

COST: 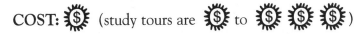 (study tours are ❀ to ❀ ❀ ❀)

 Cornell University
626 Thurston Avenue
Ithaca, NY 14850

 (607) 255-6260

www.cornell.edu

COUNTRY WORKSHOPS

"The workshop was a truly unique and enriching experience."
—*Country Workshops participant*

Traditional woodworking with hand tools is not a completely dying art, thanks to Country Workshops. This satisfying craft produces items which are both beautiful and functional.

The five-day tutorials and workshops combine hands-on experience and theory. Students predominantly use a drawknife and spokeshave at a shaving horse. The use of a wood lathe, carving knife, hewing ax, and adze is also taught. Workshops usually begin by splitting stock from a freshly felled log.

Typical courses include chairmaking, Swiss cooperage (the craft of making tapered cylindrical containers with joined staves held together by hoops, as used by traditional alpine dairy farmers), Swedish woodenware (focusing on spoons and large hollowed bowls), handcrafted furniture (producing a small Craftsman-style end table), timber framing (for loft construction), and wooden boat building. Tutorials are limited to two participants per five-day course during the winter months.

Serious woodworkers of all abilities — professionals, amateurs, and beginners — can be accommodated.

Country Workshops is located on a mountain farmstead about forty-five miles away from Asheville, North Carolina. Because they're just a few miles from the Appalachian Trail, outdoor recreational possibilities abound. Whitewater rafting and hiking are available nearby. The farm has a pond, garden, and woods for guests to use.

The closest airports are Tri-Cities, Tennessee, and Asheville, North Carolina. Airport pickups can usually be arranged with other students who pass by on their way to Country Workshops.

Tutorial participants stay in private rooms in the guest log cabins. Workshop participants in the spring, summer, and fall stay in a dormitory or bring a tent, van, or small trailer to the free camping area.

COST:

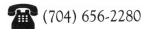 Country Workshops
90 Mill Creek Road
Marshall, NC 28753-9321

(704) 656-2280

countryworkshops.org

DILLMAN'S CREATIVE ART AND PHOTOGRAPHY WORKSHOPS

Painting is a wonderful means of self-expression, but most of us never attempt any art once we complete school. Picking up a paintbrush without formal training can be intimidating. But with the guidance and encouragement of a professional artist, almost everyone can discover the satisfaction of creating art.

Weekend or week-long courses at Dillman's can provide beginners (or advanced artists) with the knowledge and skills to pursue painting or photography as a fulfilling hobby or career. Courses range from Oil Landscapes to pastel Portraits to Wildflowers in Watercolor to Greeting Cards in Acrylic. A number of photography courses are also offered, as well as some business-related courses such as Marketing Your Art Work. Instruction is provided by nationally-known artists.

Workshops are offered during the spring, summer, and fall. A few workshops are held off-site each year (in places such as Tahiti or Paris) for participants to combine travel with art and photography.

Although the studios are open twenty-four hours a day, participants usually make some time to pursue recreational activities at the lakeside resort, such as kayaking, swimming, fishing, nature hikes, volleyball games, and cookouts. Dillman's Sand Lake Lodge is located in Lac du Flambeau, Wisconsin. Nonparticipants accompanying the person enrolled in the workshops can be easily accommodated at the lodge.

COST:

Dillman's Creative Arts Foundation
P.O. Box 98F
Lac du Flambeau, WI 54538

 (715) 588-3143

DODGE/SKIP BARBER DRIVING SCHOOL

"...will definitely make us all better drivers...I would strongly recommend this course to anyone — everyone — who plans to drive anywhere....The sooner it can be incorporated into one's driving career, the better."

—Dodge/Skip Barber Driving School participant

Participation in a two-day driving course just might change your life by saving it! It can prevent injuries and financial burdens by making you a better, more confident driver who is equipped to deal with the challenges of driving under any conditions.

As the largest racing school in the world, the Skip Barber School typically teaches race driving using race cars. But in partnership with Dodge, they offer a defensive driving course using Vipers, Stealths, and Stratus sedans. The emphasis is on enhancing overall driving ability and building confidence for everyday driving situations. As opposed to racetrack skills, participants learn "street skills" of accident evasion, skid control, emergency braking, emergency lane changing, highway manners, and vehicle dynamics theory.

Theory is taught in the classroom, while the practical application occurs on the skid pad and autocross course. Advanced car control skills in all drive-line types (rear-wheel, front-wheel, and all-wheel drive) are included. Participants learn to become better drivers in the rain, in snow, on ice...as well as in the dry, when trouble is least expected.

Anyone sixteen years or older who is comfortable with the controls of an automobile may participate.

The course is conducted year-round at the Sears Point Raceway in the San Francisco Bay area and October through April at Sebring International raceway in Central Florida.

Accommodations and meals are participants' own responsibility and are not included in the cost.

COST:

 Skip Barber Racing School
29 Brook Street
P.O. Box 1629
Lakeville, CT 06039

☎ (860) 435-1300

www.skipbarber.com

HAYSTACK MOUNTAIN SCHOOL OF CRAFTS

Each summer about eighty artists and students come together to explore craft and art, ideas and imagination. Haystack's program acknowledges tradition while enabling new frontiers in contemporary visual art.

Classes range from one to three weeks and are held June through September. Offerings include clay (wheel throwing, porcelain glazing), metals (pewtersmithing, sculpture, jewelry), surface design (fabric printing), drawing, painting, blacksmithing (sheet metal work, weldering, soldering, sculpture), wood (woodworking, finishing, turning), basketry, papermaking, glass (hot glass blowing), and fibers (weaving, quilting, needlepoint). While the course offerings appear similar to those offered at other craft schools, Haystack focuses less on the technical "how-to" and more on the creative process. In addition to hands-on instruction and practice, participants engage in conversation and exercises to foster new ways of thinking about and producing art. Most classes emphasize elements of design and address the physical, psychological, and social aspects that give value to an object. Generally any level of student can be accommodated (unless otherwise specified in the individual course description).

While the waterside setting of the school enables a number of recreational possibilities, the focus is on creating. Studios are open twenty-four hours a day, seven days a week.

Housing ranges from a dorm/open bunkhouse to single rooms with a private bath. Three meals are served each day in the dining room.

Academic credit for two- or three-week sessions is available. Students receive three undergraduate or graduate credits through the University of Southern Maine.

The school is located in Deer Isle, Maine (connected to the mainland by a bridge over Eggemoggin Reach). It is about five hundred miles from New York City, 250 miles from Boston, 150 miles from Portland, and sixty miles from Bangor. Air and bus transportation is available to Bangor, as is taxi-van service from Bangor to Deer Isle.

COST:

 Haystack Mountain School of Crafts
P.O. Box 518
Deer Isle, ME 04627

(207) 348-2306

www.craftweb.com/org/haystack/haystack.htm

THE HEARTWOOD SCHOOL FOR THE HOMEBUILDING CRAFTS

"To anyone planning to build a house, the Heartwood course is invaluable, in the end saving thousands of dollars in contractor's fees, errors, and needlessly limited possibilities."

—*Heartwood participant*

Heartwood feels that too many people are uninvolved with the building of their home. By surrendering this very important aspect of our lives to developers, realtors, and contractors, we end up buying or renting houses that are impersonal, expensive, and poorly built. But by learning how to build or improve a house, you can be assured of living in a home that's affordable, energy-efficient, and meets your needs.

A three-week housebuilding course is offered. No previous construction experience is needed. The mornings include classroom sessions, demonstrations, slide programs, and discussions. In the afternoons, students join in on the construction of a custom house involving both timber and conventional framing. The comprehensive program includes power tool use, site preparation, foundation types, building code requirements, framing systems, exterior and interior finishes, installing doors and windows, building stairs, plumbing, and electrical systems.

Specialized one-week workshops include carpentry for women, home design, cabinetmaking, and renovation. Courses are mainly offered in the summer, with a few in the fall and spring.

Participants arrange their own accommodations and meals (with the exception of weekday lunches). There are several hotels, campgrounds, and bed and breakfasts nearby.

Heartwood is located in the Berkshire Hills of western Massachusetts. The Appalachian Trail and the cultural programs of Tanglewood are nearby.

COST:

The Heartwood School for the Homebuilding
Crafts
Johnson Hill Road
Washington, MA 01235

 (413) 623-6677

www.heartwoodschool.com

INDIANA UNIVERSITY'S MINI UNIVERSITY

Indiana University holds a vacation college for five days every June. Unlike many campus vacation programs which focus on indepth study in one particular area for the week, the Mini University offers about 100 short classes lasting one to two hours. Participants may sign up for up to fifteen noncredit classes in the arts, humanities, international affairs, domestic issues, science, business and technology, human growth and development, and health/fitness/leisure.

Classes in the past have included:

- **Understanding Ballet**
- **Caring for Your Antiques and Heirlooms**
- **What the Consumer Really Does Not Want to Know About Life Insurance**
- **Introduction to Windows on the PC**
- **Racism and the Law**
- **Drugs in America**
- **What's New in First Aid**
- **Getting the Most Out of Your Leisure Time**
- **Conflict Management**
- **The Power of Positive Listening**
- **Turkish Traditional Art**
- **Middle East Update**
- **Mathematics as a Creative Art**

Leisure activities include picnics, films, plays, golf, swimming, tennis, and bowling.

Participants are housed in the campus hotel with private rooms and baths or in dorm-style housing with shared baths. Meals are taken in campus dining halls and cafeterias.

COST:

 Mini University
Indiana University Alumni Association
P.O. Box 4822
Bloomington, IN 47402

 (800) 824-3044 or (812) 855-0921

www.indiana.edu

INTERNATIONAL CENTER OF PHOTOGRAPHY

A variety of weekend workshops are offered throughout the year for amateur and professional photographers. Some are strictly technical, such as Electronic Flash Photography, Light and Style, Hand Coloring Photographs, and Printing from Negatives and Slides. Others incorporate psychological and sociological insights with the photographic process. Examples of these include:

- **Beyond the Self-Portrait: Artist as Subject**
  By using themselves as models, participants investigate their personal history, hopes, fears, rage, and passion. The process challenges notions of the self, family, society, and culture.

- **How to Open Up**
  This workshop encourages self-development through the photographic exploration of our home. By beginning at home and investigating the people and objects that are the most familiar and most important to us, creativity can be revealed and developed.

- **Photographing the Unphotographable**
  Participants attempt to access the unseen world through a number of exercises including meditation, automatic writing, and "self-remembering." They generate texts, participate in discussions, and make pictures to photograph the "unseen world" of emotion, thought, and memory.

For some workshops, participants must submit a portfolio for review when applying.

Participants arrange their own lodging in New York City.

COST:

 International Center of Photography
1130 Fifth Avenue at 94th Street
New York, NY 10128

 (212) 860-1776

www.icp.org

INTERNATIONAL MUSIC CAMP

If you're one of the many adults who rebelled against piano lessons as a child and now regrets stopping the lessons, the International Music Camp may be just what you need to get you going again. If you never had the opportunity to develop any musical skills and always wished you had, the Camp is worth your consideration.

The International Music Camp is a summer school of fine arts for both youth and adults. During June and July a variety of four- to seven-day courses are offered. All are taught by professional artist-educators.

The adult (nineteen years and up) courses include Adult Band/Orchestra, Adult Choir, and Women's Barbershop Workshop. Courses open to both youth and adults include piano, guitar, stage band and jazz ensembles, handbells, and marimba and vibes.

Besides music, there are classes in drama, dance (modern and ballet), creative writing, and art (oils, acrylics, watercolors, sketching, and portraiture).

Classes are divided into beginning, intermediate, or advanced sections. An audition tape must be submitted for the higher levels in some classes. Private lessons are also offered.

Participants are housed in dormitories.

Recreational activities are scheduled in the late afternoon and evenings. These include swimming, basketball, volleyball, movies, and, of course, concerts.

The Camp is located at the International Peace Garden between North Dakota and Manitoba, Canada. The scenic grounds contain a wild flower garden, formal garden, bell tower, hiking trail, and arboretum. Participants are picked up at the train or bus station in Rugby, North Dakota.

COST:

 August thru May
International Music Camp
1725 11th Street SW
Minot, ND 58701

 (701) 838-8472

 June and July
International Music Camp
RR1, Box 116A
Dunseith, ND 58329

 (701) 263-4211

Iowa Summer Writing Festival

"It's challenging, supportive, energetic. There is no way a writer can walk out of this program without seeing improvement in his or her work."

—*Iowa Summer Writing Festival participant*

Every summer the University of Iowa offers over one hundred noncredit writing workshops. Held May through July, the Festival's weekend and week-long programs cover every conceivable area of writing: picture books for children, poetry, letter writing, short fiction, science fiction, personal memoir writing, fiction writing for beginners, playwriting, nature essays, humor writing, screenwriting, commentary, journal writing, romance novels, mystery writing, and so on.

Workshops are open to any adult interested in writing. No previous experience is necessary. Some of the workshops are geared towards beginners, a few for advanced writers, and most for those who fall in between these two categories.

Classes are primarily based on the workshop method. A few lectures and writing exercises may be included in some of the sessions, but most focus on reading and discussing every participant's work. Fellowship is the crucial element in energizing Festival participants for learning and artistic experimentation. While writing is by nature a solitary occupation, the contact with other writers gives encouragement, helpful criticism, and stimulation to take risks and make new discoveries.

The University of Iowa campus is easily accessible by plane or bus. Shuttle service is available from the airport.

Participants may choose residence hall accommodations (two bedroom apartments with a shared bath) or hotel rooms with private baths. Except for two dinners included as part of the program, meals are not included. Recreational options include walks along the Iowa River, museums, concerts, and plays.

COST:

 Iowa Summer Writing Festival
The University of Iowa
116 International Center
Iowa City, IA 52245

 (319) 335-2534

www.uiowa.edu/~iswfest/

JOHN C. CAMPBELL FOLK SCHOOL

Individual expression and social interaction are encouraged through music, dance, crafts, and gardening in this unique school. Founded in 1925 as an alternative educational institution for the people of Appalachia, the school has updated some of the materials and methods used in its classes but still emphasizes the traditions of Southern Appalachia and other cultures of the world.

Most classes offered throughout the year are a week in length, while some are held over weekends. Offerings include basketry (ranging from natural vine to reed to white oak), blacksmithing (from basic forging to advanced sculpture), book arts (papermaking and bookbinding), broom making, calligraphy, clay (hand building, wheel throwing, porcelain) crafts business (marketing and photography), crochet, dance (square and contra, English ritual, old time couple), design/printing (batik and fabric painting, Ukranian Easter eggs), dolls, enameling, glass (stained glass, glass bead making), jewelry (clay, wire wrapped, basic metal construction), kaleidoscopes, knitting (designer fabrics, fisherman sweaters, Christmas stockings), lace (bobbin lace, Battenburg lace, Danish counted thread), marbling (fabric and paper), mountain dulcimer (making/playing), nature/garden (bonsai, fly tying, dried flower wreaths and swags, tanning leather), painting (watercolor, oil), photography, quilting, rug hooking and weaving, spinning, weaving (multiharness, floor loom, tapestry wall hanging), and woodcarving (human figure, bird, native animals, Santa and angel, ladder back chair).

Some of the courses are specifically designed for beginning or advanced students, but most can accommodate students at any level. Instruction is noncompetitive and relaxed. There are no grades or credits. Discussion, conversation, and hands-on learning takes precedence over learning through reading and writing.

Students typically attend class six hours each day. There are morning walks and stretches, evening group singing, dancing, and storytelling sessions, historical tours of the area, and other activities for relaxing and learning between formal class time. Studios are open for students to work independently on their projects between classes.

On-campus lodging is available (ranging from a dorm room with three to eight twin beds and a shared bath to a double with two twin beds and a bath). Three meals are served each day in the dining room.

The school is located in a scenic mountain valley in southwestern North Carolina (within three hours driving time from airports in Chattanooga and Knoxville, TN; Asheville, NC; Greenville, SC; and Atlanta, GA). The school provides airport pickup service from the Atlanta airport for $55 each way.

COST:

 John C. Campbell Folk School
Route 1, Box 14A
Brasstown, NC 28902-9603

☎ (800) 365-5724 or (704) 837-2775

sunsite.unc.edu/ne-abana/folksch.html

JOSEPH VAN OS PHOTO SAFARIS, SHOOTS, AND WORKSHOPS

While most vacationers take pictures as mementos of their trips, photography isn't the main point of getting away. But for beginners who are interested in developing their photographic skills or advanced/professional photographers who want to hone their photographic technique, a vacation focusing on photography may be ideal.

Photo safaris take participants on guided trips throughout the world's wild and scenic locations. Professional wildlife photographers are available for consultation. Depending on the locale, participants are lodged in luxurious inns and hotels or comfortable tented camps.

Photo workshops typically take place at a single site rather than the multiple locations of a touring safari. They provide concentrated classroom and field instruction with wildlife and scenery.

Photo shoots offer trained, captive-reared, predatory animals in ecologically realistic habitats as photo subjects. Wolves, bears, tigers, lions, leopards, coyotes, bobcats, and birds of prey are usually next to impossible to observe or photograph in the wild, but these special shoots provide a controlled environment with ample opportunities to photograph inside the enclosures without fences separating humans from animals.

Workshop and shoot participants stay at local hotels.

Joseph Van Os Photo Safaris is one of the leaders in the photo travel industry. Specializing in wildlife, they boast top outdoor photographers and experienced teachers, small groups (twenty participants or less for safaris, workshops, and shoots) and well-planned trips. Safaris and workshops may vary from year to year, but always include locations in North America (Colorado, the Southwest, Florida, New England), Africa, the Arctic, Antarctica, and Latin America.

COST: to

(depending on length & location)

Joseph Van Os Photo Safaris
P.O. Box 655
Vashon Island, WA 98070

(206) 463-5383

www.photosafaris.com

La Varenne

As the premier cooking school of French cuisine, La Varenne has taught many of the world's most famous chefs and cooking professionals. In addition to longer professional programs in Paris, La Varenne offers week-long courses in Burgundy for lovers of French cuisine who want to sharpen their kitchen skills and refine their knowledge and appreciation of fine food and wine.

The school is bilingual. Participants cook under the direction of expert French chefs after watching demonstrations. They also enjoy planned excursions to restaurants, open markets, stores, and wine tastings.

Courses are seven days in length and are held July through September. Topics include French pastry and Chocolate, Bistro Cooking, Contemporary French Cuisine, Regional Cooking, and Entertaining Menus. A week-long comprehensive gastronomic program is offered in October.

The programs are offered at a historic chateau ninety miles south of Paris. (The school provides transportation to and from Paris.) Participants stay in double-occupancy rooms. Recreational possibilities on the grounds include tennis and swimming. Golf and hot air ballooning are nearby possibilities.

COST:

 La Varenne Ecole de Cuisine
U.S. Office
P.O. Box 25574
Washington, DC 20007

☎ (800) 537-6486 or (202) 337-0073

LANGUAGE IMMERSION INSTITUTE

Affiliated with the State University of New York at New Paltz, the Language Immersion Institute provides opportunities for the adult learner to acquire proficiency in one or more foreign language(s) in the shortest possible time. Twenty foreign languages are offered: Arabic, Czech, Dutch, Chinese, English as a Second Language, French, German, Greek, Hebrew, Hungarian, Italian, Japanese, Polish, Portuguese, Russian, (American) Sign, Spanish, Swedish, Ukranian, and Yiddish. Classes are offered from elementary to advanced levels, within a natural, conversational context. Language laboratories and foreign films supplement the experience. The program benefits both people who want to acquire a foreign language for business purposes and those who want to use it for travel or social situations.

Weekend courses are held throughout the year, providing fifteen hours of language immersion. Five-day and two-week formats are also available. There are also overseas learning vacations and cruises in France, Germany, Russia, and Switzerland.

In the main locations (in New Paltz), participants are housed in residence halls with others studying the same language so they can practice at all times. Occupancy can be double or single. In other locations, participants must make their own accommodations in local hotels, bed and breakfasts, and rooms. Meals are not provided but are available on campus and within the community.

Courses are taught on the university campus, as well as in a Victorian mansion resort (both in New Paltz, about ninety minutes from Manhattan). There are also courses in New York City and Montvale, New Jersey.

COST: to $ $
(depending on length and location)

 Language Immersion Institute
JFT 916, State University of New York at
New Paltz
75 S. Manheim Boulevard
New Paltz, NY 12561

(914) 257-3500

eeserv.eelab.newpaltz.edu/lii

Language Studies International

> "The course was very good for me because it was practical and helped me with the vocabulary I need in my job. Now I can communicate with other people much better."
>
> —*Language Studies International participant*

The Language Studies International (LSI) schools provide intensive instruction in French, Spanish, and German as well as English. While other language schools may offer a greater variety of languages, the LSI schools provide indepth and individualized studies in these three important languages.

The Standard Course consists of twenty lessons a week for a two-week period (or longer). Courses are practical in nature, focusing on speaking and understanding the language. Reading and writing are addressed as well. The Standard Course is held throughout the year, but the Summer Courses in July and August have expanded social programs with many extracurricular activities to make it a true holiday abroad. In addition to the Standard Course, there are other options, such as the Intensive Standard Course (thirty lessons per week), nine-month academic courses, and executive/business courses geared for specific industries (such as travel and tourism). All courses use a variety of communicative teaching techniques including video, role play, and project work.

Any language proficiency can be accommodated, from beginners who have little or no knowledge of the language to advanced students who want to refine their skills. Students are assessed on their first day to determine their levels.

French instruction is provided in Paris and Sausset-les-Pins (a coastal resort northwest of Marseille); Spanish in Madrid and Salamanca (a medieval city in western Spain); German in Frankfurt, Nurnberg, Berlin, and Zurich.

Students may stay in hotels, but most opt to stay with a private family to economize and for the opportunity to practice the language further in an authentic setting. The schools screen all families and coordinate the arrangements.

Language Studies International is known for its success in preparing students for standardized language testing. More than 90 percent of their students pass these public examinations, enabling them to achieve certificates or diplomas acknowledging their proficiency in their chosen language.

COST: to
(depending on length and location)

U.S.A. (for more information):

 Language Studies International
45 Newbury Street, Suite 509
Boston, MA 02116

 (617) 859- 4949
(FAX) (617) 859-7545

International:

 Language Studies International
350 Rue St. Honoré
75001 Paris
France

 (1) 4260 5370

Language Studies International
Zeil 107
Postfach 10 14 16
D 60313 Frankfurt
Germany

(069) 20309

398

Language Studies International
Calle Luchana 31/1
28010 Madrid
Spain

 (1) 446 0999

 Language Studies International
Kreuzstrasse 36
CH 8008 Zurich
Switzerland

 (1) 251 5889

www.prolinguis.cn/lsi/files/lsi.html

NATIONAL GOURMET INSTITUTE FOR FOOD AND HEALTH

If you would like to cook and eat healthier but are bewildered by tofu, tempeh, or seitan, this course is for you. It provides five daily hours of hands-on cooking instruction Monday through Friday over a two-week period. This intensive includes knife skills, herbs and spices, grain identification and cooking techniques, soups, salads, whole-grain bread baking, sea vegetables, medicinal cooking, vegetable protein, and desserts.

The course is held in August in New York City. Participants arrange their own accommodations and leisure time.

COST:

 The Natural Gourmet Institute for Food and
    Health
    48 West 21st Street
    New York, NY 10010

 (212) 645-5170

New York Film Academy

"[The Academy] opened a window on a new life for me."
—New York Film Academy participant

Many film buffs have yearned to tell their own stories and communicate their ideas by making a film themselves. The vast majority never get around to it because they don't know where and how to begin. Without studying the basics, they feel lost. For those who don't have the time or money to obtain a degree from a California university, a shorter course can be ideal.

New York Film Academy offers six-week summer intensive workshops. Each individual learns to write, direct, shoot, and edit his or her own short film. All instruction is hands-on and practical. An integrated curriculum ensures that students understand the interdependent relationships of all aspects of filmmaking. The small class size (sixteen per class) allows intense interaction between students and the award-winning instructors. Celebrated film professionals provide guest lectures. A filmmaking certificate is awarded upon completion.

No previous filmmaking experience is needed. Participants come from a variety of backgrounds. Some take it as preparation for a four-year program or in hopes of breaking into the business. Others want to discover if they have the talent or the desire to pursue filmmaking further. Those individuals who are not interested in a career in filmmaking enjoy the opportunity to acquire a new skill which provides a creative outlet.

The Academy helps arrange housing. Low budget accommodations at the YMHA (private room, shared bath) are available.

COST:

New York Film Academy
375 Greenwich Street
New York, NY 10013

 (212) 674-4300

www.nyfa.com

PENLAND SCHOOL OF CRAFTS

As the nation's oldest craft school, Penland offers a variety of courses in twelve media:

- **Book arts** (designing, printing, binding, etc.)
- **Ceramics** (handbuilding, wheelthrowing, earthenware tile, teapots, etc.)
- **Drawing** (landscape, live, interpretive, representational)
- **Fibers** (weaving, dyeing, basketry)
- **Glass** (glassblowing, neon, coldworking)
- **Iron/sculpture** (blacksmithing, bronze casting, blade-smithing)
- **Metals** (jewelry, enameling, stone setting)
- **Paper** (sculptural papermaking, handmade paper decorating, art imagery with paper)
- **Photography** (Polaroid, outdoor/color photography, multi-media photography)
- **Printmaking** (etching, wood engraving, lithography)
- **Surface design** (screen-printing on fabric, machine embroidery, beading)
- **Wood** (furniture design, woodcarving, woodworking)

All classes are kept small enough so that both beginners and more experienced persons can receive individualized instruction. A few courses are geared specifically for the basics and a few others are only for advanced students, but most accommodate all levels. For all classes, the minimum age is nineteen. Classes are generally two weeks in length, but can range from one to eight weeks. Most are held in the summer, with the eight-week courses offered in the fall and spring.

The Penland campus consists of 450 acres and forty-seven

buildings in an isolated setting in the North Carolina mountains. There are no distractions of phone, television, or daily newspapers. The studios are open twenty-four hours a day to allow students to work as many hours as they want to learn or improve skills in their chosen area(s). A change of pace is available through daily movement classes, evening slide shows, visits to nearby studios, on-campus coffee house, library, volleyball games, dances, walks, and swims in the river.

Students live on campus in rustic dorm rooms housing three to fourteen persons or double- or single-occupancy rooms with a bath. The dining room serves three meals a day.

COST:

 Penland School of Crafts
P.O. Box 37
Penland, NC 28765

 (704) 765-2359

www.penland.org

Sew Week

"Every garment I've made since my first Sew Week has been a great success. My garments fit better, look better, and give me a great sense of accomplishment and pride....Even if there were nothing left to learn, I would continue to come and recharge my creativity."

—Sew Week participant

All of us feel better when we look our best. If you want a wardrobe that really fits and flatters while expressing your personality, it may be worth your while to make your own clothes. Your junior high home economics class may not have inspired you to design, sew, and tailor after you completed the course. But a Sew Week could get you going again and help you revamp your wardrobe with much less money than a shopping spree would cost.

A professional seamstress teaches a one-week course each month in her home. Participants range from beginners to advanced sewers. The mornings are devoted to lectures on topics such as couture techniques, drafting patterns, design, tailoring, or wardrobe planning. The afternoons are open lab where participants sew whatever project they choose. The small class size (four participants) assures personal attention.

The class is conducted in a house in the hills of San Jose, California. Participants stay in twin-bedded rooms with shared bath. Three meals are served each day.

COST:

 The Fabric Carr
P.O. Box 32120
San Jose, CA 95152

 (408) 929-1651

405

WRITERS RETREAT WORKSHOP

"The workshop was the most incredible experience of my life — exhilarating, challenging, and fun! My love of the craft of writing was renewed and my confidence restored."

—Writers Retreat Workshop participant

Serious writers (published or unpublished) who want to take their writing to new levels can enhance their chances of writing success by attending one of these ten-day workshops. Taught by authors, editors, and agents, the workshop provides indepth instruction, covering all aspects of the craft of writing (plotting, editing, characterization, dialogue, etc.). It includes diagnostic manuscript sessions, assignments, consultations, and personal writing time. Participants with an idea for a novel or those with a complete draft can leave the course with improved technique and increased confidence that they can develop and market their writing.

Most of the courses are geared towards fiction writing, but there are a few for nonfiction.

Workshops are held several times throughout the year.

Accommodations can range from dormitory-style lodging to single rooms and private baths in a Victorian home. Meals are included in the package.

Workshops are held in Bristol, Connecticut and Wakulla Springs, Florida.

COST: $ $ (all-inclusive)

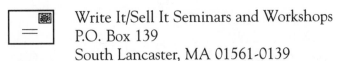
Write It/Sell It Seminars and Workshops
P.O. Box 139
South Lancaster, MA 01561-0139

 (800) 642-2494

www.channel1.com/wisi/

YESTERMORROW DESIGN/BUILD SCHOOL

For a house to really be a home, it needs to reflect the home-owner's personal vision and lifestyle. But most of us don't really know how to take charge and design, build, remodel, or upgrade a house. We leave this to architects, builders, land-scapers, and interior designers, allowing them to create the environments we live in. Or we allow our lack of knowledge and skills to intimidate us into thinking that we couldn't pos-sibly create the living environment that's right for us. Without sufficient confidence and know-how, we end up with houses and yards that leave a lot to be desired.

A course at Yestermorrow Design/Build School can change all that. Laypersons as well as professionals are empowered to shape the present and future of the built environment. The staff of professional architects, builders, artists, and craftspeople teach students to integrate their own lifestyle, priorities, and culture with home building ideas and technologies that are practical, workable, and environmentally friendly.

The heart of the Layperson Curriculum is the two-week Home Design/Build course. Through studio sessions, slide shows, lec-tures, house tours, discussion, and hands-on construction pro-jects, students learn the basics of house design and building for new construction and renovation. Three college credits are available upon completion of the course.

Other one-week courses are Renovation, Home Design, Landscape Design/Build, and Cabinetry. Timber Framing is four days. Two-day courses include Kitchen and Bathroom Design, Solar Design, Architectural Trim and Detail, Old House Assessment, Design/Build Decks, Faux Marble Painting, Ceramic Tiling, and Furniture From Found Objects. There are even some one-day courses: Electrical Wiring and Drywall Construction and Repair.

Similarly, courses within the Professional Curriculum range from one day to four weeks. These include the two-day

Community Planning, the two-week Architectural Crafts, and the four-week Design/Build: An Architectural Process.

Yestermorrow is located in the Mad River Valley (a resort area in Vermont). Recreational possibilities include hiking, swimming, bicycling, skiing, horseback riding, golf, and tennis. The area has a large number of historic buildings and scenic landscaping to tour. There are also many craft galleries, country stores, antique shops, and restaurants to visit.

Students in the Layperson Curriculum stay at a country inn about eight miles from the school. A full breakfast, bag lunch, and dinner are provided by the inn. Most rooms are doubles. Professional Curriculum students reside in one-bedroom condominiums approximately five miles from the Yestermorrow campus. Students are responsible for preparing their own meals.

Upon completion of the course, professionals have upgraded their expertise and can expand their business opportunities. At the very least, laypersons become sufficiently informed to hold a meaningful conversation with their architect or builder. Most acquire the skills and resources for creating their dream home. Some will renovate other homes for profit or may even decide that they want to pursue an architectural or building career.

COST: $\vcenter{\hbox{(\$)}}$ to $\vcenter{\hbox{(\$)}}$ $\vcenter{\hbox{(\$)}}$

> (depending on length; financial aid available for Vermont residents)

Yestermorrow School
RR1 Box 97-5
Warren, VT 05674

 (802) 496-5545

www.uestermorrow.org

Index

STATE-BY-STATE DESTINATIONS

INTERNATIONAL DESTINATIONS

About the Author

Ellen Lederman, a therapist and "vacation expert" on activities that are spiritually, mentally, and physically fulfilling, has written several books, including *Are You Ready for Love* and *The Best Places to Meet Men.*

From the Author and Publisher

A book of this nature should be considered a work in progress. Some of the programs and facilities profiled in this edition may not be included in future editions, while exciting new ones will be added.

Your input is very important! If there is a life-changing vacation you'd like to see included, please send the information to Sourcebooks at the address below. If you participate in one of the vacations profiled here, and would like to give us feedback, we'd love to hear from you.

Also, personal stories of how one of these (or similar) vacations changed your life would be most appreciated and may be included in future editions.

Your feedback will enable this book to remain as complete,

accurate, and cutting-edge as possible. By sharing your thoughts and feelings, you can help other people make a difference in their lives through a well-chosen vacation.

Please send all information and comments to:
Sourcebooks, Inc.
P.O. Box 372
Naperville, IL 60566
Attn: *Vacations That Can Change Your Life*

phone: (630) 961-3900
fax: (630) 961-2168